The Economics of Inequality, Poverty, and Discrimination in the 21st Century

Contents

PART V: POLICY

Part V

Policy

Chapter 18

Do Minimum Wages Help Fight Poverty?

David Neumark

INTRODUCTION

The federal minimum wage was last raised in three steps in 2007, 2008, and 2009, arriving at its current level of $7.25. In the past two decades, many states have also implemented or maintained minimum wages higher than the federal level (reaching a high of 29 states in 2007), which are typically binding for most workers. And most recently, a handful of states have indexed their minimum wage to the Consumer Price Index, ensuring annual minimum wage increases of the same size (in percentage terms) as the rate of inflation, although the federal minimum wage is not indexed.

The central policy goal of minimum wages is to raise incomes of low-wage workers so as to reduce poverty. Senator Edward Kennedy of Massachusetts, a perennial sponsor of legislation to increase the minimum wage, claimed that "the minimum wage was one of the first—and is still one of the best—anti-poverty programs we have" (quoted

Portions of this chapter were adapted from Neumark, D. The Economic Effects of Minimum Wages: What might Missouri expect from passage of Proposition B? *Policy Study*, no. 2, October 2, 2006. Used by permission of the Show-Me Institute. Available online at http://www.showmeinstitute.org/docLib/20070411_smi_study_2.pdf.

in Clymer 1999, 449). That minimum wages would have these salutary impacts seems, on the surface, obvious. After all, a higher minimum wage must raise the wage a worker earns, and thus increase his or her income. And minimum wage workers must—given their low wages—be in poor or low-income families. Conversely, criticism of proposals to raise the minimum wage may seem like nothing more than self-interested efforts on behalf of businesses that would foot the bill for a higher minimum wage.

However, although a higher minimum wage for low-wage workers may seem like a natural way to fight poverty, there are three reasons why raising the minimum may not help to achieve this goal. First, a higher minimum wage may discourage employers from using the very low-wage, low-skill workers minimum wage proponents are trying to help. This is the most widespread argument against minimum wages, and the most-studied question with regard to minimum wages. The disemployment effects of minimum wages are subject to some dispute. However, for the United States, the preponderance of evidence points to disemployment effects for low-wage, low-skilled workers from a higher minimum wage.

Second, a higher minimum wage may hurt poor and low-income families rather than helping them. Allowing that there are some disemployment effects, minimum wages create "winners" and "losers." The winners get a higher wage with no reduction in employment (or hours); the losers, in contrast, bear the burden of the disemployment effects—losing their job, having hours reduced, or finding it more difficult to enter employment. Furthermore, many minimum wage workers are not primary earners in poor or low-income families, but instead are secondary workers, such as teenagers in higher-income families. As a consequence, if the gains from minimum wages accrue to minimum wage workers in higher-income families, while the losses are borne by minimum wage workers in poor or low-income families, minimum wages may have perverse distributional effects—possibly increasing, rather than decreasing, the number of poor or low-income families. Research for the United States generally fails to find evidence that minimum wages help the poor, and if anything suggests that minimum wages increase the number of poor or low-income families.

Finally, there are potential adverse longer-run effects of minimum wages on the accumulation of skills that lead to higher earnings. The three principal sources of higher skills are schooling, work experience, and workplace training, and minimum wages may reduce all three of these. They may reduce training provided by employers, in response to higher labor costs. They may reduce schooling by enticing those students who can find employment at the higher minimum to leave school. And they may reduce the accumulation of work experience directly via their disemployment effects. There is some evidence of all three of these types of adverse effects on skill formation, which can prevent workers from attaining the higher-wage jobs as adults that are probably the single best means to ensure an acceptable level of family income.

In sum, much evidence for the United States indicates that minimum wages are unlikely to achieve the goals of advocates for a higher minimum wage. A higher minimum reduces employment among the least skilled. Although offset in part by higher wages paid to some workers, many of the costs are borne by poor and low-income families. And over the longer term minimum wages lead to lower skills and therefore lower wages. Thus efforts to redistribute income toward poor and low-income families should emphasize policy options other than a higher minimum wage.

The following sections provide the details on which these conclusions are based. After a brief review of the theory underlying the effects of minimum wages, empirical evidence is presented on the employment effects of minimum wages, their distributional effects, and their longer-run impact.

EMPLOYMENT EFFECTS: THEORY

The simple textbook, neoclassical economic model of the effect of the minimum wage is straightforward. There is a competitive labor market for a single type of labor, for which there is an upward-sloping aggregate labor supply curve (S) and a downward-sloping aggregate labor demand curve (D). In the absence of a minimum wage, there is an equilibrium wage w and an equilibrium quantity of labor employed L, as depicted in Figure 18.1.

If a minimum wage mw is established at a wage higher than w—so the minimum wage is "binding"—then employers reduce their use of labor for two reasons. First, there is a substitution effect, leading employers to use relatively less of the now-more-expensive labor and relatively more of other inputs (such as capital), to minimize the costs of production at the same level of output (the cost-minimization problem). Second, because marginal costs must be higher with this new

Figure 18.1
The Textbook Treatment of Minimum Wages.

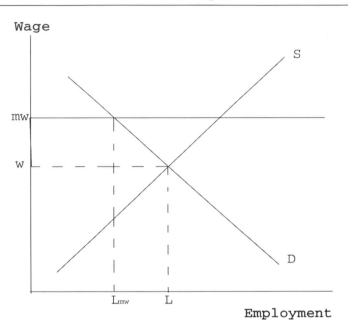

input mix (otherwise employers were not previously minimizing costs), the prices of the products firms produce rise, reducing the demand for each firm's product and leading to a reduction in the scale of operation. These substitution and scale effects lead to lower employment, say at the level $L_{mw} < L$.

Minimum wages' employment effects are typically summarized in terms of the "employment elasticity"—the ratio of the percent change in employment to the percentage change in the wage that the minimum wage induces, or in terms of the following notation:

$$\text{Employment elasticity} = \{(L_{mw} - L)/L\} \, / \, \{(mw - w)/w\}.$$

Thus, for example, an elasticity of −0.1 implies that a 10 percent increase in the wage floor reduces employment by 1 percent.

Of course the scenario depicted in Figure 18.1 is based on a model, and a simple one at that. Economists use models not because they believe they are completely accurate descriptions of reality, but because they highlight key ideas. The key idea underlying the textbook model of minimum wages is that when something becomes more expensive people use less of it, in part by substituting toward other alternatives. We see this behavior illustrated in myriad ways every day. A prime example is responses to higher gasoline prices, including reduced driving, increased demand for fuel-efficient cars (substituting alternative equipment for fuel), and increased demand for alternative fuels such as ethanol (substituting nonpetroleum for petroleum products). Similarly, employers of low-skill labor, when faced with a higher price for that labor, should be expected to substitute away from low-skill labor and toward other types of labor as well as labor-saving machinery.

However, the model depicted in Figure 18.1 may be overly simplistic, and a richer model may have different or at least more-nuanced implications. Sticking to the baseline competitive model of labor markets, there are a couple of reasons why a higher minimum wage may not produce a decline in employment, or at least not one that is large enough to be detectable. First, the minimum wage must actually be binding, so that it forces wages up above the competitive level. If there were only one type of labor, this would be trivial to check. In fact, however, Figure 18.1 is overly simplistic in an important way; although it was drawn as if there is only one kind of labor, labor is actually heterogeneous, with workers having varying skill levels. When there are different types of labor differentiated by skill level, we cannot just compare average wage levels to the minimum wage, but instead have to ask whether the minimum wage is high relative to market wages for a substantial group of workers.

A more important and challenging problem arising from heterogeneous labor is that, in this case, employers may substitute from the least-skilled to slightly more-skilled labor after a minimum wage increase. For example, at a particular firm two more-skilled workers may be able to produce the same output as three less-skilled workers. But if the price of more-skilled labor is, for example, $8 per hour, versus $5 per hour for least-skilled labor, it is more profitable to hire three of the latter workers. However, if a minimum wage of $6 is established, then because this is binding for the least-skilled workers their wage rises to $6 per hour, and it will now be more profitable to replace three least-skilled workers with two more-skilled workers (paying a total of $16 rather than $18).

Even though employment declines (by one worker, in this example), the overall employment decline (one worker) is much smaller than the employment decline among unskilled workers (three workers). And of course one can construct examples where there is a high degree of substitution and the overall employment effect is quite small. Note, however, that among the workers the higher minimum wage is intended to help—those originally earning $5 per hour—the disemployment effect is quite severe. This admittedly simple example illustrates an important point about minimum wages: one type of substitution they generate is "labor-labor" substitution—that is, substitution of one kind of labor for another. Substitution among different types of workers may mask disemployment effects for relatively broad groups of workers, while entailing sharp disemployment effects for the least-skilled.

A more fundamental challenge to the competitive model's prediction that minimum wages will reduce employment comes from models of "monopsony" power in labor markets, in which a higher minimum wage could actually increase employment. In the competitive model depicted in Figure 18.1, the aggregate labor supply curve is upward sloping, but if the labor market is assumed to be perfectly competitive, then employers are small relative to the market and hence can hire all the labor they want at the existing wage. In the classical monopsony model there is a single employer, in which case the employer faces the market-level upward-sloping labor supply curves. Employers are also assumed to have to pay workers the same wage (that is, they cannot price discriminate, paying each worker only the wage needed to entice him or her to enter the labor market). Thus when an employer wants to hire more labor, the cost of doing so is higher than the wage that is required to attract a new worker, because the wage paid to all workers increases. Hence the marginal cost of labor exceeds the wage, and because a profit-maximizing employer hires up to the point where the marginal cost of labor equals the marginal revenue product, employment is lower and wages are lower than in a competitive market. In this case a minimum wage higher than the equilibrium monopsony wage can increase employment by breaking the link between the wage and the marginal cost of labor curve.

This argument was originally developed by Stigler (1946), although he was skeptical of government's ability to predict the wage floor that would actually increase employment. More modern versions of monopsony models are based on labor market frictions that tie workers to firms even if other firms might pay higher wages, rather than the unrealistic assumption of a single employer (Manning 2003). The driving force behind monopsony—increased costs of employment of the existing workforce when a new worker is hired—can also arise from a need to supervise workers (Lang 1987) and in workplaces with tipped employees (Wessels 1997).

These more modern types of monopsony models have attracted considerable interest in recent years because there have been some studies of the employment effects of minimum wages—discussed later—that fail to find the predicted negative employment effects on low-skilled workers and sometimes even claim to find positive employment effects. As the preceding discussion makes clear, such results are difficult to reconcile with the competitive model. They can, however, be explained by monopsony models, although even in monopsony models a minimum wage set too high will lead to employment declines. Thus if there is, in fact, compelling evidence that at least over some range minimum wages do not reduce or even increase employment, then the competitive model may be called into question as a useful, if stylized, description of labor markets and the effects of minimum wages. However, the existing research on employment effects, as summarized next, provides far more compelling evidence that minimum wages lead to disemployment effects, which is consistent with the competitive model.

EMPLOYMENT EFFECTS: EVIDENCE

Labor economists have written scores of papers testing the prediction that minimum wages reduce employment. Broadly speaking, there are three types of empirical studies of the employment effects of minimum wages. The literature is extensive, so here I provide a summary of the findings from each type of study, emphasizing the studies that are most important in terms of either influencing the policy debate or presenting the best evidence. (For a comprehensive survey of the literature, see Neumark and Wascher 2007 and 2008, chapter 3.)

Aggregate Time-Series Studies

The earliest studies used aggregate time-series data for the United States to estimate the effects of changes in the national minimum wage on employment rates (the employment-to-population ratio) of young persons, typically focusing on 16- to 19-year-olds ("teens") or 16- to 24-year-olds ("young adults"), many of whom have quite low skills. These time-series studies rely on changes in the federal minimum wage to identify the effects of minimum wages. The statistical models used in these studies measure the association between employment rates of these age groups and the level of the minimum wage relative to the average wage, attempting to account for changes in the aggregate economy (the business cycle) or other influences on youth labor markets aside from the minimum wage.

"First generation" studies, extending into the 1970s, found elasticities for teen employment clustered between –0.1 and –0.3 (Brown et al. 1982); that is, for every 10 percent increase in the minimum wage, employment of teenagers falls by 1 to 3 percent. A small amount of evidence in the 1990s (most notably Wellington 1991, and Card and Krueger 1995) challenged the consensus from the earlier time-series studies. Extending the data, and using better time-series methods than many earlier studies, led to elasticities for both teenagers and young adults that were closer to zero and generally statistically insignificant (meaning that we could have very little confidence that estimates differing from zero reflected real differences rather than simply the random variation that is present in any data).

However, the most recent studies using the time-series approach with the most up-to-date time-series methods find stronger evidence of disemployment effects that are consistent with the earlier consensus. The best of these (Bazen and Marimoutou 2002; but see also Williams and Mills 2001) uses data through 1999, and estimates statistically significant teen employment elasticities of –0.12 in the short run and –0.27 in the longer run. Thus the time-series evidence confirms the negative effects of minimum wages on employment of young (and hence unskilled) individuals, and suggests that a range of the elasticity of about –0.1 to –0.3 is still a reasonable view of the likely effects of minimum wages. And the recent studies pose a clear challenge to claims that the time-series evidence for the United States does not show a detectable adverse effect of minimum wages on teenage employment (e.g., Bernstein and Schmitt 2000).

National Studies Using Both Across-State and Time-Series Variation

Beginning in the early 1990s, researchers began to reexamine the effects of the minimum wage on employment by continuing to use national data, but exploiting newly emerging state-level variation in minimum wages. The state-level variation provided researchers with more "experiments" to estimate the effects of minimum wages. And more important, state-level variation in minimum wages provides more reliable evidence. In the aggregate time-series approach, it can be hard to distinguish between the effects of a change in the federal minimum wage and the effects of the business cycle or other influences on youth employment. But with state-level data, some states where minimum wages do not increase can effectively serve as "controls" for the states where minimum wages do increase, by providing information on changes in youth employment for reasons aside from the minimum wage.

The evidence on disemployment effects from the earliest studies using this approach was mixed (Card 1992a; Card et al. 1994; Neumark and Wascher 1992, 1994). One important issue that emerged, for teenagers in particular, was how both employment *and* school enrollment of teenagers responds to the minimum wage (Neumark and Wascher 1995, 1996). Specifically, the evidence indicated that employment elasticities for teens overall understate the size of the disemployment effects on the lowest-skilled workers among these teenagers (minorities, those who have already dropped out of high school, etc.). In particular, a higher minimum wage increases the probability that some teenagers leave school to take jobs, and displace less-skilled teen workers who had already dropped out of high school—precisely the "labor-labor" substitution discussed in the previous section. Moreover, an increase in the minimum wage raises the probability that nonenrolled teenage workers become both nonenrolled and nonemployed ("idle"); these results were especially pronounced for blacks and Hispanics and for individuals who had a lower wage prior to the increase in the minimum wage.

A second issue that emerged was that the disemployment effects of minimum wages appeared more adverse once allowance is made for changes beyond the very short run. One might suspect that employment adjustments in the low-wage labor market are rapid, because workers in this labor market turn over relatively quickly, so that employment can adjust quickly via changes in hiring even if they do not fire workers when the minimum wage increases (Brown et al. 1982). However, some changes that lower employment, including shifts toward using relatively more capital or higher-skilled labor, take time. Baker et al. (1999) and Keil et al. (2001), in particular, show that the disemployment effects of minimum wages are stronger once longer-run adjustments are allowed, and muted when models focus only on short-run effects.

In sum, the evidence from the national studies of state minimum wage increases quite unambiguously points to disemployment effects of minimum wages on teens and young adults. Many of the estimates are in the range cited earlier, with elasticities between –0.1 and –0.3, although there are also many refinements in terms of the effects on the least skilled that may be sharper but masked by enrollment shifts, as well as estimates of longer-term effects that are sometimes larger.

"Case Studies" of Specific State Minimum Wage Increases

The final approach to estimating the effects of minimum wages on employment has focused on isolated examples of state minimum wage increases. The research strategy is the same as in the national studies that exploit state-level variation in minimum wages, but this "case study" approach offers the potential advantage of limiting the analysis to a state where the minimum wage increases and another very similar state (or even region of a state) that provides a more reliable control. The downside is that the results are less likely to generalize to proposed increases in other states in other time periods.

Early versions of these studies had somewhat conflicting answers (Katz and Krueger 1992; Card 1992b; Kim and Taylor 1995). The best known case study of a specific minimum wage increase—and the one cited most frequently by minimum wage advocates—is Card and Krueger's (1994) investigation of the effects of the 1992 increase in New Jersey's minimum wage. They surveyed fast-food restaurants in New Jersey and eastern Pennsylvania (bordering New Jersey) about two months before and seven months after the April 1992 increase in the New Jersey minimum wage. Their results imply that the increase in New Jersey's minimum wage led to *faster* employment growth, with an elasticity of +0.73. This evidence presented a clear challenge to the conventional theory and large body of evidence on minimum wages (including even the studies that tend to find *no* effect of minimum wages), and likely prompted the name of their book that featured this study, *Myth and Measurement* (Card and Krueger 1995).

However, subsequent research uncovered serious problems with the data used in the study (Neumark and Wascher 2000). Illustrating that small details can matter greatly in research, the Card-Krueger survey asked managers or assistant managers a very ambiguous question to measure employment: "How many full-time and part-time workers are employed in your restaurant, excluding managers and assistant managers?" This question could refer to the current shift, the day, or perhaps the payroll period; and compounding the problem, nothing forced the respondent to use the same definition of employment in the two surveys. Reflecting the inaccurate and inconsistent measurement of employment, the data collected by Card and Krueger indicated far greater variability across the two observations than was plausible for fast-food restaurants.

Reestimating the models, using actual payroll records from many of the same restaurants, yielded estimates much more consistent with the prior research, with elasticities of employment with respect to the minimum wage in the range of −0.1 to −0.25, often statistically significant. In a response to the Neumark and Wascher study, Card and Krueger (2000) turned to yet another data source that is much more reliable than their original data, and found estimated employment elasticities centered on zero. Since it might be difficult to judge between the latter two data sources, it appears that the safest conclusion is that this particular case study yields estimated elasticities between about 0 and −0.25. Moreover, recent case studies or similar approaches also point to disemployment effects (Hoffman and Trace 2009; Powers 2009; Thompson 2009). Finally, some work has studied the eating and drinking sector more broadly, to try to help resolve the dispute over the studies of the fast-food industry (Singell and Terborg 2006; Dube et al. 2010). This evidence is more mixed, with Singell and Terborg finding an employment elasticity of around −0.2 for the retail eating and drinking sector, but Dube et al. finding no effect.

Overall, what do we conclude from the case studies? The evidence appears to be most variable for the studies using this approach, likely because of the variety of cases researchers study, making it harder to draw firm conclusions. For the most part, the better studies tend to show either negative effects of minimum wages on employment, or sometimes no effect.

There is, though, one serious limitation of case studies of specific industries that calls into question their importance. In particular, economic theory makes no firm prediction about what will happen to employment in a very narrow industry. As the theory section explained, in the standard model the negative employment effects stem from cost increases for low-wage labor, which in turn increase prices and reduce labor demand. But this does not have to occur in every industry, especially in a narrow industry segment such as fast-food restaurants. As an example, suppose that fast-food restaurants compete with pizza shops, and pizza shops are more intensive users of low-wage labor, perhaps because fast-food restaurants use a fair amount of capital to produce and prepare food. In that case, costs may be pushed up more for pizza shops than for fast-food restaurants, and demand for "low-end" food could shift *toward* fast-food restaurants, raising employment at those restaurants even though combined employment of the two types of restaurants falls.

This is only hypothetical. Indeed part of the motivation for research looking at the restaurant industry as a whole (Dube et al. 2010) is to avoid this problem of shifts in employment within an industry. On the other hand, the problem with looking at a single—if broader—industry is that there can be a good deal of labor-labor substitution within the industry, masking disemployment effects for low-wage workers *within* the industry. As a result, neither case studies of narrow industries nor broader studies of particular industries may be very informative about one of the central questions policy makers ask when contemplating a minimum wage increase, and one of the central questions that determines whether minimum wages help fight poverty—namely, "Will employment of low-skilled workers fall, and by how much?"

DISTRIBUTIONAL EFFECTS

Even though minimum wages *do* reduce employment, they could have distributional effects that might be viewed as beneficial. As noted earlier, minimum wages create winners and losers; the first group are those whose wages and incomes increase, and the latter those whose incomes fall, through either job loss or hours reductions (or increased difficulty of finding a job).

If all minimum wage workers were in poor or low-income families, then it is more likely that minimum wage increases would on average help those families, as the wage gains experienced by many workers would increase incomes in many poor and low-income families, and the losses would likely fall on a much smaller share of workers and hence families. The situation is more complicated, however, because low-wage workers are in fact scattered throughout the income distribution, with many in quite high-income families. Perhaps the most important lesson from research on the distributional effects of minimum wages is that the connection between low-wage work and poverty-level family income is rather weak, leading even researchers whose work is cited by advocates for higher minimum wages to acknowledge that the minimum wage is at best a "blunt instrument" (Card and Krueger 1995, 285) for helping low-income families.

Table 18.1 illustrates vividly that *many* low-wage workers are not in poor families. It shows the distribution of all workers and low-wage workers (earning below $7.25) across family income-to-needs

Table 18.1
Low-Wage Workers and Household Income-to-Needs

Income-to-Needs Ratio	% of All Workers	% of Workers with Wages below $7.25
<1	4.2	13.2
1 to 1.25	2.1	4.9
1.25 to 1.5	2.6	6.1
1.5 to 2	6.4	10.4
2 to 3	15.7	19.0
>3	69.1	46.3

Source: Burkhauser and Sabia (2007), Appendix Table A.3. Calculations based on CPS data. The numbers are slightly different from what Burkhauser and Sabia report in the last column of their table, because they consider only those earning between $5 and $7.25, while this table uses all workers earning less than $7.25. The conclusions are very similar either way.

categories, in 2003. "Needs" is defined as the level of family income that puts a family of a given size and age structure at the poverty line, so families with income-to-needs of one are right at the poverty line, and so on. Although around 10.8 percent of families in 2003 were poor, only 4.2 percent of all workers were in poor families. In other words, well over half of poor families have no workers, and raising the minimum wage does nothing to help these families. Moreover, many minimum wage workers are in nonpoor and even relatively high-income families. Only 13.2 percent of workers earning a wage less than $7.25 were in poor families, while 46.3 percent—or nearly one-half, most of whom are likely teenagers or other secondary workers—were in families with incomes three times the poverty line (or approximately $56,000 in 2003, for a family of four) or higher. Thus, if the benefits of minimum wages are spread equally across all affected low-wage workers, then only 13.2 percent of these benefits go to poor families, and nearly half of these benefits go to families who are roughly in the top half of the income distribution.

Of course, if the winners from minimum wage increases are the low-wage workers in poor, low-income families, whereas the losers are the low-wage workers in high-income families, then minimum wages would redistribute income to low-income families. But the opposite is also plausible, in which case the distributional effects could be quite adverse. Theory makes no prediction regarding the distributional effects of minimum wages.

Some research tries to determine the distributional effects of minimum wages using simulations, first computing the distribution across the family income-to-needs distribution of low-wage workers likely to be affected by the increase, and then, based on assumptions about how these workers will be affected by the minimum wage increase, computing the effects on incomes of different types of families. Typically, such studies suggest that a good share of the gains from minimum wage increases will go to higher-income rather than lower-income families, for exactly the reasons discussed earlier—many low-income families have no workers, and many low-wage workers are in higher-income families (Burkhauser and Sabia 2007 is a recent example).

More reliable evidence, however, comes from directly estimating the effects of minimum wage increases on the family income distribution. Neumark et al. (2005) examined state and federal minimum wage increases over the period 1986–95. Their results are summarized briefly in Table 18.2, in terms of percentage point changes in response to minimum wage increases of 10 percent. The estimates indicate that a 10 percent increase in the minimum wage causes a 0.71-percentage-point *increase* in the number of poor families (or a 0.0071 increase in the proportion of poor families), representing a 3.9 percent increase in the number of poor families. If we look instead at the number of families below 1.5 times the poverty line ("poor" or "near-poor"), the estimates also indicate an increase—in this case 1.04 percentage points, so the number of families between 1 and 1.5 times the poverty line increases as well. Finally, the estimates indicate that this increase in the number of poor and near-poor families comes from families originally a bit above the poverty or near-poverty line, presumably as secondary workers in these higher-income families lose a job, have their hours reduced, or find it more difficult to enter employment. The

Table 18.2

Percentage Point Change in Proportions of Families in Ranges of Income-to-Needs Distribution, Minimum Wage Increase versus No Increase

Income-to-needs = 0 to 1 (poor)	Income-to-needs = 0 to 1.5 (poor or near-poor)	Income-to-needs = 1.5 to 3
0.71[*]	1.04[**]	−1.46[**]

Source: Neumark et al. (2005), Table 2. The dataset covers 1986–95. Reported estimates are percentage point changes in proportion of families in cell. "**" ("*") superscript indicates estimate is statistically significant at 5 percent (10 percent) level.

adverse distributional effects of minimum wages are consistent with more of the negative effects of minimum wages falling on low-skill workers in poor and low-income families, while the gains accrue more to those in high-income families. Oversimplifying, the data are more consistent with teens in middle- and high-income families getting the higher wages from minimum wage increases, while poor primary breadwinners are bearing the disemployment costs.

Other recent research also studies the distributional effects of minimum wages. Although the evidence does not always point to minimum wages *increasing* poverty, much of it does point in this direction (Gunderson and Ziliak 2004; Wu et al. 2006). The study by Wu et al. (2006) is especially revealing. The authors estimate the effects of a wide array of policies on a variety of income inequality measures, which can sometimes be given an interpretation in terms of economic welfare. They find that higher minimum wages either have no effect or increase inequality, and this occurs in such a way that when the incomes of lower-income families weigh heavily in calculating social welfare, minimum wages reduce social welfare.

Perhaps the most significant conclusion from the research literature, however, is that there is really *no* solid evidence of beneficial distributional effects of minimum wages. As a result, there is no basis for concluding that minimum wages reduce the proportion of families living in poverty or near-poverty, offsetting the negative employment effects of minimum wages. Indeed, the combined evidence is best summarized as indicating that an increase in the minimum wage largely results in a redistribution of income *among* low-income families, with some gaining as a result of the higher minimum wage and others losing as a result of diminished employment opportunities or reduced hours.

At the same time, this is an understudied question in the economics research literature, and as additional evidence accumulates, the conclusions may vary when researchers look at different time periods, different institutional settings, different countries, or even different types of minimum wages. Recall that theory makes a strong prediction about employment effects, but no prediction about distributional effects. As a reflection of this, research on what are called "living wages"—which are a narrower type of minimum wage imposed in U.S. cities—has found that these wage floors reduce employment, like minimum wages, but may have more beneficial distributional effects (Adams and Neumark 2005). For the same reason, conclusions about employment effects of minimum wages should generalize across countries, and they generally do (Neumark and Wascher 2007). But there is less reason to be sure that the conclusion that minimum wages are ineffective in reducing poverty in the United States necessarily carries over to other countries.

LONGER-RUN EFFECTS

The evidence on minimum wage effects discussed to this point focuses on short-run effects, typically looking at effects at most a year after minimum wage increases. There are, however, potential effects of minimum wages in the longer run. Why might these longer-run effects arise? First, minimum wages may lower formal training among young workers—training that would increase wages. Workers undergoing such training have lower productivity when the training is occurring. Such training is typically financed by lower wages, but if productivity while training falls below the minimum wage floor, training may be deterred (Hashimoto 1982; Feldstein 1973). There is evidence from Current Population Survey data that minimum wages reduce formal training for 20- to 24-year-olds (Neumark and Wascher 2001a), with the estimates implying that a typical higher state minimum wage reduces the incidence of training by about 0.9 percentage points, or about 9 percent. However, these results are not settled (see Acemoglu and Pischke 2003, and Fairris and Pedace 2004).

Second, given the evidence of negative effects of minimum wages on employment of teens and young adults, longer-run adverse effects could arise because of reduced accumulation of labor market experience—another source of wage growth. And finally, higher minimum wages may discourage school enrollment, as already discussed (and see also Chaplin et al. 2003).

This is the least-explored area of minimum wage research, but the implications are potentially quite serious. Policy makers may not be particularly concerned with whether minimum wages cost teenagers and young adults jobs. But if minimum wages lead to lower wages and earnings among adults, via the effects just described, then their consequences may be more serious because they last into ages when people are more likely to form families and have children. Moreover, the types of effects discussed here would not be reflected only in employment. For example, workers exposed to a high minimum wage but remaining employed may receive less training.

To assess the overall effects of these longer-run influences, Neumark and Nizalova (2007) estimate the effects of exposure to higher minimum wages at younger ages—when minimum wages were most likely to be binding—on outcomes for somewhat older individuals (25- to 29-year-olds). The estimates indicate that adults exposed to minimum wages as teens or young adults have lower wages and lower earnings, providing evidence that the net effects of reductions in training, experience, and schooling persist to disadvantage workers who were exposed to higher minimum wages when young. The effects are not trivial. For example, exposure to a typical higher state minimum wage through the teen years reduces average earnings of 25- to 29-year-olds by 0.8 percent. And exposure during ages 20–24, when training opportunities may be more prevalent, reduces average earnings of 25- to 29-year-olds by about twice this amount.

Thus this evidence, although the first of its kind, suggests that the potentially adverse effects of minimum wages extend beyond disemployment effects for the youngest individuals. This suggests that the focus of most research and policy debate on minimum wages on their contemporaneous, short-run effects on teens and young adults may be misplaced.

CONCLUSIONS

Where does all of this evidence leave us regarding the wisdom of raising the minimum wage? The evidence suggests that minimum wage increases do more harm than good. Minimum wages reduce employment of young and less-skilled workers. Although in principle the gains to those who keep their jobs could offset the losses to those who bear the disemployment effects, minimum wages deliver no net benefits to poor or low-income families, and if anything make them worse off, increasing poverty. Finally, minimum wages may also have longer-run adverse effects, lowering the acquisition of skills through various channels and therefore lowering wages and earnings even beyond the age when individuals are most directly affected by a higher minimum.

It may simply be an uncomfortable fact that trying to help low-income families through mandating a higher minimum wage has negative consequences, since such wage floors amount to a tax on the employment of these workers. Those interested in using economic policy levers to redistribute income to lower-income families should instead push for policy options that encourage work, that better target poor and low-income families, and that have a proven record of reducing poverty. Empirical evidence suggests that the Earned Income Tax Credit, which is implemented at the federal level and supplemented by many states, satisfies all of these criteria (Neumark and Wascher 2001b; Hoffman and Seidman 2003; Wu et al. 2006), and thus appears to be a better redistributive policy.

BIBLIOGRAPHY

Acemoglu, Daron, and Jorn-Steffen Pischke. 2003. "Minimum Wages and On-the-Job Training." *Research in Labor Economics*, Vol. 20, pp. 159–202.

Adams, Scott, and David Neumark. 2005. "Living Wage Effects: New and Improved Evidence." *Economic Development Quarterly*, Vol. 19, No. 1, February, pp. 80–102.

Baker, Michael, Dwayne Benjamin, and Shuchita Stanger. 1999. "The Highs and Lows of the Minimum Wage Effect: A Time-Series Cross-Section Study of the Canadian Law." *Journal of Labor Economics*, Vol. 17, No. 2, April, pp. 318–50.

Bazen, Stephen, and Velayoudom Marimoutou. 2002. "Looking for a Needle in a Haystack? A Re-examination of the Time Series Relationship between Teenage Employment and Minimum Wages in the United States." *Oxford Bulletin of Economics and Statistics*, Vol. 64, Supplement 1, August, pp. 699–725.

Bernstein, Jared, and John Schmitt. 2000. "The Impact of the Minimum Wage: Policy Lifts Wages, Maintains Floor for Low-Wage Labor Market." Economic Policy Institute Briefing Paper.

Brown, Charles, Charles Gilroy, and Andrew Kohen. 1982. "The Effect of the Minimum Wage on Employment and Unemployment," *Journal of Economic Literature*, Vol. 20, No. 2, June, pp. 487–528.

Burkhauser, Richard V., and Joseph J. Sabia. 2007. "The Effectiveness of Minimum Wage Increases in Reducing Poverty: Past, Present and Future." *Contemporary Economic Policy*, Vol. 25, No. 2 (April), pp. 262–81.

Card, David. 1992a. "Using Regional Variation in Wages to Measure the Effects of the Federal Minimum Wage." *Industrial and Labor Relations Review*, Vol. 46, No. 1, October, pp. 22–37.

Card, David. 1992b. "Do Minimum Wages Reduce Employment? A Case Study of California, 1987–1989." *Industrial and Labor Relations Review*, Vol. 46, No. 1, October, pp. 38–54.

Card, David, Lawrence F. Katz, and Alan B. Krueger. 1994. "Comment on David Neumark and William Wascher, 'Employment Effects of Minimum and Subminimum Wages: Panel Data on State Minimum Wage Laws.'" *Industrial and Labor Relations Review*, Vol. 47, No. 3, April, pp. 487–96.

Card, David, and Alan B. Krueger. 1994. "Minimum Wages and Employment: A Case Study of the Fast-Food Industry in New Jersey and Pennsylvania." *American Economic Review*, Vol. 84, No. 4, September, pp. 772–93.

Card, David, and Alan B. Krueger. 1995. *Myth and Measurement: The New Economics of the Minimum Wage*, Princeton: Princeton University Press.

Card, David, and Alan B. Krueger. 2000. "Minimum Wages and Employment: A Case Study of the Fast-Food Industry in New Jersey and Pennsylvania: Reply." *American Economic Review*, Vol. 90, No. 5, December, pp. 1397–420.

Chaplin, Duncan D., Mark D. Turner, and Andrew D. Pape. 2003. "Minimum Wages and School Enrollment of Teenagers: A Look at the 1990's." *Economics of Education Review*, Vol. 22, No. 1, February, pp. 11–21.

Clymer, Andrew. 1999. *Edward M. Kennedy: A Biography*, New York: William Morrow & Co.

Dube, Arindrajit, T. William Lester, and Michael Reich. 2010. "Minimum Wage Effects across State Borders: Estimates Using Contiguous Counties." *Review of Economics and Statistics*, Vol. 92, No. 4, November, pp. 945–64.

Fairris, David, and Roberto Pedace. 2004. "The Impact of Minimum Wages on Job Training: An Empirical Exploration with Establishment Data." *Southern Economic Journal*, Vol. 70, No. 3, January, pp. 566–83.

Feldstein, Martin. 1973. "The Economics of the New Unemployment." *Public Interest*, Vol. 33, Fall, pp. 3–42.

Gunderson, Craig, and James P. Ziliak. 2004. "Poverty and Macroeconomic Performance across Space, Race, and Family Structure." *Demography*, Vol. 41, No. 1, February, pp. 61–86.

Hashimoto, Masanori. 1982. "Minimum Wage Effects on Training on the Job." *American Economic Review*, Vol. 72, No. 5, December, pp. 1070–87.

Hoffman, Saul D., and Laurence S. Seidman. 2003. *Helping Working Families: The Earned Income Tax Credit*, Kalamazoo, MI: W. E. Upjohn Institute.

Hoffman, Saul D., and Diane M. Trace. 2009. "NJ and PA Once Again: What Happened to Employment When the PA-NJ Minimum Wage Differentials Disappeared?" *Eastern Economic Journal*, Vol. 35, No. 1, Winter, pp. 115–28.

Katz, Lawrence F., and Alan B. Krueger. 1992. "The Effect of the Minimum Wage on the Fast-Food Industry." *Industrial and Labor Relations Review*, Vol. 46, No. 1, October, pp. 6–21.

Keil, Manfred, Donald Robertson, and James Symons. 2001. "Minimum Wages and Employment." CEP Discussion Paper No. 0497, Centre for Economic Performance, London School of Economics.

Kim, Taeil, and Lowell J. Taylor. 1995. "The Employment Effect in Retail Trade of California's 1988 Minimum Wage Increase." *Journal of Business & Economic Statistics*, Vol. 13, No. 2, April, pp. 175–82.

Lang, Kevin. 1987. "Pareto Improving Minimum Wage Laws." *Economic Inquiry*, Vol. 25, No. 1, January, pp. 145–58.

Manning, Alan. 2003. *Monopsony in Motion: Imperfect Competition in Labor Markets*, Princeton: Princeton University Press.

Neumark, David, and Olena Nizalova. 2007. "Minimum Wage Effects in the Longer Run." *Journal of Human Resources*, Vol. 42, No. 2, Spring, pp. 435–52.

Neumark, David, Mark Schweitzer, and William Wascher. 2005. "The Effects of Minimum Wages on the Distribution of Family Incomes: A Non-parametric Analysis." *Journal of Human Resources*, Vol. 40, No. 4, Fall, pp. 867–917.

Neumark, David, and William Wascher. 1992. "Employment Effects of Minimum and Subminimum Wages: Panel Data on State Minimum Wage Laws." *Industrial and Labor Relations Review*, Vol. 46, No. 1, October, pp. 55–81.

Neumark, David, and William Wascher. 1994. "Employment Effects of Minimum and Subminimum Wages: Reply to Card, Katz, and Krueger." *Industrial and Labor Relations Review*, Vol. 47, No. 3, April, pp. 497–512.

Neumark, David, and William Wascher. 1995. "Minimum-Wage Effects on School and Work Transitions of Teenagers." *American Economic Review*, Vol. 85, No. 2, May, pp. 244–49.

Neumark, David, and William Wascher. 1996. "The Effects of Minimum Wages on Teenage Employment and Enrollment: Evidence from Matched CPS Surveys." *Research in Labor Economics*, Vol. 15, pp. 25–63.

Neumark, David, and William Wascher. 2000. "Minimum Wages and Employment: A Case Study of the Fast-Food Industry in New Jersey and Pennsylvania: Comment." *American Economic Review*, Vol. 90, No. 5, December, pp. 1362–96.

Neumark, David, and William Wascher. 2001a. "Minimum Wages and Training Revisited." *Journal of Labor Economics*, Vol. 19, No. 3, July, pp. 563–95.

Neumark, David, and William Wascher. 2001b. "Using the EITC to Help Poor Families: New Evidence and a Comparison with the Minimum Wage." *National Tax Journal*, Vol. 54, No. 2, June, pp. 281–318.

Neumark, David, and William Wascher. 2007. "Minimum Wages and Employment." *Foundations and Trends in Microeconomics*, Vol. 3, Nos. 1–2, pp. 1–186.

Neumark, David, and William Wascher. 2008. *Minimum Wages*, Cambridge, MA: MIT Press.

Powers, Elizabeth T. 2009. "The Impact of Minimum-Wage Increases: Evidence from Fast-Food Establishments in Illinois and Indiana." *Journal of Labor Research*, Vol. 30, No. 4, December, pp. 365–94.

Singell, Larry D., and James R. Terborg. 2006. "Employment Effects of Two Northwest Minimum Wage Initiatives: Eating and Drinking and Hotel and Lodging." Unpublished paper, University of Oregon.

Stigler, George J. 1946. "The Economics of Minimum Wage Legislation." *American Economic Review*, Vol. 36, No. 3, June, pp. 358–65.

Thompson, Jeffrey P. 2009. "Using Local Labor Market Data to Re-Examine the Employment Effects of the Minimum Wage." *Industrial and Labor Relations Review*, Vol. 62, No. 3, April, pp. 343–66.

Wellington, Alison J. 1991. "Effects of the Minimum Wage on the Employment Status of Youths: An Update." *Journal of Human Resources*, Vol. 26, No. 1, Winter, pp. 27–46.

Wessels, Walter J. 1997. "Minimum Wages and Tipped Servers." *Economic Inquiry*, Vol. 35, No. 2, April, pp. 334–49.

Williams, Nicolas, and Jeffrey A. Mills, J. A. 2001. "The Minimum Wage and Teenage Employment: Evidence from Time Series." *Applied Economics*, Vol. 33, No. 3, February, pp. 285–300.

Wu, Ximing, Jeffrey M. Perloff, and Amos Golan. 2006. "Effects of Taxes and other Government Policies on Income Distribution and Welfare." Unpublished paper, Texas A&M University.

Chapter 19

Globalization and Earnings Inequality in the United States

Keith Gunnar Bentele and Lane Kenworthy

Globalization is interaction and integration across national borders. Our interest here is in economic globalization, as opposed to cultural, political, or other types. Economic globalization includes trade (goods or services produced in one country and sold in another), foreign direct investment (a company based in one nation setting up or buying a factory or office in another), and immigration (movement of people from one country to another).

Figure 19.1 shows globalization trends for the United States according to three key measures: imports as a share of GDP, outward foreign direct investment as a share of GDP, and foreign-born persons as a share of the population. We discuss these trends and their implications in the sections that follow.

On net, economic globalization is a good thing. It tends to lift the living standards of people in poorer countries, by increasing their earnings and incomes. And it improves living standards of people in rich countries, mainly by reducing the prices of goods and services

Figure 19.1

Trends in Imports, Outward Foreign Direct Investment, and Immigration in the United States.

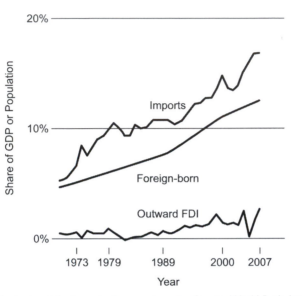

Years listed on the horizontal axis are business cycle peaks. *Sources:* World Bank, http://databank.worldbank.org; U.S. Census Bureau, http://www.census.gov/population/foreign.

they buy. Economic globalization also reduces the likelihood that nations will go to war against one another.

But the fact that globalization is good on the whole—on average—does not mean it is good for every person or household. In the world's rich countries, a particular concern is globalization's impact on low and middle earners. If an affluent nation such as the United States imports more of its cars, clothing, and other products, some Americans who produce these goods in U.S. factories may either lose their jobs or suffer stagnant or declining wages. The same is true if plants or offices move overseas, or if more immigrants enter the United States.

Globalization may thereby increase earnings inequality. And it may do so in an especially pernicious way. It is one thing if earnings are rising for everyone and inequality increases because those above the middle enjoy a faster rate of increase than those below. Arguably, it is much more worrisome if earnings in the bottom half do not even increase.

The latter is essentially what has happened in the United States since the early 1970s. Figure 19.2 shows trends in wages and salaries

Figure 19.2
Trends in Hourly Earnings at the 10th, 50th (median), and 95th Percentiles of the Distribution.

Years listed on the horizontal axis are business-cycle peaks. *Source*: Economic Policy Institute analysis of data from the U.S. Census Bureau, Current Population Survey, Outgoing rotations group, http://www.stateofworkingamerica.org.

("earnings") of employed persons, adjusted for inflation, at various points in the distribution. In 1973, a peak year in the business cycle, the median for hourly earnings was slightly less than $15 per hour (in 2009 dollars). In 2007, also a peak business-cycle year and therefore suitable for comparison, it had increased only to $15.50. Over those 34 years median earnings rose just 6 percent. That was true throughout the lower half of the earnings distribution. At the 10th percentile it rose from $7.70 per hour only to $8.06. For those at the high end of the distribution, by contrast, the rise in hourly earnings was a good bit healthier. At the 95th percentile, for instance, the increase over that period was about 33 percent.

This increase in earnings inequality is important not just for individuals but also for households. In theory, a rise in earnings inequality among employed individuals could have no effect on inequality of household incomes, because households with stagnant or declining earnings might have a second adult enter the labor force. The United States does now have more two-earner households than we used to, but that has done relatively little to blunt the impact of rising earnings inequality. Rising earnings inequality has been the principal cause of growing income inequality among American households (Burtless 1999; Mishel et al. 2009; OECD 2011).

Globalization is not the only contributor to the increase in earnings inequality in the United States. In fact, researchers have identified a wide array of causes, including the shift of employment from manu-facturing to services, technological change, stagnant educational attainment, union decline, heightened competition in many industries, changes in corporate governance, growing prevalence of winner-take-all labor markets, a shift toward pay for performance, and an erosion in the inflation-adjusted value of the minimum wage.

Some researchers conclude that economic globalization is a minor contributing factor to the rise in inequality. Studies yielding this con-clusion often use either a single measure of globalization or a fairly restricted set of measures. A researcher might, for instance, examine the impact of trade, leaving out capital mobility and immigration. Other researchers conclude that globalization has had a major impact on earnings inequality.

Globalization can have a direct effect on earnings inequality, along the lines suggested earlier. It also can increase inequality indirectly. For example, globalization might increase inequality by contributing to the weakening of labor unions. We look at both direct and indirect impacts. We then consider why globalization may have had a larger inequality-increasing effect in the United States than in other affluent nations. Finally, we briefly examine the impact of globalization on the earnings of those at the top of the distribution.

GLOBALIZATION'S DIRECT EFFECTS ON EARNINGS INEQUALITY

Trade

The United States' trade with other nations has increased substan-tially over the past four decades. As Figure 19.1 shows, imports rose from 5 percent of GDP in 1970 to 17 percent in 2007. If we add together imports and exports, they jumped from 10 percent of GDP to nearly 30 percent during this period.

For a rich country, an increase in international trade creates eco-nomic pressures that produce higher inequality in wages and salaries. This is expected by economic theory, and it has been documented widely by empirical studies (Bivens 2008a). There is little disagreement among researchers about whether trade increases inequality, but a great deal of disagreement over the magnitude of the increase.

Trade affects the labor market in complex and contradictory ways. Consider the position of firms that make products for export versus those that experience competition from products produced abroad. For export-oriented firms, access to international markets is a benefit. It is likely to lead to increased employment, profits, and wages. For firms whose products must compete with imports, on the other hand, international trade may reduce profits, wages, and employment. That is especially true when the imports originate from countries with substantially lower labor costs. In recent decades the share of U.S. imports coming from less developed nations has increased sharply. In 2006 Mexico's share of imports into the United States was 11 percent, nearly double the level of 1985. China's share in 2006 was 16 percent, more than an eightfold increase from 1985 (Cooper 2007).

Imports can have these impacts through two primary mechanisms: wage pressures and job displacement. First, the production of goods in countries with much lower labor costs can result in lower prices for products and put downward pressure on the wages of workers. These pressures materialize as domestic employers attempt to reduce production costs to remain competitive. Employers may engage in a wide array of practices with implications for wages and employment: labor costs can be reduced by eliminating benefits, resisting wage increases, undermining union strength, investing in labor saving technologies, or outsourcing production abroad. Second, as goods produced abroad are imported they may displace production that otherwise would have occurred domestically, and with it jobs.

It is possible that the countervailing costs and benefits of trade— positive impacts for exporters and negative impacts for import-competing industries—could balance out with little net effect on employment or earnings. However, since the 1970s the United States has been running an increasingly large trade deficit, meaning that the total value of U.S. imports exceeds the value of U.S. exports. As an illustration, take the trade relationship between United States and Mexico following the North American Free Trade Agreement (NAFTA) in 1994. NAFTA sharply reduced barriers to trade, primarily through the elimination of tariffs. It resulted in increases in U.S. exports to Mexico, but even larger increases in imports from Mexico into the United States. In 1993 the United States had a relatively small trade surplus with

Mexico of $1.6 billion. By 2010 the United States had a trade deficit with Mexico of $97.2 billion. According to one estimate, this displaced nearly 700,000 U.S. jobs between 1993 and 2010 (Scott 2011).

Job displacement may be temporary, as trade is likely to have offsetting positive impacts on employment in exporting industries, and trade deficits can have a simulative impact on the U.S. economy as capital flows from nations in a trade surplus relative to the U.S. return to the United States (Bivens 2008a). Trade therefore does not necessarily reduce employment. It may even increase it. Nevertheless, the different types of jobs that are displaced and created may increase earnings inequality. For example, if losses in highly compensated unionized manufacturing jobs are replaced with lower-wage jobs in retail or construction, total employment may be unaffected but earnings inequality will rise (Scott 2011).

Another way that trade can raise earnings inequality is by shifting the employment mix in favor of better-skilled workers. The United States exports a number of "advanced" goods such as aerospace or computer-related products. These industries tend to have high wages and employ better-educated workers. Industries that compete with imports, on the other hand, often are involved in the mass-production of consumer goods, products such as clothes. These industries have historically been more labor-intensive, have employed less-educated workers, and have had lower wages on average. Suppose the total volume of trade grows, both exports and imports. The rise in exports will tend to increase employer demand for high-skilled workers, while the rise in imports will tend to reduce employer demand for less-skilled workers. In its *2010 Career Guide to Industries*, the U.S. Bureau of Labor Statistics projects that employment in aerospace manufacturing will remain stable between 2010 and 2018, while employment in apparel will fall by about 50 percent. These trends will put upward pressure on wages for high-skilled workers and downward pressure on wages for low-skilled workers, increasing inequality.

Finally, it is worth emphasizing that the impact of trade on wages can spread to other industries. Less-educated workers who are displaced by imports may subsequently enter the market for low-end service jobs and thereby push down wages for other less-skilled workers. Put another way, "landscapers may not get displaced by imports, but their wages do indeed suffer from job competition with import-displaced apparel workers" (Bivens 2008b, 3).

Studies examining the relationship between trade and inequality in the 1980s and 1990s suggest that roughly 10 to 40 percent of the increase in earnings inequality can be attributed to trade. A recent effort to update these types of analyses found that trade is responsible for roughly 30 percent of the increase, between 1979 and 2005, in the difference between the wages of workers with and those without a college degree (Bivens 2008a). Further, given the geographically concentrated nature of employment in trade-sensitive industries, the experience of these impacts has been more pronounced in some areas of the country (Bentele 2009). A leading skeptic of the hypothesis that trade is a significant cause of rising earnings inequality, Paul Krugman, suggested in a recent review that "there has been a dramatic increase in manufactured imports from developing countries since the early 1990s. And it is probably true that this increase has been a force for greater inequality in the United States and other developed countries" (Krugman 2008, 134).

Capital Mobility

Technological advances and reduced trade barriers have dramatically expanded the volume of international investment. This includes both short-term investments, such as those into a nation's stock market or currency, and investments that tend to be longer term, such as the building or purchasing of factories and offices. We focus on the latter. Two important developments here are outsourcing and offshoring. Outsourcing involves a firm contracting the production of components, such as auto parts or microchips, to foreign companies and then importing them back into the United States. Offshoring refers to the complete relocation of production or service provision from the United States to another country.

Wages in many developing nations are much lower than in the United States, so the financial incentive for firms to move abroad can be quite strong. According to the U.S. Bureau of Economic Analysis, in 2008 the average hourly manufacturing wage in Mexico was only 16 percent of the average in the United States. In China, average manufacturing wages were approximately $1.30 an hour, or 4 *percent* of the U.S. average. Flows of investments from the United States to other countries, referred to as foreign direct investment outflows, have increased over the past couple of decades. In the late 1980s annual foreign direct investment outflows were $23 billion on average, less than 1 percent of GDP. By the mid-2000s outflows had risen to nearly 3 percent of GDP, totaling $393 billion in 2007.

A significant body of research has established that foreign direct investment outflows from the United States do not reduce employment domestically. While some jobs are lost, more jobs are created, resulting in an overall positive influence of investment outflows on employment (Agarwal 1997). However, very little research has examined the impact of investment outflows on earnings inequality. One study finds that foreign direct investment outflows from developed countries do increase inequality by reducing employment opportunities in lower-skill sectors (Jaumotte et al. 2008).

Investments from developed countries are generally concentrated in the low-end manufacturing and natural resource sectors in developing nations. This pattern of investment emerges not just as producers of labor-intensive goods, such as apparel, move or outsource overseas, but as companies of all types relocate the segments of production requiring the least skilled labor. Across a wide range of high-end products including computers, iPods, and semiconductors, multinational companies manufacture more sophisticated components in developed countries and locate more labor-intensive aspects, such as assembly, in developing countries (Krugman 2008). This can be considered a good thing: we export "bad" labor-intensive jobs and keep "good" skill-intensive jobs. Others argue that a union job with benefits may not be a "bad" job from the perspective of a less-educated American worker, even if the job is labor-intensive. In any event, this process will increase earnings inequality.

While much of the discussion of offshoring and outsourcing has focused on relocation of manufacturing employment, there is growing attention to offshoring of service work. The offshoring of less-skilled service work, such as the explosive growth of call center employment in India, is now so familiar as to be the setting for a sitcom—entitled, appropriately, *Outsourced*. In recent years there also has been increased offshoring of high-wage professional service work. In 2004 a minor scandal erupted as internal memos from IBM detailing the company's offshoring plans came to light. These plans involved shipping thousands of highly compensated programming jobs to China, India, and Brazil. IBM expected savings of $168 million annually as a result of the relocations. Between 2003 and 2009, IBM hired roughly 90,000 employees in India and has become India's second-largest employer (Herbst 2009).

Alan Blinder has argued that the potential for the offshoring of occupations is no longer an issue of skilled jobs versus less-skilled jobs, but rather an issue of whether or not it is possible to deliver the particular service with a high degree of quality electronically. The work of surgeons and child care workers cannot be offshored, but that of computer programmers and call center operators can. Blinder estimates that 22 to

29 percent of the jobs in the United States are potentially offshorable. Further, he finds no relationship between job skill and "offshorability" of occupations. In other words, potentially offshorable jobs are not confined to low-end or low-skilled occupations; some of the most offshorable jobs include computer programmers, IT researchers, actuaries, mathematicians, and statisticians (Blinder 2009). Of course, that these occupations can be offshored does not mean they will be. The potential impact on earnings inequality in the United States is unclear. If high- and low-skill jobs are equally represented among those offshored, there may little impact.

Immigration

Economic globalization includes cross-border movement not only of goods, services, factories, and offices but also of people. Like imports, exports, and foreign direct investment, immigration has increased substantially over the past few decades. As Figure 19.1 shows, the foreign-born share of the U.S. population was 5 percent in 1970. It then began a steady rise, reaching 12.5 percent in the late 2000s. This includes undocumented immigrants, though it likely undercounts them.

Immigration can increase earnings inequality in two main ways. First, it may increase the supply of less-skilled workers, putting downward pressure on wages in low-skill jobs (Borjas et al. 1992). Second, the immigrant population tends to have a more bifurcated education and skill distribution than do native-born Americans: many with low education and quite a few with high education, and not so many in the middle. To the extent these immigrants get employed in jobs that fit their skills, they will increase the shares of employees with low and high wages.

Recent empirical studies, however, tend to find that immigration has played a small role in rising earnings inequality in the United States, except in areas with the highest concentrations of migrants (Card and Shleifer 2009). This may be partly because the lower cost of immigrant labor increases the profits of firms that hire them, and they may then purchase more goods and/or services from other firms, who in turn can hire more native-born workers (Ottaviano and Peri 2008).

GLOBALIZATION'S INDIRECT EFFECTS ON EARNINGS INEQUALITY

We noted earlier that the increase in earnings inequality in the United States has many causes other than globalization. But globalization may affect some of these other causes, and in this way it may contribute indirectly to inequality's rise. We discuss two: the shift away from manufacturing to services (deindustrialization) and the decline in the share of American employees that are unionized (deunionization).

Deindustrialization

Manufacturing wages tend to be more compressed than wages in the service sector; the range between the lowest- and highest-paid manufacturing worker is smaller than the range in services. Consequently, as employment has shifted from manufacturing to services, wage inequality has increased.

Over 80 percent of international trade is comprised of manufactured goods. With the cost of production significantly lower abroad, it seems likely that trade and foreign domestic investment have contributed to the decline of manufacturing employment in the United States. Technological change also has played a major role. Manufacturing productivity has increased due to heightened use of labor-saving technologies including computers, automation, and robotics. The total volume of manufacturing output in the United States has thus more than doubled since the 1970s even while manufacturing employment has decreased. Technology may therefore be more important than globalization as a cause of manufacturing employment decline.

Yet globalization may contribute to technological change. The decision to outsource production overseas or to invest in labor-saving technologies are different options available to firms seeking reduced labor costs in the context of rising international competition. It has been found that increased competition raises R&D investment in British manufacturing firms and that stronger import competition is associated with higher R&D investment in U.S. high-technology industries (Blundell et al. 1999; Zietz and Fayissa 1994). Investments in technology are often explicitly cited as necessary to survive and remain competitive in the global marketplace. From this perspective the broad reductions in manufacturing employment, whether they be via technology, outsourcing, or closure, are a response to increased international competition and related efforts to reduce labor costs (Hytrek and Zentgraf 2008).

Deunionization

A second major change in the U.S. labor market with direct implications for inequality is the steady and substantial erosion of union membership. The share of the American workforce in unions has fallen from nearly 25 percent in 1973 to roughly 12 percent in 2010 (Hirsch and Macpherson 2011). Unions have both direct and indirect impacts on earnings inequality. In addition to raising the wages of their members, and in particular raising the wages of less-educated workers, unions may have broader political impacts that also impact wages and benefits. For example, U.S. states with stronger unions tend to have higher state minimum wages (Cox and Oaxaca 1982; Zavodny 1996).

The factors driving deunionization are various and include declining employment in the manufacturing sector, a shift of employment from union-friendly northeastern and midwestern states to the South and Southwest, deregulation of highly unionized industries, a probusiness shift in the political climate since the 1980s, and efforts by employers to reduce union strength and membership. Globalization has contributed in two ways (Cappelli et al. 1996; Piven and Cloward 1998; Shulman 2003; Freeman 2007; Baccaro 2011). First, heightened international competition has encouraged employers to reduce labor costs. Second, globalization has shifted the balance of power between workers and employers. The ability of employers to credibly threaten to relocate has weakened the bargaining position of established unions and that of workers attempting to form unions. A study conducted in the mid-1990s found that in just over half of all union certification elections, employers threatened to close the plant if the union was successful: "According to the organizers, specific unambiguous threats ranged from attaching shipping labels to equipment throughout the plant with a Mexican address, to posting maps of North America with an arrow pointing from the current plant site to Mexico, to a letter directly stating that the company will have to shut down if the union wins the election" (Bronfenbrenner 1997, 2).

U.S. EXCEPTIONALISM?

Earnings inequality has increased more in the United States than in other rich countries. But many of those other nations are equally or even more exposed to global pressures. If globalization is a key contributor to the rise of earnings inequality, why has that rise been larger in the United States than elsewhere?

The most likely reason has to do with pay-setting arrangements and the size of the public sector (Wallerstein 1999; Rueda and Pontusson 2000; Oskarsson 2005; Kenworthy 2007). Among the rich democratic nations, the United States has the smallest share of its workforce with pay determined by collective bargaining. It also has one of the smallest shares in public employment, where pay is less likely to be affected by global pressures. Globalization has exerted downward pressure on wages for the least skilled and perhaps upward pressure on wages for the best skilled, but these "market" pressures were muted to a much greater extent in countries with strong collective bargaining institutions and/or high public employment than in the United States. Additionally, it has been suggested that social norms regarding earnings inequality have changed more in the United States than elsewhere (Piketty and Saez 2006).

TOP EARNERS

We have focused on globalization's impact on earnings in the middle and lower parts of the distribution. However, this leaves out one of the most striking aspects of inequality's rise in the United States: the growing separation between the top 1 percent and the rest of the population.

Though important, this aspect of earnings inequality is less studied because data have become available only recently. The earnings data shown in Figure 19.1 are from surveys of households conducted each year by the Bureau of Labor Statistics. Those survey data are quite good for the bulk of the population, but not so good for those with very high earnings. For the latter, researchers must turn to tax records. Recent work by Anthony Atkinson, Thomas Piketty, and Emmanuel Saez (2011) and by the Congressional Budget Office (2010) provides data on the pretax incomes of households in the top 1 percent. These data indicate a sharp and steady rise in those incomes, both in an absolute sense and relative to the pretax incomes of households in the bottom 99 percent. The Congressional Budget Office calculates that the share of pretax income going to the top 1 percent of American households ballooned from 9 percent in 1979 to 19 percent in 2007.

Globalization has contributed to this development by dramatically expanding the size of markets for goods and services. U.S.-based firms are able to sell far more soda and software in a worldwide market of 6 billion people than in a domestic market of 300 million. This increases their revenues, facilitating rising pay for their chief executives and other top officers. Similarly, entertainers and athletes now perform on a worldwide stage, generating far greater revenues than a generation ago.

On the other hand, globalization is just one of a number of hypothesized causes of rising top income shares. Others include technological change, shifts in corporate governance practices, tax cuts, deregulation in finance, union decline, and the rise of winner-take-all markets (Frank and Cook 1995; Piketty and Saez 2006; Roine, Vlachos, and Waldenström 2009; Bakija et al. 2010; Hacker and Pierson 2010; Kenworthy 2010).

Here too we observe a degree of U.S. exceptionalism. The rise in inequality between the top and the rest has been greater in the United States than in other affluent nations (Atkinson et al. 2011). Inequality at the top has increased in some other countries, such as the United Kingdom and Canada, but to a lesser degree than in the United States. And in continental European nations such as Germany and France, there has been little or no rise. This suggests either that globalization has been a minor contributor or that domestic institutions and policies have moderated globalization's impact.

CONCLUSION

Globalization is a multifaceted phenomenon, the individual dimensions of which may have unique and complex effects on the U.S. labor market. Consequently, it is nearly impossible to quantify the aggregate contribution of globalization to rising earnings inequality. Some of the processes involved, such as the impact of threat effects on the bargaining position of labor, are largely immeasurable. Further, how can we distinguish the impact of global competition from that of other motives for adoption of labor-saving technology? Among the factors on which we do have more of an empirical handle, such as trade and immigration, immigration appears to be a minor player while trade appears to have made a significant contribution to rising earnings inequality. The impacts of outsourcing and offshoring are more difficult to estimate, but they are expected to have affected earnings by reducing demand for less educated workers, one of the major drivers of rising earnings inequality. Even if we were to take the most conservative estimate of the impact of trade or offshoring, we would still likely conclude that globalization has been a significant contributor to inequality's growth.

Given the increasing volume of trade, the magnitude of investment outflows from United States, and the growing prominence of low-wage countries as a source of imports, we can expect globalization to continue to exert upward pressure on inequality of earnings in the United States. Then again, the example of other nations, which have also experienced globalization without witnessing substantial increases in inequality, suggests that this not a foregone conclusion.

BIBLIOGRAPHY

Agarwal, J. P. 1997. "Effect of Foreign Direct Investment on Employment in Home Countries." *Transnational Corporations* 6: 1–28.

Atkinson, Anthony B., Thomas Piketty, and Emmanuel Saez. 2011. "Top Incomes in the Long Run of History." *Journal of Economic Literature* 49: 3–71.

Baccaro, Lucio 2011. "Labour, Globalization and Inequality: Are Trade Unions Still Redistributive?" *Research in the Sociology of Work* 22: 213–85.

Bakija, Jon, Adam Cole, and Bradley T. Heim. 2010. "Jobs and Income Growth of Top Earners and the Causes of Changing Income Inequality: Evidence from US Tax Return Data." Working Paper Williams College (November).

Bentele, Keith G. "Rising Earnings Inequality in the United States: Determinants, Divergent Paths, and State Experiences" (PhD diss., University of Arizona, 2009).

Bivens, Josh. 2008a. *Everybody Wins, Except for Most of Us: What Economics Teaches about Globalization*. Washington, DC: Economic Policy Institute.

Bivens, L. Josh. 2008b. "Trade, Jobs, and Wages: Are the Public's Worries About Globalization Justified?"Issue Brief #244, Economic Policy Institute. http://www.epi.org/publication/ib244/. May 6, 2008.

Blinder, Alan S. 2009. "How Many US Jobs Might Be Offshorable?" *World Economics* 10: 41–78.

Blundell, Richard, Rachel Griffiths, and John van Reenen. 1999. "Market Share, Market Value and Innovation in a Panel of British Manufacturing Firms." *Review of Economic Studies* 66 (3): 529–54.

Borjas, George, Richard Freeman, and Lawrence Katz. 1992. "On the Labor Market Impacts of Immigration and Trade." In *Immigration and the Work Force: Economic Consequences for the United States and Source Areas*, edited by George Borjas and Richard Freeman, 213–44.

Bronfenbrenner, Kate. 1997. "We'll close! Plant closings, plant-closing threats, union organizing and NAFTA." *Multinational Monitor*, 18(3), 8–14.

Burtless, Gary. 1999. "Effects of Growing Wage Disparities and Changing Family Composition on the U.S. Income Distribution." *European Economic Review* 43: 853–65.

Cappelli, Peter, Laurie J. Bassi, and Harry Charles Katz. 1996. *Change at Work*. New York: Oxford University Press.

Card, David and Andrei Shleifer. 2009. "Immigration and Inequality." *American Economic Review* 99: 1–21.

Congressional Budget Office. 2010. "Average Federal Tax Rates and Income, by Income Category, 1979–2007." www.cbo.gov/publications/collections/collections.cfm?collect=13.

Cooper, William H. 2007. *U.S. Trade with Developing Countries Trends, Prospects, and Policy Implications*. Washington, DC: Congressional Research Service, Library of Congress.

Cox, James C. and Ronald L. Oaxaca. 1982. "The Political Economy of Minimum Wage Legislation." *Economic Inquiry* 20 (4): 533–55.

Frank, Robert H. and Philip J. Cook. 1995. *The Winner-Take-All Society*. New York: Penguin.

Freeman, Richard B. 2007. *America Works: The Exceptional U.S. Labor Market*. New York: Russell Sage Foundation.

Hacker, Jacob and Paul Pierson. 2010. "Winner-Take-All Politics: Public Policy, Political Organization, and the Precipitous Rise in Top Incomes in the United States." *Politics and Society* 38: 152–204.

Herbst, Moira. 2009. "IBM Cuts Jobs as It Seeks Stimulus Money." *Bloomberg Businessweek*, March 25.

Hirsch, Barry, and David Macpherson. 2011. *Union Coverage and Data Book*. Washington, DC: BNA.

Hytrek, Gary J. and Kristine M. Zentgraf. *America Transformed*. New York: Oxford University Press.

Jaumotte, Florence, Subir Lall, and Chris Papageorgiou. 2008. "Rising Income Inequality: Technology, or Trade and Financial Globalization?" International Monetary Fund Working Paper No. WP/08/185

Kenworthy, Lane. 2007. "Inequality and Sociology." *American Behavioral Scientist* 50 (5): 584.

Kenworthy, Lane. 2010. "Business Political Capacity and the Top-Heavy Rise in Income Inequality: How Large an Impact?" *Politics & Society* 38 (2): 225–65.

Krugman, Paul R. 2008. "Trade and Wages, Reconsidered." *Brookings Papers on Economic Activity*, Spring: 103–54.

Mishel, Lawrence R, Jared Bernstein, and Heidi Shierholz. 2009. *The State of Working America: 2008–2009*. Ithaca, NY: ILR Press.

OECD. 2011. *The Causes of Growing Inequalities in OECD Countries*. Paris: OECD.

Oskarsson, Sven. 2005. "Divergent Trends and Different Causal Logics: The Importance of Bargaining Centralization When Explaining Earnings Inequality across Advanced Democratic Societies." *Politics and Society* 33: 359–85.

Ottaviano, I. P. and Giovanni Peri. 2008. "Immigration and National Wages: Clarifying the Theory and the Empirics." Working Paper 14188. National Bureau of Economic Research.

Piketty, Thomas and Emmanuel Saez. 2006. "The Evolution of Top Incomes: A Historical and International Perspective." *American Economic Review: Papers and Proceedings* 96: 200–205.

Piven, Frances F. and Richard A. Cloward. 1997. *The Breaking of the American Social Compact*. New York: New Press.

Roine, Jesper, Jonas Vlachos, and Daniel Waldenström. 2009. "The Long-Run Determinants of Inequality: What Can We Learn from Top Income Data?" *Journal of Public Economics* 93 (7–8): 974–88.

Rueda, David and Jonas Pontusson. 2000. "Wage Inequality and Varieties of Capitalism." *World Politics* 52: 350–83.

Scott, Robert E. 2011. "Heading South: US-Mexico Trade and Job Displacement after NAFTA." Economic Policy Institute Briefing Paper 308.

Shulman, Beth. 2003. *The Betrayal of Work: How Low-Wage Jobs Fail 30 Million Americans and Their Families.* New York: New Press.

Wallerstein, Michael. 1999. "Wage-Setting Institutions and Pay Inequality in Advanced Industrial Societies." *American Journal of Political Science* 43: 649–80.

Zavodny, Madeline. "The Minimum Wage: Maximum Controversy over a Minimal Effect?" (PhD diss. Massachusetts Institute of Technology, 2006).

Zietz, Joachim and Bichaka Fayissa. 1994. "The Impact of Exchange Rate Changes on Investment in Research and Development." *The Quarterly Review of Economics and Finance* 34: 195–211.

Chapter 20

Immigration and Inequality: Why Do High-Skilled Immigrants Fare Poorly in Canada?

Laura J. Templeton and Sylvia Fuller

INTRODUCTION

Originally proposed 40 years ago, and enacted in 1988, Canada's Multicultural Act ensures all Canadians "equal access and full partici-pation [in] social, political, and economic spheres."[1] Canada's official commitment to an egalitarian society is particularly relevant today given the volume of immigrants arriving each year and their cultural diversity. Canada admits more immigrants per capita than any other country (Reitz 2005). In 2010, approximately 280,000 newcomers were granted permanent residency.[2] No one source country dominated, with the top three (Philippines, India, and the People's Republic of China) together accounting for only one-third of newcomers.[3]

Commitment to multiculturalism is not simply Canadian govern-ment policy; it also enjoys wide public support, as does immigration generally. And while anti-immigrant sentiment has increased in recent years in much of Europe, Australia, and the United States, support for immigration has grown over time in Canada, stabilizing at comparatively high rates since the early 2000s (Wilkes and Corrigall-Brown 2011). By 2002, approximately three-quarters of Canadians approved of multiculturalism (Dasko 2003). Compared to earlier survey years, Canadians surveyed in 2002 were also more likely to believe that multicultural policies promote greater understanding between different groups, provide greater equality of opportunity, and foster greater national unity (Dasko 2003). A Pew Global attitudes survey from the same year found that the majority of Canadian respondents (77%) had a positive view of immigrants. By comparison, 49 percent of American respondents felt immigrants were good for the country while European citizens (with the exception of Bulgarians) were more likely to see immigrants as having a bad influence on the country (Pew Global 2002). Despite an already impressive intake, 29 percent of Canadians feel immigrant allotments should increase (Simon and Sikich 2007). Despite a per capita intake one-third of Canada's, only 10 percent of Americans support increased immigration.

Running in direct opposition to the collective values of Canadians, however, are persistent economic inequalities. Immigrants do not fare as well as native-born Canadians in the labor market. Moreover, although public approval of immigration has increased, the economic gap between immigrants and the native-born has widened for more recent cohorts (Frenette and Morissette 2005). This has occurred despite an increasing emphasis in Canadian immigration policy on selecting immigrants presumed most suited to the Canadian labor market (Green and Green 1999). Figure 20.1, which compares educational levels by nativity and immigrant cohort, reveals that Canadian immigrants are actually more likely to have a university degree than the native-born. Furthermore, each successive immigrant cohort is more highly educated than the last. Indeed, the percentage of immigrants with a university degree is roughly twice as high for the most recent cohort compared to those who arrived prior to 1991 (45% vs. 22% for men, and 39% vs. 18% for women).

Given Canada's apparently welcoming reception of newcomers and increasingly skilled immigrants, declining immigrant fortunes are troubling. Many countries are looking to skilled immigration as a means of maintaining the labor force against a backdrop of aging populations and declining fertility (UN Department of Economic and Social Affairs 2004). We therefore believe Canada's experience should

Figure 20.1
Percentage of Canadians with University Credentials by Gender and Immigrant Status, 2006.

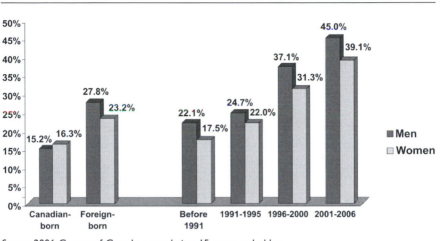

Source: 2006 Census of Canada—population 15 years and older.

be of international interest. In what follows, we document economic inequalities affecting immigrants to Canada and probe possible causes. We focus particular attention on the situation of the university educated, who are both the most sought-after immigrant group and, in Canada, the group suffering the greatest disadvantage compared to their native-born counterparts. The chapter proceeds in three sections. First, we discuss the economic performance of recent immigrants to Canada, highlighting disparities in earnings/income, unemployment, underemployment, and occupational status. Second, we review key explanations for the underperformance of highly skilled immigrants, focusing on both immigrant characteristics and aspects of the receiving context. The third section compares highly skilled immigrants in Canada to their counterparts in Australia and the United States, countries that share high levels of historical and contemporary immigration but employ different practices for selecting economic migrants. We conclude by discussing inequalities more broadly. We argue that greater economic inequalities for highly skilled immigrants in Canada relative to Australia and the United States in part reflect a more inclusive immigration system that allows a greater range of global citizens to call Canada home.

PART I: THE ECONOMIC WELFARE OF IMMIGRANTS IN CANADA

The falling economic position of highly skilled immigrants to Canada has been well documented since the mid-1990s (Bloom, Grenier, and Gunderson 1995). Evidence of this decline is apparent in three key dimensions tied to well-being: earnings, unemployment rates, and occupational status.

Earnings and Income

Even though Canada's immigrants are increasingly highly skilled (Akbari 1999; Galarneau and Morissette 2004, 2008; Li 2003; Reitz 2005), the earnings gap at time of entry between immigrant and Canadian-born workers is widening, while the speed at which this gap narrows is slowing (Aydemir and Skuterud 2005; Frenette and Morissette 2005; Hum and Simpson 2004; Picot and Sweetman 2005; Warman and Worswick 2004). Picot and Sweetman (2005) show that although immigrant cohorts from the 1970s initially earned less than native-born Canadians, they were able to catch up within 20 years. However, immigrants who entered Canada during the 1980s still earned approximately 15 percent less than native-born workers 16 to 20 years later. Frenette and Morissette (2005) calculate that initial earnings gaps have widened so greatly in recent decades that immigrant earnings will have to grow at unusually high rates for eventual convergence to occur. Because earnings are the largest component of income for most Canadians, overall income gaps have also increased between immigrants and the Canadian-born.

Canadian Census data reveal that the median individual income for university-educated immigrant men who arrived in Canada within the past 5 years dropped from $30,731 in 2000 to $25,334 in 2005 (Figure 20.2). During the same period the median income of university-educated Canadian-born men grew from $58,253 to $58,843. As shown in Figure 20.2, this corresponds to a roughly 10-percentage-point increase in the gap in median incomes between highly educated Canadian-born men and recently arrived immigrant men (from 47% to 57%). The income gap relative to the Canadian-born increased as well for immigrant men who had been in Canada for 5 to 10 years, although not to the same degree (from 35% to 38%).

The income gap between university-educated immigrant and Canadian-born women also worsened between 2000 and 2005.

Figure 20.2
Median Income Gap between University-Educated Immigrant and Canadian-Born Men.

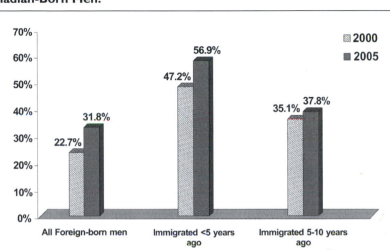

Source: 2006 Census of Canada—population 15 years and older.

Immigrant women who had been in Canada for less than 5 years earned $17,756 in 2000, but only $16,303 in 2005. Meanwhile, median incomes grew for university-educated Canadian-born women from $40,633 in 2000 to $41,875 in 2005, increasing the income gap from 56 percent to 61 percent (Figure 20.3). The income gap widened from 37 percent to 43 percent for immigrant women who had lived in Canada for 5 to 10 years.

Low earnings of recent immigrant cohorts contribute to dispro-portionate rates of chronic low income[4] for immigrant households (Picot, Hou, and Coulombe 2007). Approximately 19 percent of immigrant families who entered Canada between 1992 and 2000 experienced low income for at least four of the first five years (i.e., "chronic low income") in Canada. This is 2.5 times the rate (7.5%) of the Canadian-born who experienced poverty for at least four of the previous five years. Immigrants with higher levels of education are less likely to experience chronic poverty. However, the propor-tion of chronically poor immigrants with university credentials is growing. Over 40 percent of chronically poor immigrants in the 2000 cohort had a university degree, compared to 13 percent in the 1993 cohort (Picot et al. 2007).

Figure 20.3
Median Income Gap between University-Educated Immigrant and Canadian-Born Women.

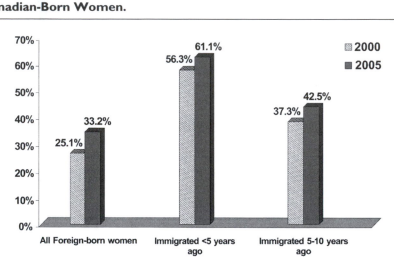

Source: 2006 Census of Canada—population 15 years and older.

Unemployment

In addition to lower earnings and income, recent immigrants also experience higher unemployment rates than native-born Canadians, even when comparisons are restricted to those with high levels of education (Galarneau and Morissette 2004; Hawthorne 2008). Immigrant/native-born unemployment rates among the university educated, however, are negligible for older immigrant cohorts, suggesting that immigrants may overcome this disadvantage as they become more settled. Figure 20.4 reveals that although there is a 6.8-percentage-point gap in the unemployment rate for the most recent cohort of university-educated immigrant men and their Canadian-born counterparts, this shrinks to less than a percent for those who have been in the country for 20 years. The same pattern holds for university-educated women. The 10.6-point gap in unemployment rates between the most recent arrivals and the Canadian-born shrinks to a mere 0.2 points for the most established immigrant women.

In contrast to patterns for income gaps, the unemployment gap between recent university-educated immigrants and the Canadian-born improved somewhat between 2001 and 2006. Foreign-born men holding

Figure 20.4
Point Differences in Unemployment Rates for University-Educated Immigrants and Their Canadian-Born Counterparts by Gender, 2006.

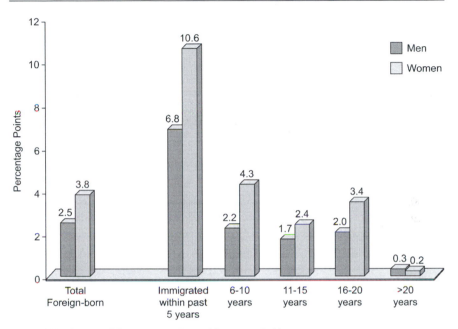

Source: 2006 Census of Canada—population 15 years and older.

university credentials who had immigrated to Canada within the five years leading up to the 2001 Canadian Census experienced unemployment rates 7.5 points higher than their Canadian-born counterparts (10.9% vs. 3.4%).[5] By 2006, both groups had lower unemployment rates, but the improvement was slightly more marked for immigrant men, reducing the gap by 0.7 percentage points (to 6.8%). A small improvement in the unemployment gap also occurred for recent immigrant women with university degrees, who saw the difference in their unemployment rate relative to native-born women drop from 10.8 to 10.6 percent.

Of course it is important to remember that unemployment rates reveal very little about the *quality* of a job. The convergence in unemployment rates between native and foreign-born Canadians may indicate nothing more than increasing financial pressures faced by newcomers, with highly skilled immigrants accepting whatever employment they can secure, no matter the quality.[6]

Underemployment and Occupational Status

Another important indicator of economic well-being for university-educated immigrants is underemployment[7] and occupational status. Jobs that are not commensurate with past education and experience not only contribute to low earnings, they also represent a potentially demoralizing rupture in career progress and identity. As with earnings, the immigrant/native-born underemployment gap continues to increase (Galarneau and Morissette 2008). While the underemployment rate for Canadian-born men improved from 12 percent to 10 percent between 2001 and 2006, it worsened from 25 percent to 28 percent for immigrant men. Women experienced the same trends. Canadian-born women saw their underemployment rate drop from 13 percent to 12 percent, while immigrant women experienced an increase from 38 percent to 40 percent. This means the underemployment gap for men increased from 13 percent to 18 percent in a span of five years while the female underemployment gap increased from 25 percent to 28 percent (Galarneau and Morissette 2008).

Growing underemployment rates mean university-educated immigrants are increasingly likely to work in low-skill, low-status jobs in Canada, a pattern that has been noted since the 1990s. In 1995, approximately a quarter of recent immigrants with university degrees worked in sales or services, twice the rate of the Canadian-born (Badets and Howatson-Leo 1999). More recently, data from the 2006 Canada Census show that of immigrants with degrees related to regulated occupations (i.e., engineering, health fields, teaching) who were not working in their intended field, 16 percent were working in clerical occupations, with another 10 percent working in sales and service. This compares to 6 percent and <1 percent of the Canadian-born (Zietsma 2010). As with income and unemployment, immigrant women with university credentials fare worse with respect to underemployment than their male counterparts. Approximately half of recent immigrant women with foreign engineering credentials secured engineering or managerial work in engineering in Canada in 2001 (Hawthorne 2008). By comparison, 62 percent of male recent immigrant engineers with foreign credentials found work in their field. Similar trends are apparent in medicine (62% success rate for foreign-trained immigrant women compared to 81% for immigrant men), accounting (54% vs. 68%), architecture (45% vs. 58%), and information technology (66% vs. 71%) (Hawthorne 2008).

PART II: WHY ARE CANADA'S HIGHLY SKILLED IMMIGRANTS FARING SO POORLY IN THE CANADIAN LABOR MARKET?

Explanations for the declining economic position of highly skilled immigrants relative to the native-born typically center on changes in the characteristics of recent immigrant cohorts, the characteristics of native-born workers, or more general labor market trends and macroeconomic conditions. Explanations centering on changes in the characteristics of recent immigrant cohorts generally consider the implications of changes in source countries and what this means in terms of the quality and transferability of immigrants' education, work experience, and language skills, as well as risk of discrimination. Explanations focusing on changes in the characteristics of Canadian-born workers highlight changes in the educational endowments of workers against whom immigrants are most likely to be competing for positions (i.e., young workers in urban centers). Finally, a focus on labor market and macroeconomic changes underscores the impact of broader changes that create greater difficulties for all new labor market entrants.

Immigrant Characteristics

Foreign Credentials and Work Experience

A critical component of the employment disadvantages faced by recent immigrants is the devaluation of their human capital by Canadian employers (Alboim, Finnie, and Meng 2005; Aydemir and Skuterud 2005; Buzdugan and Halli 2009; Ferrer and Riddell 2008; Green and Worswick 2004; Reitz 2001). Indeed, 37 percent of immigrants who encountered difficulties securing employment in Canada felt that their troubles were due to nonrecognition of their foreign work experience by Canadian employers (Schellenberg and Maheux 2007), and 35 percent cited difficulties with recognition of foreign educational credentials (Schellenberg and Maheux 2007). Recent calculations show that foreign work experience is worth approximately one-third of Canadian work experience (Ferrer and Riddell 2008). For each year of work experience, Canadian-born men receive an average 3.6 percent increase in earnings up until the 10-year mark. Immigrant men receive only a 1.0 percent increase in earnings for each year of foreign work experience. Canadian-born women receive similar (although slightly lower) returns to work experience as Canadian-born men while immigrant women's returns to foreign work experience are negligible (Ferrer and Riddell 2008). Similarly, the labor market value of foreign university credentials is less than one-third of Canadian credentials (Alboim et al. 2005).

Poor returns to foreign university degrees may stem from concern about educational quality. Sweetman (2004) finds that immigrant earnings in Canada are highly correlated with source country educational quality; immigrants from countries with low educational quality scores earn substantially less in the Canadian labor market than those coming from countries with higher educational quality scores. He suggests that part of the downturn in immigrant economic fortunes may be because more recent immigrants are more likely to originate from countries with low-quality education systems than older immigrant cohorts. It is notable however that the educational quality scores used by Sweetman reveal East Asian education (i.e., Hong Kong, China, Japan, Korea) to be of the highest quality (Hanushek and Kimko 2000). Yet immigrants with degrees from Asia receive an earnings penalty of roughly $5,400 despite controlling for a host of other immigrant characteristics such as field of study, official languages proficiency, work experience, and settlement city.[8]

Another possibility is that employers are less able to evaluate the worth of non-Canadian credentials. Lack of familiarity with educational systems in other countries adds a layer of uncertainty that can make hiring immigrants appear more risky (Esses, Dietz, and Bhardwaj 2006). Consistent with this interpretation, immigrants who received their degrees in countries perceived to be more economically and socially similar to Canada, notably the United States, Australia, and Europe, have higher employment rates than those who received their degrees in Asia, Latin America, and Africa (Adamuti-Trache and Sweet 2005; Gilmore and Le Petit 2008). Shifts in source countries away from the former and toward the latter may contribute to the worsening of immigrant fortunes.

Lack of information can also undermine the transferability of foreign experience. Work technologies and practices as well as informal norms governing workplace interactions can vary from place to place. This undermines the value of foreign work experience and can also create uncertainty about whether skills will transfer to the Canadian context even in cases where they are, in fact, applicable. The perception that source countries for newer immigrant cohorts are more culturally distant from Canada can contribute to this dynamic. For immigrants seeking to work in fields requiring technical or professional accreditation, official recognition of their credentials by professional bodies can ease information problems. However, in practice, gaining credential recognition is difficult in Canada and often involves costly and time-consuming retraining (Bauder 2003).

Language Proficiency

The majority of immigrants today come from countries where the main language is neither English nor French, Canada's official languages (Boyd and Cao 2009; Chiswick and Miller 2003). Perhaps not surprisingly, one-third of immigrants who report difficulties finding suitable employment in Canada identify language proficiency as a problem (Schellenberg and Maheux 2007). Language proficiency is essential for basic communication on the job. The consequences of lack of facility in English and French can be circumvented by finding a job where most communication is with others who speak the same language. However, Canadian immigrant men who work in ethnically homogeneous settings tend to earn less as a result, in part because ethnic niches are concentrated in relatively low-paying occupations and industries (Hou 2009). Jobs at the upper end of the occupational spectrum are particularly likely to require high levels of fluency, without which degrees may be of little use (Chiswick and Miller 2001, 2003). Lack of fluency can also hamper immigrants' ability to communicate effectively about their educational credentials or work experience. Indeed, the earnings penalty for poor language skills is more pronounced for those in the upper end of the earnings distribution compared to those working low-paying jobs (Boyd and Cao 2009). Lack of proficiency in English or French explains part of the devaluation of foreign education (although not the discounting of foreign experience) (Ferrer, Green, and Riddell 2006).

Labor Market Competition

Increasing educational attainment among Canadian-born workers also contributes to poor outcomes for recent immigrant cohorts (Reitz 2001). Although immigrant educational attainment has been increasing, university completion rates have risen even faster for the Canadian-born population. As a result, the education gap that favors immigrants has narrowed (Reitz 2007). This convergence is especially pronounced in large urban centers such as Toronto, Montreal, and Vancouver, where immigrants are most likely to settle (Grant and Sweetman 2004).

Deteriorating Prospects for All New Labor Market Entrants

The worsening position of subsequent cohorts of immigrants in Canada can also be explained in terms of deteriorating prospects for all new labor market entrants (Frenette and Morissette 2005; Green and Worswick 2004). Regardless of age or number of years of work experience in their home country, immigrants are new to the Canadian labor market. Green and Worswick (2004) argue that recent immigrants should not be compared to all native-born Canadians, but rather to recent Canadian-born university graduates as the latter group is also inexperienced in the Canadian labor market. Further, macroeconomic conditions should impact both groups in similar ways.

Almost half of the worsening entry position noted for recent immigrants relative to the Canadian-born can be explained when recent immigrants are compared to recent graduates and not the Canadian-born average (Green and Worswick 2004). Frenette and Morissette (2005) determine that when these two groups are compared the earnings gap for recent immigrant cohorts increases by only 5 percentage points, from 7 percent (1980 earnings year) to 12 percent (2000 earnings year). This compares to original estimates of a 23 percent decline in relative earnings for the same time period (Frenette and Morissette 2005).

Discrimination

Although each of the explanations reviewed thus far offers compelling reasons for the deteriorating economic situation of recent immigrants, none, whether considered alone or in combination, are able to fully account for the disadvantage faced by immigrants relative to the native-born or for the decline in economic prospects for more recent cohorts of Canadian immigrants (Reitz 2001). This "unexplained" effect is particularly noticeable for immigrants from racial minority groups (called "visible minorities" in Canada). This suggests that more recent immigrant cohorts, who are predominately nonwhite, may be encountering labor market discrimination (Galabuzi 2006; Reitz and Banerjee 2007).

University-educated nonwhite immigrants are at a significant disadvantage in the Canadian labor market compared to their white counterparts (Boyd and Yiu 2009; Buzdugan and Halli 2009). Buzdugan and Halli (2009) show that visible minority immigrants receive an additional earnings penalty of approximately $3,000 per year compared to white immigrants. High rates of unemployment and underemployment for nonwhite immigrants, particularly those from Eastern, Southern, and Southeastern Asia, have also been documented (Boyd and Schellenberg 2007; Galarneau and Morissette 2004, 2008; Hawthorne 2008). Unemployment rates are much lower for university-educated immigrants originating from South Africa (5.2%), the United States (5.3%), and Australia/New Zealand (6.3%) compared to immigrants from China (18.7%) or India (12.8%; Hawthorne 2008). Canadian Census data from 2001 also show immigrant men who originated from South Asia or Southeast Asia had underemployment rates of 37 percent and 48 percent compared to only 12 percent for those originating from North America, 10 percent for Northern/Western Europe immigrants, and 10 percent for those arriving from Oceania (Galarneau and Morissette 2004). These differences are net of between-group differences in work experience, language, education, field of study, and region of residence. Similarly women from South and Southeast Asia show particularly high underemployment rates compared to immigrant women from Oceania and Northern/Western Europe (South Asia: 55%, Southeast Asia: 61%, Oceania: 17%, and Northern/Western Europe: 18%; Galarneau and Morissette 2004). Boyd and Schellenberg (2007) find as well that foreign-trained physicians born in Southeastern Asia and Eastern Asia are least likely to secure work as a physician in Canada.

While institutional barriers act as a major deterrent to the acceptance of foreign human capital by employers within regulated fields (Hall and Sadouzai 2010), inequalities are also apparent within unregulated sectors (Templeton 2011). White information technology (IT) specialists with non-Western foreign credentials, such as those from Romania, Russia, and the Ukraine, regain their foothold in the Canadian labor market much more quickly than IT specialists from China, South Asia, or the Philippines, even when matched along other key labor market characteristics (Templeton 2011). Further, white immigrants with *non-Western* IT credentials are more likely to experience occupational status recovery following migration to Canada than nonwhite immigrants with *Western* IT credentials, a finding that supports claims that nonwhite immigrants face discrimination in the labor market (Templeton 2011).

Recent field studies demonstrate how disadvantage for highly skilled nonwhite immigrants can transpire. Using fictitious resumés, Dietz et al. (2009) asked undergraduate students to evaluate and rank different types of job applicants who varied with respect to place of birth, visible minority status, and whether or not foreign credentials had been recognized. While job seekers who had Canadian or recognized credentials were ranked similarly, a bias in favor of white immigrants appeared when students rated resumés where the job applicant had nonrecognized credentials. This suggests that the availability of apparently nonprejudicial justifications (i.e., the perceived inferior quality of non-Canadian education or experience) can facilitate behavioral manifestations of subtle prejudice, which may account for at least part of the devaluation of immigrant credentials and experience despite high levels of overt support for immigration in the population at large. Although this bias was demonstrated with university students, a recent field study shows that Canadian employers may also use cues from resumés to determine applicant suitability. Oreopoulos (2009) finds that not only did otherwise equivalent resumés with non-Canadian education and experience result in fewer calls for interviews with Canadian employers, but that callback rates also decreased when the only difference was a Chinese, Indian, or Pakistani (vs. a British) name.

PART III: CAN THE OUTCOMES OF SKILLED IMMIGRANTS IN AUSTRALIA AND THE UNITED STATES INFORM OUR UNDERSTANDING OF IMMIGRANT ECONOMIC INEQUALITIES IN CANADA?

The falling economic position of highly skilled immigrants relative to native-born workers does not appear to be universal. Immigrants in the United States and Australia have fared better in recent years than their Canadian counterparts (Bonikowska, Hou, and Picot 2011; Borjas and Friedberg 2009; Hawthorne 2008). In addition to earning higher salaries overall, university-educated immigrants who migrated to Australia at the turn of the 21st century were more likely than similar immigrants to Canada to find a professional or managerial job and to find employment consistent with their degree (Hawthorne 2008). American immigrants as a whole have also experienced an upswing in economic performance in recent years. Following 30 years of earnings deterioration, earnings comparisons between the native-born and immigrants who arrived in the United States between 1995 and 2000 were on par with foreign-born/native-born comparisons from 20 years earlier (Borjas and Friedberg 2009).

Although it is possible that the improvement in immigrant economic outcomes in Australia and the United States is due to a selection effect, with more competitive immigrants opting to immigrate to the United States (Bonikowska et al. 2011) or Australia, it is also possible that structural differences related to how each country selects economic migrants are at play.

Do Different Economic Immigrant Selection Practices Explain the More Favorable Economic Performance of American and Australian Immigrants?

Unlike economic immigrants who apply to Canada's skilled workers program, the United States does not use a points system.[9] Instead, the United States takes a demand-driven approach (Papademetriou, Somerville, and Tanaka 2008). After establishing a need to hire a foreign worker, an American employer can sponsor the migration of a skilled foreigner to fill a particular job via the H-1B visa program. During the 1990s, the burgeoning needs of the high-tech industry placed pressure on employers, resulting in sudden growth of the H-1B program (Zavodny 2003). While roughly 60,000 highly skilled workers migrated to the United States in 1989 via employer sponsorship, this had swelled to approximately 135,000 by 1999 (Lowell 2000). Almost 60 percent of those who entered the United States with an H-1B in 2001 worked computer-related jobs (Borjas and Friedberg 2009).

This rapid expansion of the H-1B category in the 1990s meant that a higher proportion of newcomers had jobs waiting for them when they arrived, bypassing a major hurdle facing other skilled migrants. Indeed, Borjas and Friedberg (2009) show that the influx of H-1B workers explains roughly 30 percent of the increase in the relative earnings of new immigrants in the 1990s. Unlike the American program, the Canadian points system does not insist that skilled immigrants prearrange employment. Even though arranged employment is listed as one of the six ways immigrants are assessed by officials, it is awarded fewer points (10) than maximums for level of education (25), proficiency in Canada's official languages (24), and work experience (21). It is not uncommon for Canadian-bound immigrants to arrive without any job leads, a circumstance that has detrimental effects for long-term economic well-being (Templeton 2011).

Similar to the Canadian context, Australian skilled immigrants also experienced poor labor market outcomes in the early 1990s (Hawthorne 2005). In response, the Australian Department of Immigration and Multicultural Affairs revised the skilled migration selection policy to address barriers stemming from credential recognition problems and poor language proficiency (Hawthorne 2005). Unlike the Canadian points system, which awards the same points to all university-degree holders regardless of where the credential is from, Australia's new points system, in effect since 1999, awards bonus points to international students who graduated from an Australian college or university (Papademetriou et al. 2008). This ensures that these migrants avoid barriers related to concerns about the quality of foreign credentials. The revised Australian points system also requires all skilled immigrants to pass a mandatory English-proficiency test (Hawthorne 2005). This too departs from the Canadian system. Although the Canadian system awards a large share of the total points possible for full fluency in Canada's official languages, it does not bar entry to those who do not meet a minimum standard of proficiency.

CONCLUSION

The poor economic position of highly skilled immigrants in the Canadian labor market has been well documented. However, the best approach to ameliorating this disadvantage is not always clear. The American and Australian experiences suggest that changing selection practices might improve the situation of highly educated immigrants. It is important to acknowledge however that inequalities manifest at various points in the migration process. The selection processes in Australia and the United States may improve postmigration economic inequalities, but at the cost of less equal opportunities for migration in the first place. For example, highly skilled foreigners interested in migrating to the United States under the H-1B program may be vulnerable to premigration racial stereotyping and discrimination by American employers (Somerville and Walsworth 2009). In the case of IT workers, risk-averse employers may focus their recruiting efforts on workers from India instead of considering highly skilled workers from other areas of the world as Indians have become symbolic of the successful foreign IT worker (Banerjee 2006; Zavodny 2003). This certainly seems to be the case given that half of all H-1B workers admitted into the United States in 2001 were from India (Borjas and Friedberg 2009). The favoring of Indian IT workers consequently restricts opportunities for high-tech workers from other areas of the world as employer sponsorship is a necessary requirement of the H-1B program.

Although Australian selection practices do seem to be beneficial to the economic welfare of newcomers, they can inadvertently strengthen the privilege already experienced by particular groups. By emphasizing the worth of Australian university credentials, Australian selection practices ultimately reward those who can afford to obtain an Australian university degree. Due to the substantial tuition[10] that foreign students must pay in Australia (Hawthorne 2010), this selection criterion can strengthen global economic inequalities, facilitating the movement of the wealthy. Further, due to its premigration screening for English proficiency, Australia's policies also inadvertently privilege immigrants from English-speaking countries, the majority of whom migrate from traditional source countries, such as the United Kingdom, Ireland, South Africa, and New Zealand (Hawthorne 2008). In this case, insistence upon minimum English-speaking capabilities may reinforce the dominance of English-speaking cultural groups in Australia. Canada's program on the other hand is more likely to recruit skilled immigrants from nontraditional source countries given the more lenient assessment of language proficiency.

Ultimately, officials within each of these host countries struggle to balance the economic needs of the nation with the successful economic integration of immigrants while attending to social justice concerns. Recently, Citizenship and Immigration Canada unveiled a new economic migration scheme, the Canadian Experience Class (CEC),[11] which may do just that. Borrowing elements from both the Australian and American models, the CEC program facilitates the permanent migration of international students upon completion of a Canadian program as well as temporary foreign workers who were recruited to Canada to fill specific jobs. By opening the CEC to temporary foreign workers, Canada facilitates the migration of workers who might not be able to afford a university education in Canada or elsewhere. Although it is too early to tell whether immigrants who enter under the CEC fare better than those who enter under the traditional points system, this new migration program may provide a useful way to balance the needs of a host country with those of newcomers.

NOTES

1. Retrieved June 4, 2011, from http://www.parl.gc.ca/Content/LOP/researchpublications/936-e.htm.

2. Retrieved October 17, 2011, from: http://www.cic.gc.ca/english/resources/statistics/facts2010/permanent/index.asp.

3. In 2010, 35 percent of Canada's newcomers originated from these three countries, with 13 percent coming from the Philippines, 11 percent from India, and 11 percent from the People's Republic of China. Retrieved October 17, 2011, from: http://www.cic.gc.ca/english/resources/statistics/facts2010/permanent/10.asp.

4. Defined by Picot, Hou, and Coulombe (2007) as families who have incomes "below 50% of median income of the total population, adjusted for family size" for "at least four of the first five years in Canada."

5. 2001 unemployment data retrieved June 4, 2011, from: http://www12.statcan.ca/english/census01/home/index.cfm.

6. Point-in-time comparisons of different immigrant cohorts that suggest improvement over time in income, unemployment, and other indicators can be overly optimistic insofar as immigrants who face the greatest barriers may opt to leave Canada. This is particularly likely in the case of unemployment—while persistent low income may be bearable in light of other perceived advantages of life in Canada (such as better opportunities for one's children), remaining in Canada may be less appealing for highly educated immigrants who face ongoing difficulty securing any employment at all.

7. Galarneau and Morissette (2004) define underemployment as a situation that arises when a person with university credentials works a job that requires at most a high school diploma.

8. When compared to immigrants who received their highest degree from the United States, the United Kingdom, Australia, or Western/Northern Europe (Buzdugan and Halli 2009).

9. Canada's points system assesses applicants along six selection criteria: education, language proficiency, work experience, age, arranged employment, and adaptability. Under the current system, it is possible for an applicant to receive a passing mark despite possessing minimal language proficiency and without prearranging work.

10. According to Hawthorne (2010), tuition fees for international students are much greater in the United States, the United Kingdom, and Australia when compared to fees in Canada. For example, international students enrolled in business/management in 2007 paid US$18,383 at the University of Sydney in Australia while students enrolled in a similar program at Laval University in Canada paid US$10,634.

11. Full details of the *Canadian Experience Class* can be obtained from: http://www.cic.gc.ca/english/immigrate/cec/index.asp.

BIBLIOGRAPHY

Adamuti-Trache, Maria and Robert Sweet. 2005. "Exploring the Relationship between Educational Credentials and the Earnings of Immigrants." *Canadian Studies in Population* 32(2): 177–201.

Akbari, Ather H. 1999. "Immigrant Quality in Canada: More Direct Evidence of Human Capital Content." *International Migration Review* 33(1): 156–75.

Alboim, Naomi, Ross Finnie and Ronald Meng. 2005. "The Discounting of Immigrants' Skills in Canada: Evidence and Policy Recommendations." *Institute for Research on Public Policy Choices*, 11(2): 1–26.

Aydemir, Abdurrahman and Mikal Skuterud. 2005. "Explaining the Deteriorating Entry Earnings of Canada's Immigrant Cohorts." *Canadian Journal of Economics* 38(2): 641–72.

Badets, Jane and Linda Howatson-Leo. 1999. "Recent Immigrants in the Workforce." *Canadian Social Trends* 52: 16–22.

Banerjee, Payal. 2006. "Indian Information Technology Workers in the United States: The H-1B Visa, Flexible Production, and the Racialization of Labor." *Critical Sociology* 32(2–3): 425–45.

Bauder, Harald. 2003. " 'Brain Abuse', or the Devaluation of Immigrant Labour in Canada." *Antipode* 35: 699–717.

Bloom, David. E., Gilles Grenier and Morley Gunderson. 1995. "The Changing Labour Market Position of Canadian Immigrants." *Canadian Journal of Economics* 28(4b): 987–1005.

Bonikowska, Aneta, Feng Hou and Garnett Picot. 2011. "A Canada-US Comparison of Labour Market Outcomes among Highly Educated Immigrants." *Canadian Public Policy* 37(1): 25–48.

Borjas, George and Rachel Friedberg. 2009. "Recent Trends in the Earnings of New Immigrants to the United States." *National Bureau of Economic Research Working Paper, No. W15406.*

Boyd, Monica and Xingshan Cao. 2009. "Immigrant Language Proficiency, Earnings, and Language Policies." *Canadian Studies in Population* 36(1–2): 63–86.

Boyd, Monica, and Grant Schellenberg. 2007. "Re-accreditation and Occupations of Immigrant Doctors and Engineers." *Canadian Social Trends* 84: 2–10.

Boyd, Monica and Jessica Yiu. 2009. "Immigrant Women and Earnings Inequality in Canada." In *Racialized Migrant Women in Canada*, edited by Vijay Agnew, 208–32. Toronto: University of Toronto Press.

Buzdugan, Raluca and Shiva Halli. 2009. "Labor Market Experiences of Canadian Immigrants with Focus on Foreign Education and Experience." *International Migration Review* 43(2): 366–86.

Chiswick, Barry R. and Paul W. Miller. 2001. "A Model of Destination-Language Acquisition: Application to Male Immigrants in Canada." *Demography* 38 (3): 391–409.

Chiswick, Barry R. and Paul W. Miller. 2003. "The Complementarity of Language and Other Human Capital: Immigrant Earnings in Canada." *Economics of Education Review* 22: 469–80.

Dasko, Donna. 2003. "Public Attitudes towards Multiculturalism and Bilingualism in Canada." Paper presented at the Canadian and French Perspectives on Diversity Conference, Gatineau, Quebec, October 16.

Dietz, Joerg, Victoria Esses, Chetan Joshi and Caroline Bennett-AbuAyyash. 2009. "The Evaluation of Immigrants' Credentials: The Roles of Accreditation, Immigrant Race, and Evaluator Biases." *Canadian Labour Market and Skills Researcher Network, No. 18.*

Esses, Victoria, Joerg Dietz and Arjun Bhardwaj. 2006. "The Role of Prejudice in the Discounting of Immigrant Skills." In *Cultural Psychology of Immigrants*, edited by Ramaswami Mahalingam, 113–30. Mahwah, NJ: Lawrence Erlbaum.

Ferrer, Ana, David Green and Craig Riddell. 2006. "The Effect of Literacy on Immigrant Earnings." *Journal of Human Resources* 41(2): 380–410.

Ferrer, Ana and Craig Riddell. 2008. "Education, Credentials and Immigrant Earnings." *Canadian Economics Association* 41(1): 186–216.

Frenette, Marc and René Morissette. 2005. "Will They Ever Converge? Earnings of Immigrant and Canadian-Born Workers over the Last Two Decades." *International Migration Review* 39(1): 228–58.

Galabuzi, Grace-Edward. 2006. *Canada's Economic Apartheid: The Social Exclusion of Racialized Groups in the New Century*. Toronto: Canadian Scholars' Press.

Galarneau, Diane, and René Morissette. 2004. "Immigrants: Settling for Less?" *Perspectives* 5(6): 5–16.

Galarneau, Diane, and René Morissette. 2008. "Immigrants' Education and Required Job Skills." *Perspectives* 5(6): 5–18.

Gilmore, Jason and Christel Le Petit. 2008. "The Canadian Immigrant Labour Market in 2007: Analysis by Region of Postsecondary Education." *Immigrant Labour Force Analysis Series*. Ottawa: Statistics Canada.

Grant, Hugh, and Arthur Sweetman. 2004. "Introduction to Economic and Urban Issues in Canadian Immigration Policy." *Canadian Journal of Urban Research* 13(1): 1–24.

Green, Alan and Green, David. 1999. "The Economic Goals of Canada's Immigration Policy: Past and Present." *Canadian Public Policy* 25(4): 425–51.

Green, David and Christopher Worswick. 2004. "Immigrant Earnings Profiles in the Presence of Human Capital Investment: Measuring Cohort and Macro Effects." *Institute for Fiscal Studies Working Paper, No. WP04/13*.

Hall, Peter V. and Tulin Sadouzai. 2010. "The Value of 'Experience' and the Labour Market Entry of New Immigrants to Canada." *Canadian Public Policy* 36(2): 181–98.

Hanushek, Eric and Dennis Kimko. 2000. "Schooling, Labor Force Quality, and the Growth of Nations." *American Economic Review* 90(5): 1184–1208.

Hawthorne, Lesleyanne. 2005. "Picking Winners: The Recent Transformation of Australia's Skilled Migration Policy." *International Migration Review* 39(2): 663–96.

Hawthorne, Lesleyanne. 2008. "The Impact of Economic Selection Policy on Labour Market Outcomes for Degree-Qualified Migrants in Canada and Australia." *Institute for Research on Public Policy* 14(5): 2–50.

Hawthorne, Lesleyanne. 2010. "Demography, Migration and Demand for International Students." In *Globalisation and Tertiary Education in the Asia-Pacific: The Changing Nature of a Dynamic Market*, edited by Christopher Findlay and William Tierney, 93–119. River Edge, NJ: World Scientific Publishing Company.

Hou, Feng. 2009. "Immigrants Working with Co-ethnics: Who Are They and How Do They Fare?" *International Migration* 47(2): 69–100.

Hum, Derek and Wayne Simpson. 2004. "Economic Integration of Immigrants to Canada: A Short Survey." *Canadian Journal of Urban Research* 13(1): 46–61.

Li, Peter S. 2003. *Destination Canada*. Don Mills, ON: Oxford University Press.

Lowell, B. Lindsay. 2000. "H-1B Temporary Workers: Estimating the Population." *The Center for Comparative Immigration Studies Working Paper, No. 12.*

Oreopoulos, Philip. 2009. "Why Do Skilled Immigrants Struggle in the Labor Market? A Field Experiment with Six Thousand Résumés." *Metropolis British Columbia Working Paper Series, No. 09-03*: 50 pages.

Papademetriou Demetrios G., Will Somerville and Hiroyuki Tanaka. 2008. *Hybrid Immigrant-Selection Systems: The Next Generation of Economic Migration Schemes*. Washington, DC: Migration Policy Institute.

Pew Global. 2002. "What the World Thinks in 2002." Retrieved August 20, 2011, from: http://pewglobal.org/files/2011/04/2002-Report-Final-Updated.pdf.

Picot, Garnett, Feng Hou, and Simon Coulombe. 2007. "Chronic Low Income and Low-Income Dynamics among Recent Immigrants." *Analytical Studies Branch Research Paper Series, No. 294*. Ottawa: Statistics Canada.

Picot, Garnett, and Arthur Sweetman. 2005. "The Deteriorating Economic Welfare of Immigrants and Possible Causes: Update 2005." *Analytical Studies Branch Research Paper Series, No. 262*. Ottawa: Statistics Canada.

Reitz, Jeffrey G. 2001. "Immigrant Success in the Knowledge Economy: Institutional Change and the Immigrant Experience in Canada, 1970–1995." *Journal of Social Issues* 57(3): 579–613.

Reitz, Jeffrey G. 2005. "Tapping Immigrants' Skills: New Directions for Canadian Immigration Policy in the Knowledge Economy." *Choices* 11(1): 3–18.

Reitz, Jeffrey G. 2007. "Immigrant Employment Success in Canada, Part 1: Individual and Contextual Causes." *Journal of International Migration and Integration* 8(1): 11–36.

Reitz, Jeffrey G., and Rupa Banerjee. 2007. "Racial Inequality, Social Cohesion and Policy Issues in Canada." In *Belonging? Diversity, Recognition and Shared Citizenship in Canada*, edited by Thomas Courchene, Keith Banting, and Wanda Wuttunee, 1–56. Montréal: Institute for Research on Public Policy.

Schellenberg, Grant, and Hélène Maheux. 2007. "Immigrants' Perspectives on Their First Four Years in Canada: Highlights from Three Waves of the Longitudinal Survey of Immigrants to Canada." *Canadian Social Trends*: 2–34.

Simon, Rita J., and Keri W. Sikich. 2007. "Public Attitudes toward Immigrants and Immigration Policies across Seven Nations." *International Migration Review* 41(4): 956–62.

Somerville, Kara and Scott Walsworth. 2009. "Vulnerabilities of Highly Skilled Immigrants in Canada and the United States." *American Review of Canadian Studies* 39(2): 147–61.

Sweetman, Arthur. 2004. "Immigrant Source Country Educational Quality and Canadian Labour Market Outcomes." *Analytical Studies Branch Research Papers Series, No. 234*. Ottawa: Statistics Canada.

Templeton, Laura. 2011. "When Skills Don't Matter: Occupational Status Recovery Inequalities within Canada's Highly Skilled Immigrant Population" (Doctoral dissertation, University of Alberta).

United Nations, Department of Economic and Social Affairs (2004). World Economic and Social Survey 2004: International Migration (United Nations, ST/ESA/291/Add.1).

Warman, Casey and Christopher Worswick. 2004. "Immigrant Earnings Performance in Canadian Cities: 1981 through 2001." *Canadian Journal of Urban Research* 13(1): 62–84.

Wilkes, Rima and Catherine Corrigall-Brown. 2011. "Explaining Time Trends in Public Opinion: Attitudes towards Immigration and Immigrants." *International Journal of Comparative Sociology* 52(1–2): 79–99.

Zavodny, Madeline. 2003. "The H-1B program and Its Effects on Information Technology Workers." *Federal Reserve Bank of Atlanta, Economic Review.*

Zietsma, Danielle. 2010. "Immigrants Working in Regulated Occupations." *Perspectives*: 13–28.

Chapter 21

Educational Inequality and Children: The Preschool and Early School Years

David T. Burkam

Americans simultaneously believe that schools are places where social inequalities should be equalized, where the advantages or disadvantages that children experience in their homes and families should not determine what happens to them in school, and that school is a place where children should have equal chances to make the most of their potential. There is widespread faith among Americans in the value of education for social betterment for everyone, for both individuals and the nation. Among the many institutions in U.S. society, schooling is seen by most Americans as the embodiment of meritocracy. They believe—or at least hope—that children's experiences in our nation's elementary and secondary schools allow them to succeed without regard to their family circumstances, their race or ethnicity, or their gender. Such beliefs are hardly new. At the beginning of the

Portions of this chapter were adapted from David T. Burkam and Valerie E. Lee, "Inequality at the starting gate: Social background differences in achievement as children begin school." EPI Book, September 2002. Available online at http://www.epi.org/publication/books _starting_gate/

20th century, it was common to think of our public schools as "the best friend of the children of the poor" (Colgrove 1911, 80).

THE CRITICAL YEARS

Children neither begin nor end their education on an equal footing, and their early experiences in school represent an "especially critical but generally neglected period in research on child development" (Alexander and Entwisle 1988, 1). Although many children have informal educational experiences early in their lives—in preschool, Head Start, or child care—kindergarten is the point where virtually all children begin their formal education. Most children enroll in kindergarten when they are five years old, yet their cognitive status when they begin kindergarten varies enormously (Alexander and Entwisle 1988; Comer 1988; Duncan et al. 1998; Entwisle, Alexander, and Olsen 1997; Lee and Burkam 2002; National Center for Education Statistics 2000; Ramey and Campbell 1991; Zill 1999).

Third-grade achievement scores are already strong predictors of future academic success—including high school graduation and college enrollment—suggesting that on average schools may do little to ameliorate preexisting social inequalities (Annie E. Casey Foundation 2010; Lesnick et al. 2010). The prospects for postsecondary education, a well-paying job, and the good life may already be shrinking for many children, only four years after starting school and before most have reached their 10th birthday.

INEQUALITY IN THE EARLY YEARS

Among scholars who investigate early schooling, there is considerable and long-standing debate about whether social background differences in academic performance are a result of "cultural deprivation" (also called "social deprivation") or "educational deprivation" (Natriello, McDill, and Pallas 1990). Current sociological language includes descriptors such as "risk" and "educational disadvantage," factors that may inhibit individuals from fulfilling their potential (Fantini and Weinstein 1968). These factors include race and ethnicity, poverty, single-parent family structure, poorly educated mothers, and limited English proficiency (Natriello, McDill, and Pallas 1990).

Research using data from the National Assessment for Educational Progress has documented substantial differences by race for elementary school children (e.g., Applebee, Langer, and Mullis 1988), and at least one study documents substantial cognitive differences between black and white children at as early as three and four years old (Jencks and Phillips 1998). Natriello, McDill, and Pallas (1990) estimate that about 40 percent of school-age children are "at risk." Although large numbers of children have trouble learning to read, such difficulties are much more likely to occur among poor children, nonwhite children, and non-native speakers of English (Snow, Burns, and Griffin 1998).

A distressing pattern, known as the *Matthew effect*, emerges from the work of some social scientists who study the influence of prior achievement on children's subsequent learning. The name derives from a biblical proclamation in Matthew 13:12: "To all those who have, more will be given, and they will have an abundance; but from those who have nothing even what they have will be taken away" (Walberg and Tsai 1983). The Matthew effect has been called a "rich get richer" framework. Many decades ago, Merton (1968) applied the phenomenon to scientific productivity; already-prestigious scientists receive more recognition than their lesser-known rivals for similar scientific innovations.

The Matthew effect in education leads to ever-widening performance gaps. Children who enter school at higher performance levels acquire new skills faster than children at lower levels. Children with richer vocabularies read more, learn more words, and as a consequence read even better. Poor readers read slowly and without enjoyment, and so tend to read less frequently and advance more slowly (Stanovich 1986). What is it about the structure and content of the early grades that inhibits learning rates for initially low-achieving children? What is it about schools that enroll more-able children that leads to increased learning? Could it be that the way instruction is typically structured in the early grades works best for children who come in with stronger reading and mathematics skills? Of course, one likely factor is the simple fact that children who already know their ABCs are able to move on to new material sooner. Some scholars suggest that the Matthew effect helps to explain why performance disparities widen over time and why such disparities may be so difficult to close. In the race to the top, no matter how fast the trailing children run, the leading children are always running faster.

INEQUALITY AT THE STARTING GATE

There is substantial social inequality in the cognitive performance of U.S. kindergarten children as they begin their formal schooling. Using data from the current and nationally representative data from the

U.S. Department of Education's *Early Childhood Longitudinal Study–Kindergarten Cohort* (ECLS-K), Lee and Burkam (2002) report substantial differences in young children's achievement scores in literacy and mathematics by race, ethnicity, and socioeconomic status (SES) as they begin kindergarten. Moreover, family conditions (e.g., single- or dual-parent households, number of books in the home) and prior child care experiences are also related to race, ethnicity, and SES. The impact of these race and social class differences is reinforced by the strong relationship between race and SES. The parents of children who are members of certain minority groups—particularly blacks and Hispanics—occupy the lowest rungs on the income and education ladders in the United States.

When differences in SES, family, and home conditions are taken into account, a substantial proportion of the observed test-score differences between black, Hispanic, and white children is "explained away." In other words, much of these group differences are easily explainable by the larger economic, social, and cultural setting in which these children spend the first years of their lives. Accounting for SES explains about half of the race gap in entering achievement, and activities outside the home also explain an additional large proportion. Although the influence of SES is ameliorated when other family factors are accounted for, the differentiation in achievement by SES is substantial even when a wide array of family demographics and behaviors were included.

Although researchers may use statistical methodology to "explain away" the links between children's race, ethnicity, and social class and their achievement scores, this approach simply reveals that race and class are associated with other phenomena that are related to achievement. Both race and class alone are incomplete in describing social disadvantage in cognitive competence. Such statistical entities are not how children present themselves to schools. The multiple disadvantages of minority status, low income, low parental education, perhaps single-parent status, and a lack of educational resources in the home are the realities that their kindergarten teachers and schools must confront. Exactly how teachers and schools respond to these incoming disparities determines the education trajectories of all children.

INEQUALITY BETWEEN SCHOOLS

The quality of the schools these children attend is as disparate as the skill levels of the enrollees, but the link between children's social background and school quality is often assumed rather than subjected to empirical scrutiny. Typically, research that considers these links describes them in very general terms. Natriello, McDill, and Pallas (1990) conclude that U.S. children from poor families usually receive their education in the nation's worst schools. Several assumptions underlie the vast amount of research on child development and schooling experiences of poor children. Low-income children are often misclassified as low-ability, because so many of them perform poorly on cognitive tests administered early in kindergarten. The link between background and school quality means that disadvantages derived from the lack of home resources to stimulate cognitive growth are reinforced frequently by a lack of school resources (both financial and human). The low resource base of these schools makes it difficult for them to compensate for poor children's weak preparation. Like Natriello, McDill, and Pallas (1990), Edmonds (1986) claims that disadvantaged children do not perform well in school, not due to innate deficiencies but to inadequate school quality. The Matthew effect seems to operate partially through the reality of which children attend which schools.

Although race/ethnicity and socioeconomic status (particularly defined by poverty or economic need) are not equally strongly associated with broad measures of school quality, the patterns of association are themselves strikingly consistent (Lee and Burkam 2002). Black, Hispanic, and lower-SES children begin school at kindergarten in systematically lower-quality elementary schools than their more advantaged and white counterparts. Whether defined by less favorable social contexts, larger kindergarten classes, less outreach to smooth the transition to first grade, less well prepared and experienced teachers, less positive attitudes among teachers, fewer school resources, or poor neighborhood and school conditions, the least advantaged U.S. children begin their formal schooling in consistently lower-quality schools. The consistency of these findings, across aspects of school quality that are themselves very different from one another, is both striking and troubling. In addition, there is a strong association between the type of communities where schools are located (large or medium city, suburbs, small town, or rural area) and the quality of their public schools. The lowest-quality schools are in the United States' large cities; the highest-quality schools are located in the suburbs, where our most affluent citizens reside. Those findings translate into a sobering conclusion: the children who need the best schooling actually start their education in the worst of our nation's public schools.

There is, however, some difference of opinion about the importance of school factors in determining children's achievement. Although the Coleman Report led social scientists for several decades to conclude that school factors matter less to student achievement than home factors (Coleman et al. 1966), researchers more recently have shown that differences in school structure and organization lead to significant differences in young children's achievement (Duncan, Brooks-Gunn, and Klebanov 1994; Elliott 1998). There is a strong research strand demonstrating school effects in the last few decades, although most of this research has focused on high schools. Coleman and his colleagues (1966; Coleman 1987) cautioned that schools prove more effective for children from strong family backgrounds than for children from weak ones. If families can offer only limited resources to their children, they might hope the school could compensate for their disadvantages. However, weak resource bases of schools attended by low-income children do not allow for such compensations.

This raises a perennial question associated with social policy: If more resources (defined here quite broadly) went to schools serving disadvantaged children, would learning gaps shrink? If the children who need high-quality schooling the most actually attended the United States' highest-quality schools, would race- and class-based learning deficits disappear? Definitive causal claims are always open to debate, but the empirical trends suggest that school resources do make a difference. In the face of such evidence, surely we could reevaluate "what goes where" in light of "who goes where."

ADDRESSING INEQUALITY IN KINDERGARTEN

When young children in the United States should begin their formal schooling, what the nature of that schooling should be, and how long the kindergarten school day should last have all been debated for almost two centuries. Although the availability of publicly funded preschool education (including Head Start) in this country is far from universal, and is typically restricted to low-income children, virtually all U.S. children now experience kindergarten (National Center for Education Statistics 2000). Despite its almost universal availability, the nature and length of the optimal kindergarten experience is widely debated among educators, early childhood specialists, parents, and researchers (Balaban 1990; Graue 1999; Karweit 1988, 1992; Spodek 1986; Vecchiotti 2001). At its inception in the mid-19th century, kindergarten was viewed as a nurturing, protected place where young children would spend time developing all dimensions of the self before their introduction to the formal academic rigors of the educational system (Shapiro 1983). Reinforcing and perpetuating the idea of development through play were the ideas of such early 20th-century developmentalists as G. Stanley Hall and Arnold Gessell (Chung and Walsh 2000). Early formal academic instruction was then viewed as detrimental to the development of young children. Dominating the educational landscape at that time was the view that education was a process of *development* rather than a process of *instruction* (Bryant and Clifford 1992; Meisels and Shonkoff 2000). Since the 1960s, however, experts have called for more than "self-directed play." In the early childhood field, the expression "early intervention" typically refers to introductory activities that focus on both play and academics. Pressure has mounted among policy makers, however, to increase the cognitive demands made on kindergarten students (Gullo 1990; Shepard and Smith 1988; Walsh 1989).

Several demographic and sociocultural factors explain the growing implementation of full-day kindergarten over half-day kindergarten. First, the number of working mothers with children under six years old is growing; over 60 percent of these mothers are now in the workforce (Children's Defense Fund 1996). To serve the child care and scheduling needs of these parents, many schools offer full-day kindergarten programs (although kindergarten must be supplemented with other child care arrangements for mothers who work full-time). Second, for growing numbers of children, kindergarten is rarely the first school experience. Rather, it fits into a continuum that routinely begins with day care and/or a prekindergarten or preschool experience and moves through elementary school (Olsen and Zigler 1989). Since the mid-1970s, more and more children under five have attended preschool programs: private and public preschools, Head Start, and child care. Proponents of full-day kindergarten believe that children, as a result of their various child care and preschool experiences, are ready for more demanding and cognitively oriented educational programs (Gullo 1990; Helmich 1985; Herman 1984; Humphrey 1980; Naron 1981). Third, recent scientific, technological, and economic developments have thrust into the forefront of social discourse the critical importance of academic success, especially literacy and numeracy skills. Public and political forces collectively impose enormous pressures on schools to focus on children's academic achievement, and this focus begins earlier and earlier.

Full-day kindergarten advocates suggest that a longer school day provides educational support that ensures a productive beginning school experience and increases the chances of future school success, particularly for poor children (Evansville-Vanderburgh School Corporation 1988; Karweit 1989; Ohio State Legislative Office of Education Oversight 1997; Weast 2001). The growing diversity among today's kindergarten children in terms of their racial, ethnic, cultural, social, economic, and linguistic backgrounds challenges educators to serve children well in increasingly complex classrooms. Full-day advocates suggest several advantages for the longer kindergarten day: (1) it allows teachers more opportunity to assess children's educational needs and individualize instruction; (2) it makes small-group learning experiences more feasible; (3) it engages children in a broader range of learning experiences; (4) it provides opportunities for in-depth exploration of curriculum; (5) it provides opportunities for closer teacher-parent relationships; and (6) it benefits working parents who may need a longer school day.

However, not all educators, researchers, and parents favor full-day kindergarten. Detractors argue that children who attend full-day kindergarten are at risk of stress and fatigue due to the long day. However, research reveals that children attending full-day kindergarten demonstrate less frustration than children in half-day programs and do not show evidence of fatigue (Elicker and Mathur 1997; Snyder and Hoffman 2001). Others argue that full-day kindergarten increases the chance that children will be expected to achieve and perform beyond their developmental capabilities.

Using national data from the Early Childhood Longitudinal Study–Kindergarten Cohort, Lee, Burkam, and their colleagues (2006) report that full-day programs in public schools are more likely to enroll less advantaged children (children from families of lower SES and disadvantaged minority status). Moreover, full-day programs are more commonly found in public schools located in large cities, which enroll less affluent and more minority children. A logical explanation for these trends focuses on public efforts to induce social equity. Despite the higher cost of operating full-day kindergarten programs, they may be implemented to achieve a compensatory aim. Schools with disadvantaged populations may be able to offer such programs because their Title I funds could cover the added costs.

The relative impact of full-day and half-day kindergarten programs has been subjected to considerable empirical scrutiny, with the majority of studies conducted in the 1980s and again in the 2000s. Studies from the 1990s reveal that the topic continues to be an important focus of early childhood education. Many of the more recent studies include a focus on children's social and behavioral outcomes as well as teachers' and parents' perceptions of full-day kindergarten. In general, research findings favor full-day (or extended-day) kindergarten over half-day programs for academic performance (Alber-Kelsay 1998; Lee et al. 2006; Cryan et al. 1992; Harman 1982; Humphrey 1980; Koopermans 1991). Furthermore, some of this research suggests that full-day kindergarten is especially effective for socially and educationally disadvantaged children (Holmes and McConnell 1990; Eliker and Mathur 1997). Some studies document long-term benefits from full-day kindergarten (Humphrey 1983; Weiss and Offenberg 2002), whereas others report no long-term positive effects. No study demonstrates academic advantages for children in half-day kindergarten.

Cryan et al. (1992) concluded that teachers rated full-day children higher than half-day children on dimensions of classroom behavior. Similarly, children who attend full-day kindergarten were found to engage in more child-to-child interactions (Hough and Bryde 1996), experience greater improvement in social skills (da Costa and Bell 2000; Eliker and Mathur 1997), and have better self-concepts (Anderson 1983; Humphrey 1983) than children who attend half-day kindergarten. Several studies demonstrate positive parent and teacher attitudes toward full-day kindergarten (Anderson 1985; Graja 1984; Eliker and Mathur 1997; Evansville Vanderburgh School Corporation 1988; Humphrey 1983; Hough and Bryde 1996; Johnson 1993; Terens 1984).

INEQUALITY BEYOND THE STARTING GATE

Despite widespread faith in the role of schooling to address or ameliorate these social inequalities, there is substantial evidence that our nation's schools sometimes play a major role in magnifying such inequalities. Virtually all researchers agree that social background factors are associated with school success. Moreover, there is general agreement that social stratification in educational outcomes increases as children move through school (Entwisle, Alexander, and Olsen 1997; Phillips, Crouse, and Ralph 1998). Teachers' blatant preferential treatment of children by social class was documented in such seminal works as Hollingshead's Elmtown study (Hollingshead 1949/1975) and Ray Rist's exploration of a single group of children as they moved from kindergarten through second grade (Rist 1970). Hollingshead offered rich details on the lives of mostly white adolescents in a typical midwestern town in the 1940s; Rist documented the emerging social caste system within a group of all-black children in an urban ghetto school in the 1960s. Both researchers unveiled the consistent teacher biases against lower-class students and the negative impact of that treatment.

Such blatant preferential treatment is probably less common than the school structures that accomplish many of the same results. Social inequalities in school achievement increase as children advance through school mainly because of differentiation in these educational experiences that begin as early as kindergarten and first grade (with reading groups, special education placement, and retention), extend through elementary school (as ability grouping, special education, and gifted and talented programs continue), and are well recognized by high school (with formal and informal tracking, advanced placement, and the like) (Oakes 1985).

SUMMER LEARNING AND THE FAUCET THEORY

For almost a century, the impact of lost instructional time over the summer months has captured researchers' attention (Cooper et al. 1996). Early studies focused on what students retained or lost but overlooked crucial factors in children's learning processes. Concern for social inequality in the 1960s and 1970s led researchers to explore achievement differences across SES levels. One study investigated learning differences between schools with differing SES and racial composition (Hayes and Grether 1969, cited in Cooper et al. 1996). Children in schools serving low-income and largely minority populations showed average summer losses in reading, whereas schools serving more advantaged clienteles reported summer gains.

The most influential early research on summer learning centered on a small number of landmark studies in two U.S. cities. One study, focusing on sixth- and seventh-graders in Atlanta (Heyns 1978), reported that achievement gaps between black and white students, and between lower- and higher-income children, widened over the summer. The Heyns study motivated policy makers and educational researchers to investigate the benefits of summer school and compensatory education programs (Carter 1984). The multiyear longitudinal study by Entwisle, Alexander, and their colleagues (Entwisle and Alexander 1992, 1994; Entwisle et al. 1997) reported findings similar to the Heyns study among younger children in the Beginning School Study in Baltimore.

The authors of the Baltimore study generalized their findings into a popular and influential model of early learning: *the faucet theory*. Under the faucet theory, "when school is in session, the faucet is turned on for all children, the resources children need for learning are available to everyone, so all children gain. When school is not in session, children whose families are poor stop gaining because for them the faucet is turned off. The resources available to them in summer (mainly family resources) are not sufficient to promote their continued growth" (Entwisle et al. 1997, 37).

As the faucet theory gained empirical support, many researchers have attempted to identify exactly what resources—summer school, home and family activities, cultural capital—are most effective in promoting summer learning (Burkam et al. 2004). However, the full range of mechanisms through which SES influences children's learning in the summer remain unclear. Richard Rothstein (2002, 2004) emphasizes the many aspects of children's lives *besides* school that might influence achievement, including health care, employment, lead exposure, housing conditions, child-rearing practices, mobility, and family stability. Such conditions are clearly linked to social class, and probably also to academic achievement. These conditions would endure throughout the year, whether children were or were not in school. However, their role may be more important during the summer because of the lack of additional resources and regularity in children's lives when they are not in school.

THE CRITICAL YEARS REVISITED

Minority and low-SES children start kindergarten academically behind their white and middle-class peers. Moreover, these children tend to enroll in our nation's worst schools. Their initially lower status often reduces their learning rates in kindergarten as children with lower entering skills tend to lag behind their more cognitively prepared peers. Seemingly small month-by-month learning differences add up to something larger when we recognize that some children lose ground every single one of the 9.5 months they are in school over the two school years. After only four years of schooling, the academic status of children is beginning to harden into well-defined trajectories.

Who will graduate from high school, who will continue into college, these key targets are already easily predicted from children's third-grade school performance.

The importance of entering achievement provides a major explanation for social differences in learning as children move through the early grades. Although all children are learning, as time moves on learning differences by race and class increase because certain children are more likely to start out at an academic disadvantage. Many would like to believe that the nation's schools could and would decrease such learning differences, or at the very least hold them constant. Yet there is much evidence that schools have a minimal impact on reducing inequality in academic performance by race and class. Indeed, race and class disparities increase during the early years. At the same time, however, the substantial variation in school quality or resources—in particular the lower-quality schools attended by socially disadvantaged children—does seem to exacerbate the problem. Consequently, any potential for schools to ameliorate these cognitive disparities may be masked by assigning the least advantaged children to the least advantaged schools. Many admit that schools should be held fully accountable for righting the wrongs of our society. On the other hand, many also find it truly troubling that initial disadvantages in achievement increase as low-SES and minority children move into and through school, especially given how quickly early performance seems to lock children into life trajectories. Truly, "to all those who have, more will be given, and they will have an abundance; but from those who have nothing even what they have will be taken away."

BIBLIOGRAPHY

Alber-Kelsay, Krista. 1998. "Full-day kindergarten vs. half-day kindergarten: The outcome of first grade reading achievement." ERIC Document Reproduction Service No. 417-380.

Alexander, Karl, & Doris Entwisle. 1988. "Achievement in the first two years of school: Patterns and processes." *Monographs of the Society for Research in Child Development*, 53(2), Serial No. 218.

Anderson, Eleanor V. 1983. "Increasing school effectiveness: The full day kindergarten." Paper presented at the Annual Meeting of the American Educational Research Association 68th New Orleans, LA. ERIC Document Reproduction Service No. 248 036.

Anderson, Eleanor V. 1985. "Comparing full-day and half-day kindergartens." *ERS Spectrum*, 3(1), 3–10.

Annie E. Casey Foundation, 2010. *Kids Count Special Report: Early Warning! Why Reading by the End of Third Grade Matters*. Baltimore: Annie E. Casey Foundation.

Applebee, Arthur N., Judith A. Langer, & Ina V. S. Mullis. 1988. *Who reads best? Factors relating to reading achievement in grades 3, 7, and 11*. Princeton, NJ: Educational Testing Service.

Balaban, Nancy. 1990. "Statement to the Montgomery County Council." *Young Children*, 45(3), 12–16.

Bryant, Donna M., & Richard M. Clifford. 1992. "150 years of kindergarten: How far have we come?" *Early Childhood Research Quarterly, 7*, 147–54.

Burkam, David T., Douglas D. Ready, Valerie E. Lee, & Laura LoGerfo. 2004. "Social class differences in summer learning between kindergarten and first grade: Model specification and estimation." *Sociology of Education, 77*(1), 1–31.

Carter, Launor F. 1984. "The sustaining effects study of compensatory and elementary education." *Educational Researcher, 13*: 4–13.

Children's Defense Fund. 1996. *The State of America's Children: Yearbook 1996*. Washington, DC.

Chung, Shunah, & Daniel J. Walsh. 2000. "Unpacking child-centeredness: A history of meanings." *Curriculum Studies, 32*(2), 215–34.

Coleman, James S., Earnest Q. Campbell, Carol J. Hobson, James McPartland, Alexander M. Mood, Frederic D. Weinfeld, & Robert L. York. 1966. *Equality of Educational Opportunity report*. Washington, DC: U.S. Government Printing Office.

Coleman, James S. 1987. "Families and schools." *Educational Researcher, 16*(32–38).

Colgrove, Chauncey P. 1911. *The Teacher and the School*. New York: Charles Scribner's Sons.

Comer, James P. 1988. "Educating poor minority children." *Scientific American, 259*, 42–48.

Cooper, Harris, Barbara Nye, Kelly Charlton, James Lindsay, & Scott Greathouse. 1996. "The effects of summer vacation on achievement test scores: A narrative and meta-analytic review." *Review of Educational Research 66*(3): 227–68.

Cryan, John R., Robert Sheehan, Jane Wiechel, & Irene G. Bandy-Hadden. 1992. "Success outcomes of full-day kindergarten: More positive behavior and increased achievement in the years after." *Early Childhood Research Quarterly, 7*, 187–203.

da Costa, Jose L., & Susan Bell. 2000. "Full-day kindergarten at an inner city elementary school: Perceived and actual effects." Paper presented at the annual meeting of the American Educational Research Association, New Orleans. ERIC Document Reproduction Service No 440 751.

Duncan, Greg J., Jeanne Brooks-Gunn, & Pamela Kato Klebanov. 1994. "Economic deprivation and early childhood development." *Child Development*, 65, 296–318.

Duncan, Greg, W. Jean Yeung, Jeanne Brooks-Gunn & Judith K. Smith. 1998. "How much does childhood poverty affect the life chances of children?" *American Sociological Review, 63*(3), 406–23.

Edmonds, Ronald. 1986. "Characteristics of effective schools." In Ulric Neisser (Ed.), *The School Achievement of Minority Children: New Perspectives*. Hillsdale, NJ: Lawrence Erlbaum Associates.

Eliker, James & Sangeeta Mathur. 1997. "What do they do all day? Comprehensive evaluation of full-day kindergarten." *Early Childhood Research Quarterly*, 12, 459–80.

Elliott, Marta. 1998. "School finance and opportunities to learn: Does money well spent enhance students' achievement?" *Sociology of Education*, 71(3), 223–45.

Entwisle, Doris R., and Karl L. Alexander. 1992. "Summer setback: Race, poverty, school composition, and mathematics achievement in the first two years of school." *American Sociological Review* 57: 72–84.

Entwisle, Doris R., and Karl L. Alexander. 1994. "Winter setback: The racial composition of schools and learning to read." *American Sociological Review* 59(3): 446–60.

Entwisle, Doris R., Karl L. Alexander, & Linda S. Olson. 1997. *Children, Schools, and Inequality*. Boulder, CO: Westview.

Evansville-Vanderburg School Cooperation. 1988. *A Longitudinal Study of the Consequences of Full School Day Kindergarten: Kindergarten through Grade Eight*. Evansville, Indiana; Evansville-Vanderburg School Cooperation.

Fantini, Mario D., & Gerald Weinstein. 1968. *The Disadvantaged: Challenge to Education*. New York: Harper and Row.

Graja, Richard C. 1984. "An analysis of full-day kindergarten programs." Dissertation Abstracts International, 45(02). (UMI no. 8411603).

Graue, M. Elizabeth. 1999. "Diverse perspectives on kindergarten contexts and practices." In R. C. Pianta & M. J. Cox (Eds.), *The Transition to Kindergarten* (pp. 109–42). Baltimore, MD: Paul H. Brookes.

Gullo, Dominic F. 1990. "The changing family context: Implications for the development of all-day kindergartens." *Young Children*, 45(4), 35–39.

Harman, Deborah L. 1982. "Extended day kindergarten vs. half-day kindergarten achievement differences." ERIC Document Reproduction Service No. 215 784.

Helmich, Edith. 1985. "Kindergarten schedules: Status of patterns in Illinois and a review of research. Springfield IL: Illinois State Board of Education." ERIC Document Reproduction Service No. 260 828.

Herman, Barry E. 1984. "The case for the all-day kindergarten. Bloomington, IN: Phi Delta Kappa Educational Foundation." ERIC Document Reproduction Service No. 243 592.

Heyns, Barbara. 1978. *Summer Learning and the Effects of Schooling*. New York: Academic Press.

Hollingshead, August B. 1949/1975. *Elmtown's Youth and Elmtown Revisited*. New York: John Wiley & Sons, Inc.

Holmes, C. Thoms, & Barbara M. McConnell. 1990. "Full-day versus half-day kindergarten: An experimental study." ERIC Document Reproduction Service No. 369 540.

Hough, David, & Suzanne Bryde. 1996. "The effects of full-day kindergarten on student achievement and affect." ERIC Document Reproduction Service No. 395 691.

Humphrey, Jack W. 1980. "A study of the effectiveness of full-day kindergarten. Evansville, IN: Evansville-Banderburgh School Corporation." ERIC Document Reproduction Service No. 190 224.

Humphrey, Jack W. 1983. "A comparison of full day kindergarten and half-day kindergarten." *Spectrum Journal of School Research and Information,* 1(2), 11–16.

Jencks, Christopher, & Meredith Phillips. 1998. "The black/white test score gap: An introduction." In Christopher Jencks & Meredith Phillips (Eds.), *The Black/White Test Score Gap* (pp. 1–51). Washington, DC: Brookings.

Johnson, Jessie. 1993. "Language development component: All day kindergarten program 1991–1992. Final Evaluation Report." ERIC Document Reproduction Service No. 345 834.

Karweit, Nancy L. 1988. "A research study: Effective preprimary programs and practices." *Principal,* 67(5), 18–21.

Karweit, Nancy. 1989. "Effective kindergarten programs and practices for students at risk." In Robert E. Slavin, Nancy L. Karweit, & Nancy A. Madden (Eds.), *Effective Programs for Students at Risk* (pp. 103–42). Boston: Allyn & Bacon.

Karweit, Nancy L. 1992. "The kindergarten experience." *Educational Leadership* 49(6), 82–86.

Koopermans, M. 1991. "A study of the longitudinal effects of all-day kindergarten attendance on achievement." ERIC Document Reproduction Service No. 336 494.

Lee, Valerie E. & David T. Burkam. 2002. *Inequality at the Starting Gate: Social Background Differences in Achievement as Children Begin School.* Washington, DC: Economic Policy Institute.

Lee, Valerie E., David T. Burkam, Douglas Ready, Joann J. Honigman, & Samuel J. Meisels. 2006. "Full-day vs. half-day kindergarten: In which program do children learn more?" *American Journal of Education,* 112(2), 163–208.

Lesnick, Joy, Robert M. Goerge, Cheryl Smithgall, & Julia Gwynne 2010. *Reading on Grade Level in Third Grade: How Is It Related to High School Performance and College Enrollment?* Chicago: Chapin Hall Center for Children at the University of Chicago.

Meisels, Samuel J., & Jack P. Shonkoff. 2000. "Early childhood intervention: A continuing evolution." In J. P. Shonkoff and S. J. Meisels (Eds.), *Handbook of Early Childhood Intervention* (pp. 3–31). New York: Cambridge University Press.

Merton, Robert K. 1968. "The Matthew effect in science." *Science,* 5(1), 56–63.

Naron, Nancy K. 1981. "The need for full-day kindergarten." *Education Leadership,* 38, 306–9.

National Center for Education Statistics. 2000. *America's Kindergartners.* Washington, D.C.

Natriello, Gary, Edward L. McDill, & Aaron M. Pallas. 1990. *Schooling Disadvantaged Children: Racing against Catastrophe.* New York: Teachers College Press.

Oakes, Jeannie. 1985. *Keeping Track: How Schools Structure Inequality.* New Haven: Yale University Press.

Ohio State Legislative Office of Education Oversight. 1997. "An overview of full-day kindergarten." ERIC Document Reproduction Service No. 408 046

Olsen, Deborah, & Edward Zigler. 1989. "An assessment of the all-day kindergarten movement." *Early Childhood Research Quarterly*, 4, 167–86.

Phillips, Meredith, James Crouse, & John Ralph. 1998. "Does the black/white test score gap widen after children enter school?" In Christopher Jencks & Meredith Phillips (Eds.), *The Black/White Test Score Gap* (pp. 229–72). Washington, DC: Brookings.

Ramey, Craig T., & Francis A. Campbell. 1991. "Poverty, early childhood education, and academic competence: The Abecedarian experiment." In A. C. Huston (Ed.), *Children in Poverty* (pp. 190–221). Cambridge, MA: Harvard University Press.

Rist, Ray C. 1970. "Student social class and teacher expectations: The self-fulfilling prophecy in ghetto education." *Harvard Educational Review*, 40, 411–51.

Rothstein, Richard. January 25, 2002. "Out of balance: Our understanding of how schools affect society and how society affects schools." Chicago, IL: The Spencer Foundation. Paper presented at the 30th Anniversary Conference, "Traditions of Scholarship in Education."

Rothstein, Richard. 2004. *Class and Schools: Using Social, Economic, and Educational Reform to Close the Black-White Achievement Gap.* Washington, DC: Economic Policy Institute.

Shapiro, Michael S. 1983. *Child's Garden: The Kindergarten Movement from Froebel to Dewey.* State College, PA: The Pennsylvania State University Press.

Shepard, Lorrie A., & Mary Lee Smith. 1988. "Escalating academic demand in kindergarten: Counterproductive policies." *Elementary School Journal*, 89(2), 134–45.

Snow, Catherine E., M. Susan Burns, & Peg Griffin. (Eds.). 1998. *Preventing Reading Difficulties in Young Children.* Washington, DC: National Academy Press.

Snyder, Thomas D., & Charlene M. Hoffman. 2001. Digest of Education Statistics, NCES 2001-034. Washington, DC: National Center for Education Statistics.

Spodek, Bernard. 1986. "Introduction." In Bernard Spodek (Ed.), *Today's Kindergarten: Exploring the Knowledge Base, Expanding the Curriculum* (pp. vii–xi). New York: Teachers College Press.

Stanovich, Keith E. 1986. "Matthew effects in reading: Some consequences of individual differences in the acquisition of literacy." *Reading Research Quarterly*, 21(4), 360–407.

Terens, Sheila. 1984. "Second year full day kindergarten program evaluation, Lawrence Public Schools, number four school." Paper presented at the Annual Meeting of the American Educational Research Association 68th New Orleans, LA. ERIC Document Reproduction Service No. ED 251 177.

Vecchiotti, Sara. 2001. *Kindergarten: The Overlooked School Year.* New York: Foundation for Child Development.

Walberg, Herbert J., and Shiow-Ling Tsai. 1983. "Matthew effects in education." *American Educational Research Journal*, 20(3), 359–73.

Walsh, Daniel J. 1989. "Changes in kindergarten: Why here? Why now?" *Early Childhood Research Quarterly*, 4, 377–91.

Weast, Jerry D. 2001. "Why we need full-day kindergarten." *Principal*, 80(5), 6–9.

Weiss, Andrea Del Gaudio, & Robert M. Offenberg. 2002. *Enhancing Urban Children's Early Success in School: The Power of Full-day Kindergarten.* Philadelphia, PA: Office of Research and Evaluation.

Zill, Nicholas. 1999. "Promoting educational equity and excellence in kindergarten." In Robert C. Pianta & Martha J. Cox (Eds.), *The Transition to Kindergarten* (67–105). Baltimore, MD: Paul H. Brookes.

Chapter 22

School Choice

Patrick J. Wolf and Anna M. Jacob

Many families in the United States have been choosing their child's school since the 19th century. Until recently, this choice has been driven by wealth, as families of means have paid a premium to live in a neighborhood with high-quality public schools or have self-financed private schooling for their children. Most suburban schools in the United States are well resourced and filled with predominantly middle-class, educationally advantaged, white students. Low-income families who lack the capital to purchase a home in a neighborhood with excellent public schools or pay for private schooling often are left trapped in chronically failing neighborhood schools, perpetuating a cycle of intergenerational poverty. Such schools, most common in urban and some rural areas, are populated by other low-income, disadvantaged minority students. Their students miss out on the superior resources and positive peer effects their suburban counterparts are experiencing. Such contrasting schooling experiences likely contribute to the black-white test score gap in the United States and inhibit the upward economic and social mobility of disadvantaged members of society.

The racial achievement gap has been a robust empirical observation and the focal point for numerous education reform efforts since the latter half of the 20th century. The Elementary and Secondary Education Act as reauthorized by the No Child Left Behind Act of 2001 maintained this focus, requiring that test scores be disaggregated by racial subgroups of black and Hispanic students so that the performance of each group could be tracked separately. Test scores on the National Assessment of Educational Progress Long-Term Trend Assessments reveal a persistent gap between white and black students since the 1970s. Roland Fryer estimates the black-white test score gap in eighth grade math to be 0.4 standard deviations, with similar magnitudes observed in English, history, and science (Fryer 2010, Table 16). The achievement gap has been persistent across time, prompting scholars to theorize that its primary cause is the transmission of social capital, access to high-quality schools, peer group effects, or competitive effects (Jencks and Phillips 1998, 1–51). School choice by residence or by financing a private school education has impacted these four areas in a number of ways, resulting in altered educational conditions for the students involved. If the black-white achievement gap is to be closed anytime soon, the educational environments and outcomes of the most disadvantaged students need to be positively altered. Evidence suggests that targeting school choice policies to underprivileged children accomplishes that goal.

In recent years, students in the United States that are disadvantaged by income, disability, or educational environment have been able to access school choice options through a variety of policy reforms. These programs may operate within the existing public school structure, such as magnet schools, interdistrict and intradistrict choice options, and transfer opportunities to higher-performing public schools. They also may permit students to attend charter schools, which are public schools that operate independent of the local school district. Other initiatives provide public assistance in the form of a voucher or "opportunity scholarship" for students to attend private schools. These various choice options all share a commonality: they free students from forced attendance at their residentially assigned public school. To what extent can freedom from this constraint increase educational equality?

EXTENT OF SCHOOL CHOICE IN THE UNITED STATES

Reliable enrollment data are available regarding five distinct forms of school choice in the United States: choice within public school districts, charter schools, homeschools, direct voucher programs, and

Figure 22.1
Extent of School Choice in the United States.

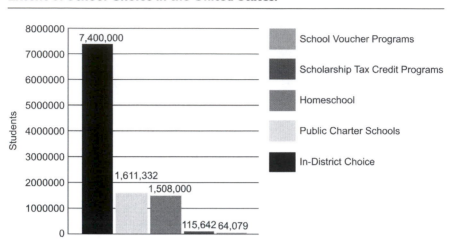

Note: Enrollment figures are for 2010, with the exception of "Homeschool" and "In-District Choice" for which the most current estimates are from 2007.
Sources: NCES Digest of Education Statistics 2009; The Alliance for School Choice: School Choice Yearbook 2009–10.

tax-credit scholarship programs (Figure 22.1). The oldest and most common form of school choice policy allows parents to select a school for their child while keeping that student within the public school system. Such internal choice mechanisms include interdistrict and intradistrict public school choice plans, open-enrollment policies, magnet schools, and public school transfer options as mandated by No Child Left Behind. In 2007, 16 percent of school-age children were attending a public school other than their assigned neighborhood school, up five percentage points from 1993 (Planty et al. 2009).

Magnet schools were the first distinctive form of public school choice, emerging largely in response to demands for desegregation in the late 1960s and early 1970s. Magnet schools are characterized by a distinguishing school-wide theme, curriculum, or pedagogical approach. Admissions policies aim to achieve racially balanced schools by attracting students from across a school district or retaining existing (mostly white) students who might otherwise abandon the public schools. Between 1976 and 1981, the federal government allocated $30 million a year for magnet programs, spending an additional $739 million between 1985 and 1991 (Blank, Levine, and Steel 1996). By 2009, more than 2.3 million schoolchildren were enrolled in 3,021 magnet schools across the United States (Snyder and Dillow 2011, 165).

Magnet schools have been mainly an urban phenomenon, designed to stem "white flight" to the suburbs. By 1991, over half of magnet schools and 80 percent of magnet programs were located in urban areas (Blank, Levine, and Steel 1996). Despite their origins as vehicles of desegregation, magnet schools have had only limited success in promoting racial and ethnic integration. While many magnet schools appear to be racially heterogeneous on paper, their internal operations often permit substantial segregation by race (Blank 1991). African American students are more likely to be assigned to the lowest academic tracks in many magnet schools, limiting contact with their white classmates. Whole-school magnets, which do not assign students to separate academic tracks, currently are viewed as the more authentic form of magnet schooling (Christenson et al. 2003).

Besides magnet schools, choice options within the traditional public school system include interdistrict school choice plans that permit students to attend a public school district other than the one in which they reside. Intradistrict choice plans, on the other hand, allow students to attend a school within their district other than their assigned neighborhood school. Such plans are sometimes referred to as "open enrollment." In addition, No Child Left Behind has a public school choice provision that allows students attending Title I schools designated in need of improvement, corrective action, or restructuring for two years in a row to transfer to a higher-performing public school within their district.[1]

A charter school is another public school choice option. Charter schools are governed by an independent group or organization operating under a charter or contractual agreement with the state legislature or other government authority. That agreement provides the school with funding and autonomy from the regulatory burden imposed by the state on traditional public schools. In exchange, the school must meet or exceed certain accountability standards. Although some public school districts manage charter schools, charter schools typically operate outside of the governance structure of the local district and are considered their own Local Educational Agency. Charter schools represent vehicles of school choice that are public but external to any traditional public school system.

Admission to most charter schools is not determined by residential address and, in the case of oversubscription, an admissions lottery typically is held. A school's charter is reviewed every three to five years, and can be revoked if performance standards, fiscal accountability procedures, curriculum guidelines, or other requirements are not being met. Since the first charter school opened in 1992, this public school choice option has grown exponentially. From the 1999–2000 school year to the 2008–9 school year, the number of students enrolled in charter schools increased from 340,000 to 1.4 million, a 312 percent increase over a nine-year period (Aud et al. 2011). Today, more than 5,400 charter schools operate in 40 states and the District of Columbia.[2] About 61 percent of the students in charter schools in 2008–9 were minorities compared to 44 percent of traditional public school students. Charter school students are also more likely to be poor (Aud et al. 2011, 147) and to be behind academically.[3]

School voucher programs assist parents in sending their children to participating private schools of their choosing. A school voucher is an arrangement whereby parents who meet certain eligibility criteria can qualify to have public dollars finance some or all of the expenses associated with a private school education (Wolf 2008b, 635). In some states, government tax credits induce corporations or individuals to donate money to nonprofit organizations that distribute tuition scholarships to needy students in elementary or secondary schools. Privately funded scholarships like this are not school vouchers, although both are used to help underprivileged students gain access to private schools. School vouchers are public monies provided by government to fund a private school education of the parent's choosing. Prior to the start of the most recent state legislative sessions, there were 10 school voucher programs enrolling 67,267 students and nine tax-credit scholarship programs enrolling 123,544 students in the United States (Campanella et al. 2011, 24). In the spring of 2011, dubbed "The Year of School Choice" by the *Wall Street Journal*, 5 states created new school voucher programs, 3 enacted new tax-credit scholarship programs, and 10 expanded existing voucher or tax-credit initiatives. For example, Arizona launched an innovative voucher program that places a portion of the government funding for a student with a disability switching from a public to a private or homeschool into an education savings account that parents can use to pay for private school tuition, tutoring, or future college expenses.

School voucher programs vary by the eligibility requirements imposed on applicants, the number of vouchers granted, the value of the voucher, the types of schools that are allowed to participate in the program, and the regulations imposed on those schools (Table 22.1).

Table 22.1
Publicly Funded School Voucher Programs in the United States in 2011

Location	Eligibility	Initiated	Students in 2010–11
Milwaukee, WI	Means test	1990	20,189
Cleveland, OH	Means test	1996	5,264
Florida	Disability	1999	21,054
Ohio	Disability-autism	2003	1,672
D.C.	Means test	2004	1,012
Utah	Disability	2005	624
Ohio	Need improvement public school	2006	13,195
Georgia	Disability	2007	2,550
New Orleans, LA	Means test	2009	1,697
Oklahoma	Disability	2010	10
Racine, WI	Means test	2011	N/A
Arizona	Disability	2011	N/A
Colorado	Residency of DCSD	2011	N/A
Indiana	Means test	2011	N/A
Ohio	Disability	2011	N/A

Note: N/A means figures are not yet available.
Sources: The Alliance for School Choice; State Departments of Education.

A growing number of parents are enrolling their children in virtual schools, online classes, homeschooling, or some combination of the three. The number of students being homeschooled has risen to about 1.5 million in 2007 compared with 1.1 million in 2003 and 850,000 in 1999 (Bielick 2008). The 2007 figure represented 2.9 percent of the school-age population that year, a 71 percent increase from 1999. White students constitute the majority of homeschooled students (77 percent), and students in two-parent households comprise 89 percent of the homeschooled population (Planty et al. 2009). The three most common reasons for homeschooling cited by parents are a desire to provide religious or moral instruction (36%), concerns about the school environment, such as drugs, safety, or negative peer pressure (21%), and dissatisfaction with the academic instruction offered at other schools (17%). Due to the increased affordability and sophistication of online options, homeschooling parents can easily customize their child's education. High-quality resources and personnel no longer need to be located in the same building, city, or even country as the student who is being educated (Moe and Chubb 2009).

Even parents who choose to send their children to traditional public high schools have the option of supplementing that education with online providers. For example, Florida Virtual School (FLVS) became the country's first statewide, online, public high school when it was founded in 1997. Initially working to fill gaps at traditional public high schools, the Florida legislature established FLVS as an independent, diploma-granting educational entity in 2000. FLVS served over 97,000 students in the 2009–10 school year, offering more than 90 courses including core subjects, electives, world languages, honors, and Advanced Placement courses.[4] The school receives per-pupil funds only for those students who successfully pass their courses.

Online courses can be coordinated either entirely over the Internet or through a hybrid schooling model. While still attending a brick-and-mortar school structure, students in hybrid schools spend all or some of the day taking online classes or utilizing instructional software under the supervision of school staff. Rocketship Education, a charter school network currently operating three campuses in San Jose, California, is a hybrid school that successfully uses technology for part of the school day to deliver curriculum to students. Rocketship Mateo Sheedy Elementary earned a 2010 achievement score of 925 (out of 1,000), making it the fifth-highest-performing low-income elementary school in California.

MARKET THEORY AND SCHOOL CHOICE

In his 1955 article, "The Role of Government in Education," economist Milton Friedman proposed supplementing publicly operated schools with a school voucher system that would allow for schools to be privately run yet publicly funded. Chubb and Moe (1990) echoed that call, recommending a total restructuring of American school governance from democratic to market control in *Politics, Markets, and America's Schools*. Their theory identifies the institutions of direct democratic governance as the root cause of the predicament of the United States' poor academic performance. The political institutions of public education discourage school autonomy and, in turn, school effectiveness because they are driven by the interests of legislators and elected school board officials. Four key areas of school organization are unduly constrained by the bureaucratic system of governance: personnel, goals, leadership, and practice. These constraints have pervasive consequences for schools, disrupting the authority of the principal to choose and motivate teachers, overwhelming schools with watered-down and frequently changing goals imposed from above, limiting effective school leadership, and fragmenting curricula and pedagogy. Under such conditions, schools are limited in their ability to improve student performance through innovation.

Chubb and Moe recommend a move to a competitive market system for the supply of educational services. They assert that fundamentally new institutions of educational governance based on free-market principles, competition, and choice are necessary to ensure academic excellence in our schools. Market-based educational bureaucracies are held accountable to parents and students who can signal their dissatisfaction with the school by choosing to exit (Hirschman 1970). This uniquely powerful threat negates the need for extensive front-end procedural rules and regulations, freeing schools to focus on the task of successfully educating students. According to this theory, the increased flexibility, combined with the threat of losing students to more appealing schools, induces schools to improve their structure and operations. With all schools forced to compete for students, the most successful models thrive, others emulate them, and the least effective schools are forced to close, to the benefit especially of disadvantaged students.

Proponents of market-based school reforms view school choice as a means of leveling disparities in race, class, and performance in public school systems (Viteritti 1999; Chubb and Moe 1990). Under a system of targeted school choice, disadvantaged populations are targeted directly, through eligibility requirements, or indirectly, by constraining the admissions criteria of participating schools to favor at-risk populations. Under a system of universal parental school choice, all students would bring equivalent financial resources to a choice school. Low-income minority children would be as valuable to a school as rich white students. As such, the principles of equality of opportunity and competition are both central to market theory as it applies to education.

Market theory predicts that schools will be motivated to specialize in order to serve a niche market. By implicitly empowering parents to allocate resources across schools, the market model of governance incentivizes schools to offer diverse pedagogical approaches to match the different needs and preferences of the students for which they are competing. This should result in allocative efficiency (Schneider, Teske, and Marschall 2000, 35), with parents experiencing greater satisfaction with their distinctive educational options while schools improve productive efficiency by competing among themselves for students.

Finally, market theory predicts that schools of choice will serve as fertile ground for the development of "social capital." James Coleman first referred to social capital as the set of resources that inhere in schools "that are useful for the cognitive or social development of a child or young person" who freely chooses to be there (Coleman 1990, 300). When a student actively chooses to attend a school, she freely commits to the traditions and values that reflect the school's mission. The voluntary nature of application to the school further bestows a sense of ownership and investment on the choosing family.

To summarize, market theorists propose that a market-based educational system premised on school choice might produce superior student achievement relative to a traditional, residentially assigned, and politically directed system because of the positive effects of competition for students and resources, school autonomy, consumer equality, efficiency, superior matches between students and school environments, and social capital development.

Critics of market-oriented reforms, however, worry that such an approach simply does not apply to education and could have negative effects. They argue that increasing choice options is likely to increase segregation, with students separating themselves by race, social class, religion, and cultural background (Fuller and Elmore 1996). According to their reasoning, school choice programs create an uneven playing field, institutionalizing an unequal, two-tier system consisting of those who escape the traditional public schools and those who do not. Opponents of school choice claim that choice options exacerbate the disparities in school systems by draining public schools of the best and brightest students, leaving behind low-achieving poor and minority children most likely to be English-language learners and to display physical or learning disabilities (Shanker 1991, 8–15, 40–41). This phenomenon is referred to as "cream skimming." As a result, traditional public schools are put at a competitive disadvantage, forced to serve the most challenging students while competing for scarce education funds. Existing resources are redirected into advertising budgets instead of educational programs (Smith and Meier 1995). Other commentators contend that parents, uneducated on how to choose an effective school and lacking sufficient information or experience, make poor educational choices (Fuller and Elmore 1996). Schools tend to converge on the one best model of education so the diversity of options under school choice would be severely limited and any "choice" would be artificial (Harris 2004, 91–130). Procedural constraints on schools would not necessarily be relaxed easily, despite the market environment (Hess 2002).

To resolve this debate, we examine the available scientific evidence on the outcomes of various choice programs enacted in this country in the past several decades to determine if they have lived up to the hopes of market theory enthusiasts or succumbed to market failure as critics predicted.

PUBLIC SCHOOL CHOICE IMPACTS

Well-designed studies tend to show that charter schools produce academic achievement outcomes that are equal or superior to traditional public schools, even though most charter schools are less than five years old, generally receive only 60 to 80 percent of the per-pupil operational funding of traditional public schools, and receive no capital funding from government sources. The major exceptions to this pattern are a national study of charter middle schools by Mathematica Policy Research that found no net achievement benefits of charter schools and a multistate evaluation by CREDO that concluded that 17 percent of charter schools in the study outperformed their traditional public school matched twin, 46 percent performed similarly to their twin, and 37 percent performed below their twin (Gleason et al. 2010; CREDO 2009).

Evaluations that follow students over time are more valid than single point-in-time studies that must statistically adjust for preexisting differences among students. The National Alliance for Public Charter Schools (2009) singled out 33 studies that met modest eligibility criteria by using longitudinally linked, student-level data to look at change over time in student or school performance while controlling for prior achievement as well as school and student characteristics. The studies that use the most recent data show that charter schools produce more instances of higher achievement gains than traditional public schools. Narrowing the eligibility criteria even further, the 13 most rigorous studies show that charter schools clearly outperformed traditional public schools. Additionally, longitudinal studies of high school graduation and college matriculation results all favor charter schools over traditional public schools.

Well-designed charter school studies are settling the cream-skimming dispute largely in favor of school choice supporters. A 2009 report by RAND analyzed transfers to charters in five metropolitan areas—Chicago, Denver, Milwaukee, Philadelphia, and San Diego.

The authors followed students who switched from traditional public schools to charter schools and concluded that "it does not appear that charter schools are systematically skimming high-achieving students or dramatically affecting the racial mix of schools for transferring students" (Zimmer et al. 2009, 19).

There have been fewer studies of the systemic or competitive effects of charter schools on the achievement of students who remain in traditional public schools and these tend to vary dramatically in quality. The most rigorous studies generally show that competition by charter schools boosts achievement in traditional public schools. Gray analyzed school-level data from Ohio to determine if traditional public schools suddenly threatened by charter school competition responded with test score gains and found a small, positive effect (Gray 2009). Other studies of the systemic effects of charter schools have found positive effects on the political knowledge and voluntarism of students in traditional public schools (Godwin and Kemerer 2002; Greene 1998, 83–106).

PRIVATE SCHOOL CHOICE IMPACTS

Fortunately, a sufficiently large number of school voucher programs have been established and evaluated in the United States to answer pressing policy questions related to vouchers targeted to underprivileged students. The highest-quality studies are those that randomly assign participants to receive the offer of a voucher or serve in the study control group. Experimental methods of analysis are often referred to as the "gold standard" of research design because the randomly generated voucher and nonvoucher groups are, on average, statistically similar in all relevant respects except for the school voucher opportunity. Of the 10 separate analyses of data from "gold standard" experimental studies of school voucher programs in six cities reviewed by Wolf (2008a), 9 conclude that some or all of the participants benefited academically from using a voucher to attend a private school of their choice. On average, the academic growth equals about an extra month of learning per year, with all or some subgroups of students showing gains eventually. Although the exact pattern of positive results varies by study, no negative achievement effects of vouchers have been found.

Consider the D.C. Opportunity Scholarship Program (OSP). The OSP serves a highly disadvantaged student population that was performing in the lower third of the national test-score distribution on average at the start of the program, is 99 percent minority, and is 100 percent eligible for the federal lunch program. Four years after the random assignment of students to the treatment and control groups, the researchers concluded that the program significantly improved reading test scores and dramatically increased students' chance of graduating from high school. The use of an Opportunity Scholarship raised students' probability of completing high school by 21 percentage points, from 70 percent to 91 percent (Wolf et al. 2011, 25).

Voucher programs also generate increased parental satisfaction with schools, particularly regarding curriculum, safety, parent-teacher relations, academics, and religion. This result has been confirmed by all five gold standard studies that asked these questions (Wolf et al. 2010). These impacts tend to be large and decrease only slightly over time. For example, after one year, 80 percent of DC parents graded their voucher schools A or B, compared to 50 percent of the control group. After four years, 78 percent of voucher users gave an A or B grade to their child's school compared to 68 percent of the control group.

A comprehensive review examined 21 quantitative studies regarding the effects of school choice on seven civic outcomes for students: political tolerance, voluntarism, political knowledge, political participation, social capital, civic skills, and patriotism. All but 3 of 59 analyses within those studies revealed that choice schools did as well or better than traditional public schools at promoting civic values, suggesting that increasing parental school choice does not undermine the public goals of education and may actually advance them (Wolf 2007).

CHALLENGES OF BEING A GOOD CHOOSER

Most studies of school choice have focused on the quality and availability of choice schools and their effect on student outcomes—the supply side of the school choice market. Comprehensive educational reform initiatives have often neglected to mention or simply assume quality on the demand side of school choice transactions. For example, the latest major education initiative by the U.S. Department of Education, Race to the Top, pays scant attention to the vital role that families play in the transformation of the educational ecosystem. The final Race to the Top application includes over 30 criteria with differing point values and funding priorities. The only one that touches on the demand side is Priority Six, which invites states to "engage families and communities" but does not lead to any additional application points if they do so (U.S. Department of Education 2009).

As educational policy in the United States evolves and the number of school choice options continues to expand, especially for otherwise disadvantaged families, we must consider how prepared most parents are to shoulder the responsibilities associated with making high-impact educational decisions for their children. The shift from residentially assigned, neighborhood public schools to an arena of choice options is a dramatic change for many families accustomed to a default schooling model. Families are differentially equipped with the necessary resources for the effective exercise of school choice and, consequently, the ability of low-income families to make good choices can vary considerably (Henig 1994). Focus group research on the D.C. Opportunity Scholarship Program revealed a link between families that function as effective education consumers and higher levels of family and programmatic resources (Stewart et al. 2009). Family resources such as a two-parent household or access to a personal support network seem to be important for successfully navigating the school choice system. Similarly, access to independent, reliable information for comparing schooling options is a key programmatic resource that empowers parents to make informed decisions. Parents denied access to these resources tend to struggle to take full advantage of the options available to them in a burgeoning choice environment.

As school choice options in the United States and elsewhere continue to expand, policy makers would do well to consider the extent to which the targets of these reforms are adequately prepared to operate efficiently in an educational marketplace. New parental consumers of education may not automatically flock to the highest-quality schools, eliminating the poorest, most dysfunctional options via the process of creative destruction that market theory confidently predicts (Bast and Walberg 2003). Attentive policy makers and other stakeholders will recognize the need to assist parents in developing the necessary aptitudes, information, and experience to research, select, and acquire the highest-quality educational opportunity available for their son or daughter. Some parents will need to be actively coached through what otherwise might seem to be a daunting task of making an effective school choice for their child.

CONCLUSIONS

Nearly 11 million students in the United States participate in school choice through out-of-boundary public school choice programs, charters, tax-credit scholarships, vouchers, homeschooling, or other formal choice mechanisms. Millions of others participate informally by deliberately choosing homes in neighborhoods that host desirable public schools or by using personal financial resources to access a quality private school education. The vast majority of students, however, are by default assigned to schools based on where they live. This situation tends to work to the disadvantage of low-income, minority students, particularly African Americans. The findings of the rigorous school choice evaluations presented here point to the potential of school choice policies to narrow the enduring and alarming achievement gap between black and white students in the United States. While no single, comprehensive study has confirmed all the aspects of a transformational school choice policy that would completely correct the imbalance in student achievement and attainment levels that currently exists between advantaged and disadvantaged groups of students, it is possible to draw certain conclusions about the impact of policy-enabled school choice based on the evidence to date.

The core logic that has emerged from school choice research is straightforward. The conventional system of residentially assigning students to neighborhood public schools or permitting private school choice through self-financing disproportionately works to the advantage of white students. The same students who tend to lose out educationally under the conventional system of residential assignment—low-income minority students—seem to benefit from school choice policies targeted to them. These benefits range from neutral to modestly positive. An insufficient number of studies have been conducted thus far to assess longer-term impacts such as the intergenerational effects of school choice, but no rigorous empirical study has demonstrated negative effects of public or private school choice programs on student outcomes in the United States. Given this body of evidence, it seems that expanding school choice options for disadvantaged families while continuing to learn about and refine policies through rigorous evaluations of their effects is the most reasonable path to pursue if we hope to someday completely realize the goal of educational equality.

NOTES

1. For more information, see No Child Left Behind Act of 2001, Title 1, Section 1116 (b) (E).

2. National charter school and enrollment statistics for each state are provided by The Center for Education Reform at http://www.edreform.com/_upload/CER_charter_numbers.pdf.

3. Witte et al. (2010) found that students in Grade 3 of independent charters in Milwaukee start out about seven percentiles lower in reading and math.

4. Enrollment data available from http://www.flvs.net.

BIBLIOGRAPHY

Aud, Susan, William Hussar, Grace Kena, Kevin Bianco, Lauren Frohlich, Jana Kemp, Kim Tahan, Katie Mallory, Thomas Nachazel, and Gretchen Hannes. 2011. *The Condition of Education 2011*. Washington, DC: National Center for Education Statistics, Institute of Education Sciences, U.S. Department of Education.

Bast, Joseph L., and Herbert J. Walberg. 2003. *Let's Put Parents Back in Charge!* Chicago: Heartland Institute.

Bielick, Stacey. 2008. 1.5 Million Homeschooled Students in the United States in 2007.Washington, DC: National Center for Education Statistics, Institute of Education Sciences, U.S. Department of Education.

Blank, Rolf K. 1991. "Educational Effects of Magnet High Schools." In *Choice and Control in American Education*, Vol. 2, edited by William Clune and John Witte. New York: Falmer.

Blank, Rolf K., Roger E. Levine, and Lauri Steel. 1996. "After 15 Years: Magnet Schools in Urban Education." In *Who Chooses? Who Loses? Culture, Institutions and the Unequal Effects of School Choice*, edited by Bruce Fuller and Richard F. Elmore. New York: Teachers College Press.

Campanella, Andrew, Malcom Glenn, and Lauren Perry. 2011. *School Choice Yearbook 2010–11*. Washington D.C.: The Alliance for School Choice.

Campbell, David. E., Martin R. West, and Paul E. Peterson. 2005. "Participation in a National, Means-Tested School Voucher Program." *Journal of Policy Analysis and Management* 24(3).

Christenson, Bruce, Marian Eaton, Michael S. Garet, Luke C. Miller, Hiroyuki Hikawa, and Phyllis DuBois. 2003. Evaluation of the Magnet Schools Assistance Program, 1998 Grantees. Washington, DC: U.S. Department of Education, Office of the Under Secretary.

Chubb, John E., and Terry M. Moe. 1990. *Politics, Markets and America's Schools*. Washington, DC: Brookings Institution Press.

Coleman, James S. 1990. *Foundations of Social Theory*. Cambridge, MA: The Belknap Press of Harvard University.

CREDO. 2009. *Multiple Choice: Charter School Performance in 16 States*. Palo Alto: Stanford University Press.

Fleming, D. J., Cowen, J. M., Witte, J. F., and Wolf, P. J. 2011. "Who Chooses Private Schools? An Analysis of Voucher Participants in Milwaukee." Unpublished working paper, Furman University.

Friedman, Milton. 1955. "The Role of Government in Education." In *Economics and the Public Interest*, edited by Robert A. Solo. New Brunswick, NJ: Rutgers University Press.

Fryer, Roland G. 2010. "Racial Inequality in the 21st Century: The Declining Significance of Discrimination." NBER Working Paper Series, Vol. w16256.

Fuller, Bruce, and Richard F. Elmore. 1996. *Who Chooses? Who Loses? Culture, Institutions, and the Unequal Effects of School Choice*. New York: Teachers College Press.

Gleason, Philip, Melissa Clark, Christina Clark Tuttle, and Emily Dwoyer. 2010. The Evaluation of Charter School Impacts: Final Report. Washington, DC: Institute of Education Sciences, U.S. Department of Education.

Godwin, R. Kenneth, and Frank R. Kemerer. 2002. *School Choice Tradeoffs: Liberty, Equity, and Diversity*. Austin: University of Texas Press.

Gray, Nathan. 2009. "The Systemic Effects of the Ohio Charter School Policy." PhD diss. University of Arkansas.

Greene, Jay P. 1998. "Civic Values in Public and Private Schools." In *Learning from School Choice*, edited by Paul E. Peterson and Bryan C. Hassel. Washington, DC: Brookings Institution Press.

Harris, Neville. 2004. "Regulation, Choice, and Basic Values in Education in England and Wales: A Legal Perspective." In *Educating Citizens: International Perspectives on Civic Values and School Choice*, edited by Patrick J. Wolf and Stephen Macedo. Washington, DC: Brookings Institution Press.

Henig, Jeffrey R. 1994. *Rethinking School Choice: Limits of the Market Metaphor*. Princeton, NJ: Princeton University Press.

Hess, Frederick M. 2002. *Revolution at the Margins*. Washington, DC: Brookings Institution Press.

Hirschman, Albert O. 1970. *Exit, Voice and Loyalty: Responses to Decline in Firms, Organizations, and States*. Cambridge, MA: Harvard University Press.

Howell, William G. 2004. "Dynamic Selection Effects in Means-Tested, Urban School Voucher Programs." In *Journal of Policy Analysis and Management* 23(2).

Jencks, Christopher, and Meredith Phillips. 1998. "The Black-White Test Score Gap: An Introduction." In *The Black-White Test Score Gap*, edited by Christopher Jencks and Meredith Phillips, 1–51. Washington, DC: Brookings Institution Press.

Moe, Terry M., and John E. Chubb. 2009. *Liberating Learning: Technology, Politics, and the Future of American Education*. San Francisco: Jossey-Bass.

National Alliance for Public Charter Schools. 2009. Charter School Achievement: What We Know, Fifth Edition. Accessed August 15, 2011. http://www .publiccharters.org/data/files/Publication_docs/Summary_of_ Achievement_Studies_Fifth_Edition_2009_Final_20110402T222331 .pdf.

"Opinion: The Year of School Choice." 2011. *The Wall Street Journal*, July 5. Accessed August 15, 2011. http://online.wsj.com/article/SB100014240 52702304450604576420330972531442.html.

Planty, M., William Hussar, Thomas Snyder, Grace Kena, Angelina KewalRamani, Jana Kemp, Kevin Bianco, and Rachel Dinkes. 2009. *The Condition of Education 2009*. Washington, DC: National Center for Education Statistics, Institute of Education Sciences, U.S. Department of Education.

Schneider, Mark, Paul Teske, and Melissa Marschall. 2000. *Choosing Schools: Consumer Choice and the Quality of American Schools*. Princeton, NJ: Princeton University Press.

Shanker, Albert. 1991. "Do Private Schools Outperform Public Schools?" *American Educator* 15(2).

Smith, Kevin B., and Kenneth J. Meier. 1995. *The Case against School Choice: Politics, Markets, and Fools.* Armonk, NY: M.E. Sharpe.

Snyder, Thomas D., and Sally A. Dillow. 2011. *Digest of Education Statistics 2010.* Washington, DC: National Center for Education Statistics, Institute of Education Sciences, U.S. Department of Education.

Stewart, Thomas, Patrick Wolf, Stephen Cornman, Kenann McKenzie-Thompson, and Jonathan Butcher. 2009. Family Reflections on the District of Columbia Opportunity Scholarship Program. Arkansas: School Choice Demonstration Project.

U.S. Department of Education. 2009. "Race to the Top Program Executive Summary." Accessed July 11, 2011. http://www2.ed.gov/programs/racetothetop/executive-summary.pdf.

Viteritti, Joseph P. 1999. *Choosing Equality: School Choice, the Constitution, and Civil Society.* Washington, DC: Brookings Institution Press.

Witte, John F., Patrick J. Wolf, Alicia Dean, and Deven Carlson. 2010. Milwaukee Independent Charter Schools Study: Report on One Year of Student Growth. Arkansas: School Choice Demonstration Project.

Wolf, Patrick J. 2007. "Civics Exam: Schools of Choice Boost Civic Values." *Education Next* 7(3).

Wolf, Patrick. 2008a. "School Voucher Programs: What the Research Says about Parental School Choice." *Brigham Young University Law Review* 2.

Wolf, Patrick. 2008b. "Vouchers." In *Routledge International Encyclopedia of Education*, edited by Gary McCulloch and David Crook. London: Routledge.

Wolf, Patrick J., Babette Gutmann, Nada Eissa, and Michael Puma. 2005. Evaluation of the DC Opportunity Scholarship Program: First Year Report on Participation. Washington, DC: Institute of Education Sciences, U.S. Department of Education.

Wolf, Patrick, J., Babette Gutmann, Michael Puma, Brian Kisida, Lou Rizzo, Nada Eissa, Matthew Carr, and Marsha Silverberg. 2010. Evaluation of the DC Opportunity Scholarship Program Final Report. Washington, DC: Institute of Education Sciences, U.S. Department of Education.

Wolf, Patrick, J., Babette Gutmann, Michael Puma, Brian Kisida, Lou Rizzo, and Nada Eissa. 2011. "School Vouchers in the Nation's Capital: Summary of Experimental Impacts." In *School Choice and School Improvement*, edited by Mark Berends, Marisa Cannata, and Ellen B. Goldring. Cambridge, MA: Harvard Education Press.

Zimmer, Ron, Brian Gill, Kevin Booker, Stephane Lavertu, Tim R. Sass, and John Witte. 2009. *Charter Schools in Eight States: Effects on Achievement, Attainment, Integration, and Competition.* Santa Monica: RAND Corporation.

Chapter 23

The Link between Nonmarital Births and Poverty

Laura Argys and Susan Averett

INTRODUCTION

Over 15 percent of the U.S. population faces the challenge of living below the federally established poverty threshold (DeNavas-Walt et al. 2011). Children in particular face substantially elevated poverty rates; one in five children lives in a household with income below the official poverty level. High rates of poverty are especially pronounced for children of color; more than one-third of African American children and over one-quarter of Hispanic children live below the poverty line, compared with only 10 percent of white children (National Center for Children in Poverty 2011).

Children living in single-parent homes are particularly at risk. In 2010, children living with an unmarried mother were five times more likely to live in poverty than children in two-parent (intact) families (DeNavas-Walt et al. 2011). These single mothers are often teens with limited access to important social networks and economic resources. Teen mothers are likely to come from low-income families and have low levels of education, and the fathers of their children typically face similar circumstances. Teen pregnancy, particularly outside of marriage, may impede the efforts of young fathers and mothers to lift themselves out of poverty. As a result of their parents' initial circumstances and the difficulties that young, poor parents face, children born to unmarried parents often experience food insecurity, health problems, and substandard housing, and may grow up in neighborhoods characterized by high crime rates, low labor market attachment, and financially strapped public schools. This environment can lead to adverse cognitive, behavioral, and educational outcomes in childhood and adolescence that can carry through to adulthood.

In testimony before Congress, prominent researcher and policy advisor Isabel Sawhill (1999) suggests that nonmarital childbearing is a significant cause of poverty in the United States: "I have become convinced that early out-of-wedlock childbearing is bad for parents, bad for society, and especially bad for children born into such families." Because unmarried mothers are often less educated, are less likely to marry, receive limited support from the fathers of their children, and rely heavily on public assistance, they face challenges in providing adequate support for their children. To design and implement appropriate policies to combat poverty, it is important to understand whether the outcomes for these parents and children would have been different if the birth had been delayed until after marriage. In this chapter we document the trends in nonmarital childbearing (with a focus on teen motherhood) and explore its causes, consequences, and the effectiveness of efforts to mitigate the impact of nonmarital childbearing on parents, their children, and society.

TRENDS IN BIRTHS TO UNMARRIED MOTHERS

Nonmarital births in the United States climbed steadily throughout the latter half of the 20th century but slowed and began a gradual decline at the end of the century. As shown in Figure 23.1, the nonmarital birthrate (the number of nonmarital births per 1,000 unmarried women between the ages of 15 and 44) rose from less than 10 births per thousand women at risk in 1940 to over 40 births per thousand by the mid-1990s. Between 1994 and 2002, the nonmarital birthrate declined by nearly 5 percent (from 46.9 to 43.9). The decline in nonmarital births at the beginning of the 21st century was not sustained, however. In 2002, the nonmarital birth trend resumed its steep climb, exceeding 50 births per 1,000 women at risk by 2007. As a result of both the increase in nonmarital births and a decrease in fertility

Figure 23.1
Number of Births, Birthrate, and Percentage of Births to Unmarried Women: United States, 1940–2007.

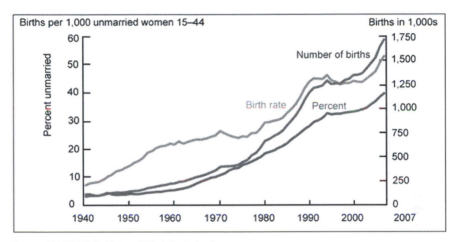

Source: CDC/NCHS, National Vital Statistics System.

within marriage, births to unmarried women rose from less than 5 percent of all births in the 1940s and 1950s to over one-third of all births by 2007. The increase in nonmarital births has been especially pronounced among minority women. In 2006, 70.7 percent of births to African American women and 49.9 percent of births to Hispanic women were nonmarital. These proportions far exceeded those for white (26.6%) and Asian (16.3%) women.

Nonmarital births have been implicated as a primary cause of children living in poverty. This generalization obscures the fact that not all births to unwed mothers are equally likely to result in adverse economic circumstances for mothers and unhealthy developmental environments for children. Not surprisingly, unmarried teen mothers and their children face disproportionately negative consequences among all single-parent families. Two-thirds of children born to unmarried young mothers live in poverty (Urban Institute 2011), and only 38 percent of young mothers go on to complete high school (Perper, Peterson, and Manlove 2010).

There is, however, some reason for optimism. While the overall nonmarital birthrate rose dramatically over the past few decades, the birthrate to teen mothers between the ages of 15 and 19 fell steadily, as seen in Figure 23.2.

Figure 23.2
U.S. Teen Fertility Rate, 1940–2008.

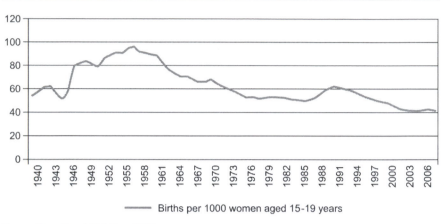

— Births per 1000 women aged 15-19 years

Source: Santelli and Melnikas, 2010.

Figure 23.3
Birthrates Per 1,000 Women Aged 15 to 19 Years, 2005–2009.

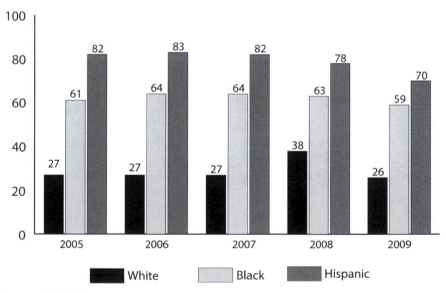

 White ▢ Black ▮ Hispanic

Source: CDC, 2011.

From 1991 through 2006, the teen birthrate fell 32 percent from 56 births per 1,000 teen women to 42 births per 1,000, but increasingly these births occurred outside of marriage (Ventura 2009). Very recently, teen birthrates began to track upward. By 2007 the overall teen birthrate had risen back to its 2002 level (National Campaign to Prevent Teen and Unplanned Pregnancy 2011), though in 2008 it resumed its downward path (Centers for Disease Control and Prevention 2010). Teen births to Hispanic and black women have fallen steadily since 2006 (Figure 23.3).

ARE THERE CONSEQUENCES OF TEENAGE CHILDBEARING?

Economic models of nonmarital childbearing that focus on the time costs of child rearing provide explanations for the disproportionate representation of young women from disadvantaged backgrounds among unmarried mothers (e.g., Becker 1960). Sociologists extend this line of thinking to examine the role played by the economic and cultural environment within a community (Wilson 1987, 1997; Edin and Kefalos 2005). The ability of women to control their fertility is interwoven with each of these explanations (Akerlof, Yellen, and Katz 1996). Though no one theoretical explanation seems able to wholly account for the substantial changes in nonmarital childbearing over the past few decades, each seems to have a role to play in our understanding of this issue. These models suggest the self-selection of poorly educated, low-income young women and men into parenthood outside of marriage, but do not address the possibility that poverty is not just a cause of teen childbearing but that teen childbearing in turn increases the probability of poverty for these parents and their children.

In his 1995 State of the Union Address, President Bill Clinton identified the most serious social problem in the United States as "teen pregnancies and births where there is no marriage" (Clinton 2005), and policy makers highlight the role that early childbearing outside of marriage plays in creating an economic underclass. Though some still focus on the morality of births to unmarried women of all ages, the motivation for most policy in this area seems to be shaped by concerns about lifelong poverty faced by teen mothers and their children. Because many teenage mothers are disadvantaged economically at the time of their pregnancy, it is difficult to isolate the effect of the teenage birth itself from other preexisting factors that cause poor economic outcomes later in life. The challenge of disentangling causation from correlation has led to a robust debate among economists regarding the consequences of early childbearing outside of marriage. What follows is a discussion of studies that attempt to disentangle the tendency of poor women to become single mothers (self-selection) from the economic consequences caused by childbearing outside of marriage.

Consequences for Mothers

Early research in this area by economists, sometimes referred to as "first-generation" studies, focused on cross-sectional regression models that compare earnings, educational attainment, and welfare use for teen mothers with mothers whose first birth occurred after her teen years. These studies statistically accounted for a host of family background and socioeconomic factors to isolate the effect of the teen birth from other factors that determine these outcomes. The evidence from these studies suggests that teen births are associated with lower wages, lower educational attainment, and a higher probability of welfare participation, after controlling for factors such as family income, age, race, parental education, and intellectual ability. As a result of these studies, the conventional wisdom for decades was that teen childbearing put a teenage mother on an irreversible path of economic deprivation. If this is the case, then policy makers have leverage—they can enact policies aimed at reducing teenage childbearing and thereby lower poverty rates and welfare receipt.

If only it were that easy. Even the best of these first-generation studies is plagued by the inevitable inability to statistically control for enough factors to capture the consequences of having a teen birth rather than the selection of disadvantaged women into teen motherhood. If the adverse consequences are not solely a result of teen childbearing, the same women, diverted from a teen birth, would still face a high risk of poverty after having children later in life and still be prone to welfare participation. Critics of the early studies note that while this research can establish a clear positive correlation between teenage childbearing and adverse economic outcomes, it does not definitively establish that the relationship is causal. In other words, there could be other unobservable factors at play. Suppose, for example, that a teen is simply not motivated and hence neither uses birth control consistently nor attends to her studies and thus struggles in school. If she ends up pregnant as a teen, empirical models that cannot adequately control for this lack of motivation will generate a spurious negative correlation between her earnings later in life and the fact that she was a teen mom, even controlling for her level of education.

In an attempt to address this problem, so called "second-generation" research used more recent statistical techniques to disentangle correlation from causation. The first studies in this group compared outcomes for sisters, one of whom had a teen birth while the other did not (Geronimus and Korenman 1992; Hoffman, Foster, and Furstenberg 1993). Because sisters share many of the same family and neighborhood characteristics, including some that are unobservable to a researcher, the differences in outcomes between the sisters should primarily represent the effect of the difference in their ages at first birth. These studies analyze samples from two different time periods—teen births occurring in the 1960s and teen births occurring in the mid-1970s through the mid-1980s. Teen sisters from the 1960s exhibited few negative effects of teen childbearing. The teen mother completed about as much schooling as her sister, had a standard of living that was no lower, and was no more likely to be poor. The analysis of the later cohort of sisters revealed consistently negative effects of a teen birth, although these negative effects were not as large as those found in first-generation studies. For example, economic well-being (measured as family income divided by the poverty line) was, on average, one-third lower for the sister who became a teen mother, as compared to first-generation studies in which the impact of teen motherhood on income was typically between 40 and 50 percent. There were substantial differences between sisters in the probability of being poor, receiving welfare, and completing education, all to the detriment of the sister experiencing a teen birth.

To address concerns that the unobservable factors causing a teenage birth may also play a role in determining educational attainment, Ribar (1994) uses an "instrumental variable" approach. This requires identifying factors outside a teen's control that might influence whether she becomes pregnant. This study relies on age at menarche as an instrument since a girl cannot become pregnant if she has not yet started menstruating. The results from this study provide no evidence that teenage childbearing alters the probability that a teen completes high school. Other researchers who used a similar approach found that girls who responded to policies that encouraged delaying births experienced increases in schooling and labor market activity (Klepinger, Lundberg, and Plotnick 1999).

Ideally, we would like to observe what would happen to a teen mother if she had not experienced a teen birth. This "counterfactual" is not observable so economists aim for the next best thing—trying to find a comparison group that is similar along all dimensions except for teen motherhood. The third generation of studies dates from the work of Hotz, McElroy, and Sanders (1997). The authors compare teen mothers to teens who became pregnant, but miscarried. This is what economists call a "natural experiment," an attempt by social science researchers to observe control and experimental groups that are the hallmark of the scientific method of inquiry. As long as groups are randomly assigned, any differences between the control (miscarriage) and treatment (teen birth) groups are assumed to be due to the effect of the treatment rather than unobservable characteristics that influence, in this case, later life socioeconomic outcomes.

The results from this study are somewhat unexpected. By their mid- to late 20s, teen mothers were found to have fared better over a number of outcomes than their counterparts who miscarried. For example, teen mothers in the study worked more regularly and earned higher wages than their counterparts, and their spouses had higher incomes. Differences in educational attainment (including receiving a GED) and welfare participation between the two groups were very small. Teen mothers did, however, have more births by age 30, and spent more time as a single mother than did the teens who miscarried.

These surprising and somewhat controversial results provided the impetus for a number of follow-up studies that tested the sensitivity of these findings to alternate specifications of the control group. Subsequent work extending the time period (Hoffman 1998), examining different cohorts (Hoffman 1998), defining the control group to include only late-term miscarriages (Ashcraft and Lang 2006), and adding additional variables to control for the social environment (Fletcher and Wolfe 2009) all found that the positive effects of a teen birth on employment and earnings became much weaker. In many cases, in fact, the newer studies confirmed earlier conclusions that there were negative effects of teen motherhood on education and employment. Hotz, McElroy, and Sanders (2005) conducted a follow-up study that addressed some of these issues, concluding there were only small, short-lived, negative economic consequences for teen mothers.

The summary of this research not only presents a succession of findings but also demonstrates the rigor and care with which economists perform their analyses and seek better techniques to try to address policy-relevant questions. In moving from first- to third-generation studies, one thing becomes clear: although there are negative consequences for women who give birth as teens, they are not nearly as severe as suggested by early research. This is an important finding from a policy perspective since it indicates that merely preventing a teenager from giving birth is not enough to place her on the path to economic prosperity. Those teenagers who do give birth are already predisposed to that trajectory. A teen birth alone is not the trigger.

Consequences for Fathers

For a number of reasons, because unmarried fathers may not be identified or informed about a birth or because they choose to disassociate themselves from the mother and child, and because information on many fathers is not often captured in survey data, far less research has been conducted to identify the impact of a birth on unmarried fathers. The data that are available indicate that unmarried fathers are younger, less educated, earn less, and face higher rates of unemployment and incarceration than married fathers (Lerman 1993; Nock 1998; Thornberry, Smith, and Howard 1997; Good and Pirog-Good 1989; Pirog-Good 1988). As was the case when examining the effects of nonmarital births on mothers, researchers must disentangle the selection of men who face economic and social obstacles into fatherhood from the causal impact of fatherhood on these same behaviors and circumstances. Though males with low aspirations and a disinclination for advanced schooling or high-paying, regular employment may be more likely to become fathers at a young age, it is also possible that the birth of a child further inhibits such accomplishments. Alternatively, some researchers suggest that fatherhood enhances one's sense of responsibility and labor market productivity. There are only a handful studies that shed light on this issue.

For parents, the arrival of a child alters the allocation of time and financial resources. One might expect, however, that the effect of becoming a father as a teen might differ from the effect of becoming a teen mother. Even in intact families, mothers tend to have greater responsibility for management of family tasks including child rearing (Parke 2000). This pattern is more pronounced for unmarried parents. Survey data suggest that only 5 percent of children born to unmarried parents lived in a single-father household, although just over 40 percent lived with both unmarried parents for some period (Lerman and Sorensen 2000). Nonresident teen fathers who devote little time to child rearing may be able to pursue their investments in schooling or work with little interruption. On the other hand, the presence of a child could cause a young father to adopt an increased sense of responsibility and work effort (Lerman and Sorensen 2000), though possibly at the expense of educational opportunities.

Increased emphasis on involving nonresident fathers in their children's lives and augmenting public transfers with child support payments has prompted data collection efforts and research focused on unmarried fathers. In *Young Unwed Fathers*, Robert Lerman (1993) was among the first to document the characteristics of young unmarried fathers. These data indicate that men who become unmarried fathers are not representative of all men. In particular, they faced substantially higher probabilities of dropping out of high school and being unemployed than men who did not have a child outside of marriage. Specifically, nearly 50 percent of unmarried fathers had dropped out of high school compared to only 10 percent of unmarried and childless white men. Lerman also reports higher rates of substance use by men who become unmarried fathers. Though the rates of substance use among unmarried fathers of all races were higher compared to men who remained childless, the prevalence of substance problems among white unmarried fathers was particularly pronounced. Nearly 50 percent of white, unmarried fathers reported using hard drugs compared to just over one-quarter of unmarried white men without children. Similarly, 31 percent of unwed white fathers reported having been arrested and charged with a crime compared to only 5.3 percent of white nonfathers.

Similar to first-generation studies on motherhood, Nock (1998) examines the impact of unmarried fatherhood on educational attainment, earnings, employment, and poverty status. He estimates models that statistically control for many characteristics that are associated with self-selection into nonmarital fatherhood: race and ethnicity, family background, cognitive ability, substance use, and criminal activity. He found that nonmarital fatherhood was associated with a reduction of nearly one-half of a year of education and a significant reduction in earnings—about $3,000 per year. A nonmarital birth before the age of 25 also reduced the probability of full-time employment by between 28 and 34 percent. These decreases in labor market productivity translated into substantial increases in the likelihood that an unmarried father lived below the poverty line. Nock extends his analysis to a comparison of brothers, one of whom fathered a child outside of

marriage, the other of whom did not. He finds a slightly larger reduction in education for unmarried fathers (one year less), which is in
keeping with a number of other studies examining the impact of nonmarital fatherhood on education.

Using approaches similar to those used in the third-generation
studies of the consequences of teen motherhood, Fletcher and Wolfe
(forthcoming) compare outcomes for male teenagers whose partners
become pregnant and miscarry with those whose partners give birth.
Their results suggest that young males who become fathers as teens
leave school 0.8 years earlier than teens whose partners' pregnancies
result in miscarriage. To partially offset the drop in schooling, these
teen fathers are more likely to pursue and obtain their GED. Fletcher
and Wolfe find no evidence that employment and earnings decline in
response to teen fatherhood, but recognize that the lower educational
attainment of teen fathers may translate into adverse labor market outcomes in adulthood.

Consequences for Children

Given that unmarried parents are, on average, younger, less
educated, less successful in the labor market, and at increased risk of
poverty, the widely held belief that there are negative consequences
to children of being born to an unwed mother is not surprising.
Although many children raised in nonintact families grow up happy,
healthy, and productive, children growing up in single-parent households, and particularly those with young mothers, face a higher risk
of poor health, low cognitive performance, low education levels,
becoming teen parents themselves, and working and earning less as
adults compared to children who spend their childhood living with
both parents in an intact family.

In *Growing Up with a Single Parent: What Helps, What Hurts?*, Sara
McLanahan and Gary Sandefur (1997) describe the potential causes
of poor outcomes for children in single-parent homes. The first is
obvious: inadequate income leads to low levels of child well-being.
Loss of income can affect the ability to invest extra resources in children's health and education. The loss of social capital resulting from
the absence of one parent can also have negative effects on child
well-being. A lack of trust between parents and weakened ties
between children and their fathers and other relatives can alter the
child's social network in important ways. Finally, the characteristics
of the community in which the child lives may affect child

development. As a consequence of low income, families may live in poorer neighborhoods with fewer institutional and social resources shown to play an important role in the development of aspirations and the transition to adulthood (Wilson 1987, 1997; Kearney and Levine 2009).

A number of studies have examined the consequences of being born to unmarried parents. Controlling for characteristics of the mother and her family, children born to unmarried parents are 37 percent more likely to drop out of school, and girls are 37 percent more likely to experience a teen birth themselves, compared to similar children living in an intact family (McLanahan and Sandefur 1997). Studies comparing outcomes for children born to teen mothers with those born to mothers in their early 20s confirm that children of teen mothers score lower on mathematics, reading, and vocabulary tests (Manlove et al. 2008) and are more likely to drop out of school (Haveman, Wolfe, and Peterson 1997). Still other researchers have compared children of teen and older mothers to examine the link between nonmarital childbearing and behavioral and health outcomes for children. The results from these studies are mixed, but many find additional disadvantages to children born to teen mothers. These children experience more chronic conditions at the same time that they have fewer doctor visits (Wolfe and Rivers 2008; Moore, Morrison, and Greene 1997; Levine, Pollack, and Comfort 2001). Boys born to teen mothers are 10 percent more likely to be incarcerated before the age of 30 (Grogger 1997; Scher and Hoffman 2008).

Finally, researchers find differences in outcomes for children born to sisters, comparing children of sisters who had births before and after the age of 19. These studies document lower test scores and increased behavior problems for children born to teen mothers in the overall sample, but a comparison of these cousins reveals much smaller and often statistically insignificant differences in outcomes, suggesting that unobserved family characteristics of teen mothers account for much of the difference found in studies comparing unrelated children (Geronimus, Korenman, and Hillemeier 1994; Turley 2003).

EFFORTS TO REDUCE NONMARITAL CHILDBEARING AND MITIGATE THE CONSEQUENCES

Over the past several decades, enormous changes have occurred in contraceptive technology and access, family formation, and childbearing in the United States. Initiation of sexual intercourse at younger ages and delays in marriage have resulted in substantial nonmarital sexual activity. Social stigma surrounding a nonmarital birth and the resulting pressure to marry when faced with a pregnancy have abated (Akerlof, Yellen, and Katz 1996). Despite an increase in contraceptive use, nonmarital birthrates remain high, especially for teens. These young mothers often come from disadvantaged families and an early nonmarital birth exacerbates an already precarious economic situation. The consequences for children born to unmarried mothers suggest a cycle of poverty. Nearly one-third of children in single-parent homes live below the poverty line, and nearly two-thirds of children born to teen mothers live in poverty (Urban Institute 2011).

Recent estimates suggest that the cost of teen nonmarital child-bearing, in the form of public expenditures on health care and child welfare, forgone tax revenue of mothers' earnings, and the cost of increases in incarceration for children born to teen mothers, exceeded $10.9 billion in 2008 (National Campaign to Prevent Teen and Unplanned Pregnancy 2011). Because of the substantial public and private costs of nonmarital childbearing, policy makers have sought to adopt policies and fund programs targeted at reducing nonmarital childbearing in general and nonmarital teen births in particular.

The high rate of fertility among the most disadvantaged teens is cause for concern among policy makers but difficult to address. For these youth, the opportunity cost of early childbearing is low. A lack of economic opportunities in the form of achievable educational goals and available jobs makes early parenthood an attractive alternative (Wilson 1987, 1997). Economic recovery that includes the revitalization of poor neighborhoods and the establishment of educational and labor market opportunities could provide important alternatives to early parenthood. The absence of such opportunities for self-sufficiency and upward economic mobility creates the breeding grounds for lifelong poverty.

The social safety net has eroded dramatically since the public has acted on the widely held belief that providing welfare to poor mothers simply provides an incentive to have more children. The combination of declining purchasing power of welfare benefits, the introduction of time limits, and restrictions on the activities of welfare recipients have been only minimally effective in reducing nonmarital births (Moffitt 1992, 1998) and leave little room for additional reforms. Although child support establishment and enforcement on behalf of the children of unmarried parents are improving, the impact of child support on the poorest children is minimal. The men who father these children are often low educated, face high unemployment rates, and have few skills, and many are incarcerated (Garfinkel, McLanahan, and Hansen 1998). Furthermore, these men frequently have children by multiple partners (Guzzo and Furstenberg 2007). As a result, the amount they can contribute in support of their families is low, and the payments that are made often are offset by dollar-for-dollar reductions in benefits with no additional increase in the standard of living for welfare recipients.

There are, however, some encouraging signs. Teenage nonmarital childbearing in the United States is now at a historic low (Santelli and Melnikas 2010; Hamilton, Martin, and Ventura 2010). The declining teen birthrate was lauded by Congress for helping lift many teens out of poverty (U.S. Congress Ways and Means Committee 2004). This low-water mark in teen birthrates, however, still leaves the United States with rates considerably higher than all Western European countries (see Figure 23.4).

Perhaps we can learn from the experiences of our European counterparts. Women in the United States are not alone in the changes that are taking place in reproductive behaviors. Adolescents in the United States initiated sexual activity at an age similar to that of adolescents in Sweden, France, Canada, and Great Britain. Abortion rates have

Figure 23.4
Teen Fertility Rates: Selected Countries, 2008.

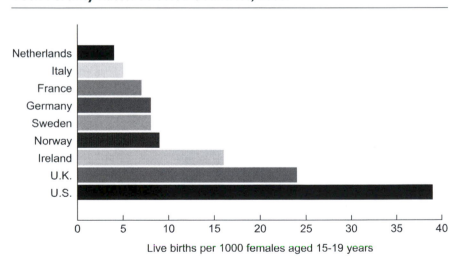

Live births per 1000 females aged 15-19 years

Source: CDC: http:/www.cdc.gov/features/dsTeenPregnancy/ (accessed August 31, 2011).

fallen and marriage rates among teen mothers are low in both the United States and Europe. The most striking difference is that European teens are much more likely to use contraception and to use more effective contraceptive methods. In the Netherlands in 2006, for example, 61 percent of sexually active 15-year-old girls reported using birth control pills at last intercourse compared to just 11 percent of 15-year-olds in the United States (Santelli and Melnikas 2010).

It is difficult to determine what prompts greater contraceptive use among European teens. The answer likely lies in some combination of attitudes about sexual activity, education regarding the effectiveness and use of contraceptives, and access to effective contraception. European attitudes toward sexuality, especially teen sexuality, differ strikingly from those guiding legislation in the United States. Europeans largely recognize that the teen years are often a time of sexual experimentation and that teenagers are likely to be sexually active. Europeans seem to take a more pragmatic approach, and rather than try to prevent sexual activity altogether, they seek solutions to protect teens from unwanted pregnancy and disease (Boonstra 2000, 2002). This recognition is slower in coming in the United States. Despite the fact that a great deal of research suggests that abstinence-only education has been largely ineffective in reducing teen sexual activity and childbearing, it is only very recently that the federal government has eliminated the mandate for abstinence-only education as the answer to dismal teen childbearing statistics (Yang and Gaydos 2010; Boonstra 2007). It is now incumbent upon researchers and educators to identify the most promising features from existing programs to develop and implement effective sex education curriculum (Kirby 2007).

Survey data collected by the Centers for Disease Control and Prevention suggests a very recent surge in contraceptive use among American teens and a shift to more efficient contraceptive methods (Guttmacher Institute 2011). Although increased contraceptive use has contributed to the reduction in teen pregnancies and births (Santelli et. al. 2007); Guttmacher Institute 2011), access to and affordability of contraceptives remain an obstacle to further reductions in the teen birthrate in the United States. Universal health care in Europe means that teens do not face access issues. In the United States, on the other hand, 36 million women had unmet contraceptive needs in 2008. Of those, 17.4 million were in need of publicly funded services either because they had an income below 250 percent of the federal poverty line or because they were teenagers (Guttmacher Institute 2008). Four in 10 poor women of reproductive age have no insurance coverage whatsoever (Gold et al. 2009). Enhancing access to effective contraception and adopting more pragmatic attitudes toward policies concerning teen sexuality may pave the way for providing effective education and comprehensive access to family planning, allowing teens to effectively avoid unwanted pregnancies.

BIBLIOGRAPHY

Akerlof, George A., Janet L. Yellen, and Michael I. Katz. 1996. "An Analysis of Out-of-Wedlock Childbearing in the United States." *Quarterly Journal of Economics*, CXI (2) (May).

Ashcraft, A., and K. Lang. 2006. "The Consequences of Teenage Childbearing." National Bureau of Economic Research Working Paper No. 12485, Cambridge, MA.

Becker, Gary S. 1960. "An Economic Analysis of Fertility." In *Demographic and Economic Change in Developed Countries*, edited by Universities National Bureau Committee for Economic Research, 209–31. Princeton, NJ: Princeton UP.

Boonstra, Heather. 2000. "Promoting Contraceptive Use and Choice: France's Approach to Teen Pregnancy and Abortion." The Guttmacher Report on Public Policy. June.

Boonstra, Heather. 2002. "Teen Pregnancy: Trends and Lessons Learned." *Guttmacher Policy Review.* 5(1): 7–10. http://www.guttmacher.org/pubs/tgr/05/1/gr050107.html (last accessed September 5, 2011).

Boonstra, Heather. 2007. "The Case for a New Approach to Sex Education Mounts: Will Policy Makers Heed the Message?" *Guttmacher Policy Review*, 10(2): 2–7. http://www.guttmacher.org/pubs/gpr/10/2/gpr100202.pdf.

Centers for Disease Control and Prevention. 2010. Table 15, December. http://www.cdc.gov/nchs/data/nvsr/nvsr59/nvsr59_01.pdf.

Clinton, William J. 1995. "State of the Union 1995," delivered version. http://www.let.rug.nl/usa/P/bc42/speeches/sud95wjc.htm.

DeNavas-Walt, Carmen, Bernadette D. Proctor, and Jessica C. Smith. 2011. "Income, Poverty and Health Insurance Coverage in the United States: 2010." U.S. Bureau of the Census, P60-239, September. http://www.census.gov/prod/2011pubs/p60-239.pdf.

Edin, Kathryn, and Maria Kefalas. 2005. *Promises I Can Keep: Why Poor Women Put Motherhood before Marriage.* Berkeley, CA: University of California Press.

Federal Register. 2009. Annual Update of the HHS Poverty Guidelines. 74(14). http://aspe.hhs.gov/poverty/09fedreg.shtml.

Fletcher, Jason M., and Barbara L. Wolfe. 2009. "Education and Labor Market Consequences of Teenage Childbearing: Evidence Using the Timing of Pregnancy Outcomes and Community Fixed Effects." *Journal of Human Resources* 44(2): 303–25.

Fletcher, Jason M., and Barbara L. Wolfe. Forthcoming. "The Effects of Teenage Fatherhood on Young Adult Outcomes." *Economic Inquiry.*

Garfinkel, Irwin, Sara S. McLanahan, and Thomas L. Hanson. 1998. "A Patchwork Portrait of Non-resident Fathers." In *Fathers under Fire*, edited by Irwin Garfinkel, Sara S. McLanahan, Daniel R. Meyer, and Judith A. Seltzer, 31–59. New York: Russell Sage Foundation.

Geronimus, Arline, and Sanders Korenman. 1992. "The Socioeconomic Consequences of Teen Childbearing Reconsidered." *Quarterly Journal of Economics*, 107: 1187–1214.

Geronimus, Arline T., Sanders Korenman, and Marianne M. Hillemeier. 1994. "Does Young Maternal Age Adversely Affect Child Development? Evidence from Cousin Comparisons in the United States." *Population and Development*, 20(3): 585–609.

Gold, R. B. et al. 2009. *Next Steps for America's Family Planning Program: Leveraging the Potential of Medicaid and Title X in an Evolving Health Care System*. New York: Guttmacher Institute.

Good, D., and M. A. Pirog-Good. 1989. "Models for Bivariate Count Data with and Application to Teenage Delinquency and Paternity." *Sociological Methods and Research*, 17(4): 409–31.

Grogger, Jeff. 1997. "Consequences of Teen Childbearing for Incarceration among Adult Children: Approach and Estimates through 1991." In *Kids Having Kids*, edited by Rebecca A. Maynard. Washington, DC: Urban Institute Press.

Guttmacher Institute. 2011. "New Government Data Finds Sharp Decline in Teen Births," New in Context, http://www.guttmacher.org/media/inthenews/2011/12/01/index.html, released December 1, 2011.

Guttmacher Institute. Contraceptive Needs and Services. 2008 Update. New York: Guttmacher Institute, 2010, http://www.guttmacher.org/pubs/win/contraceptive-needs-2008.pdf (last accessed September 1, 2010).

Guttmacher Institute. 2010. U.S. Teenage Pregnancies, Births and Abortions: National and State Trends and Trends by Race and Ethnicity. http://www.guttmacher.org/pubs/USTPtrends.pdf (last accessed September 5, 2011).

Guzzo, Karen, and Frank Furstenberg. 2007. "Multipartnered Fertility among American Men." *Demography*, 44(3): 583–601.

Hamilton, B. E., J. A. Martin, and S. J. Ventura. 2010. Births: Preliminary Data for 2009. National Vital Statistics Reports, vol. 59, no 3. Hyattsville, MD: National Center for Health Statistics. Table 2.

Haveman, Robert, Barbara Wolfe, and Elaine Peterson. 1997. "Children of Early Childbearers as Young Adults." In *Kids Having Kids*, edited by Rebecca Maynard. Washington, DC: Urban Institute Press.

Hoffman, Saul D. 1998. "Teen Childbearing Isn't So Bad After All . . . or Is It?" *Family Planning Perspectives*, 30(5): 236–39.

Hoffman, Saul D., E. Michael Foster, and Frank F. Furstenberg Jr. 1993. "Re-evaluating the Costs of Teenage Childbearing." *Demography*, 30(1): 1–13.

Hotz, V. J., S. W. McElroy, and S. G. Sanders. 1997. "The Impacts of Teenage Childbearing on the Mothers and the Consequences of Those Impacts for Government." In *Kids Having Kids*, edited by R. Maynard. Washington, DC: Urban Institute Press.

Hotz, V. Joseph, Susan Williams McElroy, and Seth G. Sanders. 2005. "Teenage Childbearing and Its Life Cycle Consequences." *Journal of Human Resources*, 40: 683–715.

Kearney, Melissa S., and Phillip B. Levine. 2009. "Socioeconomic Disadvantage and Early Childbearing." In *The Problems of Disadvantaged Youth: An Economic Perspective*, edited by Jonathan Gruber. Chicago: University of Chicago Press.

Kirby, D. 2007. *Emerging Answers 2007: Research Findings on Programs to Reduce Teen Pregnancy and Sexually Transmitted Diseases*. Washington, DC: National Campaign to Prevent Teen Pregnancy.

Klepinger, Daniel H., Shelly Lundberg, and Robert Plotnick. 1999. "How Does Adolescent Fertility Affect the Human Capital and Wages of Young Women?" *Journal of Human Resources*, 34(3): 421–48.

Lerman, Robert I. 1993. "A National Profile of Young Unwed Fathers. In *Young Unwed Fathers: Changing Roles and Emerging Policies*, edited by R. I. Lerman and T. J. Ooms. Philadelphia: Temple University Press.

Lerman, Robert I., and Elaine Sorensen. 2000. "Father Involvement with their Non-marital Children." In *Fatherhood: Research, Interventions and Policies*, edited by H. Elizabeth Peters, Gary W. Peterson, Suzanne Steinmetz, and Randal D. Day. New York: The Haworth Press.

Levine, Judith A., Harold Pollack, and Maureen E. Comfort. 2001. "Academic and Behavioral Outcomes among the Children of Young Mothers." *Journal of Marriage and the Family*, 59(2): 355–69.

Manlove, Jennifer S., Elizabeth Terry-Humen, Lisa A. Mincieli, and Kristen A. Moore. 2008. "Outcomes for Children of Teen Mothers from Kindergarten through Adolescence." In *Kids Having Kids*, 2nd Edition, edited by Saul D. Hoffman and Rebecca A. Maynard, 161–220. Washington, DC: Urban Institute Press.

McLanahan, Sara, and Gary Sandefur. 1997. *Growing up with a Single Parent: What Helps, What Hurts?* Cambridge, MA: Harvard University Press.

Moffitt, Robert A. 1992. "Incentive Effects of the U.S. Welfare System: A Review." *Journal of Economic Literature*, 30(1): 1–61.

Moffitt, Robert A. 1998. "The Effects of Welfare on Marriage and Fertility." In *Welfare, the Family, and Reproductive Behavior*, edited by Robert A. Moffitt. Washington, DC: National Research Council.

Moore, Kristen A., Donna Ruane Morrison, and Angela D. Greene. 1997. "Effects on Children Born to Adolescent Mothers." In *Kids Having Kids*, edited by Rebecca Maynard. Washington, DC: Urban Institute Press.

National Campaign to Prevent Teen and Unplanned Pregnancy. 2011. Counting It Up, the Public Costs of Teen Childbearing. http://www.thenationalcampaign .org/costs/default.aspx (last accessed July 30, 2011).

National Center for Children in Poverty. 2011. *Child Poverty*. http://www.nccp .org/topics/childpoverty.html.

Nock, Steven L. 1998. "The Consequences of Premarital Fatherhood." *American Sociological Review*, 63: 250–63.

Parke, Ross. 2000. "Father Involvement: A Developmental Psychological Per-spective." In *Fatherhood: Research, Interventions and Policies*, edited by H. Elizabeth Peters, Gary W. Peterson, Suzanne Steinmetz, and Randal D. Day. New York: The Haworth Press.

Perper, Kate, Kristen Peterson, and Jennifer Manlove. 2010. "Diploma Attachment among Teen Mothers." http://www.childtrends.org/Files/Child_Trends -2010_01_22_FS_DiplomaAttainment.pdf .

Pirog-Good, M. A. 1988. "Teenage Paternity, Child Support and Crime." *Social Science Quarterly*, 69(3): 527–46.

Ribar, David C. 1994. "Teenage Fertility and High School Completion." *Review of Economics and Statistics*, 76: 413–24.

Santelli, John, and Andrea Melnikas. 2010. "Teen Fertility in Transition: Recent and Historic Trends in the United States." *Annual Review of Public Health*, 31: 371–83.

Santelli, John S., Laura Duberstein Lindberg, Lawrence B. Finer, Susheela Singh. 2007 "Explaining Recent Declines in Adolescent Pregnancy in the United States: The Contribution of Abstinence and Improved Contraceptive Use." *American Journal of Public Health*, 97(1): 150–156.

Sawhill, Isabel V. 1999. Testimony to the U.S. House Ways and Means Committee and reprinted as "Non-Marital Births and Child Poverty in the United States." Brookings Institution. http://www.brookings.edu/testimony/ 1999/0629poverty_sawhill.aspx (last accessed July 10, 2011).

Scher, Lauren Sue, and Saul D. Hoffman. 2008. "Updated Estimates through 2002." In *Kids Having Kids: Economic Costs and Social Consequences of Teen Pregnancy*, 2nd Edition, edited by Saul D. Hoffman and Rebecca A. Maynard, 403–433. Washington, DC: Urban Institute Press.

Thornberry, T. P., C. A. Smith, and G. J. Howard. 1997. "Risk Factors for Teenage Fatherhood." *Journal of Marriage and Family*, 59(3): 505–22.

Turley, Ruth N. L. 2003. "Are Children of Young Mothers Disadvantaged Because of Their Mother's Age or Family Background?" *Child Development*, 74(2): 465–74.

Urban Institute. 2011. *Welfare Rules Database*. http://anfdata.urban.org/wrd/maps .cfm.

U.S. Congress Ways and Means Committee—Democrats. 2004. "Steep Decline in Teen Birth Rate Significantly Responsible for Reducing Child Poverty and Single-Parent Families." *Comm. Issue Brief*, April 23.

Ventura, S. J. 2009. "Changing Patterns of Nonmarital Childbearing in the United States." NCHS data brief number 18, Hyattsville, Maryland.

Wilson, William Julius. 1987. *The Truly Disadvantaged: The Inner City, the Underclass, and Public Policy*. Chicago: University of Chicago Press.

Wilson, William Julius. 1997. *When Work Disappears*. New York: Vintage Books.

Wolfe, Barbara, and Emilie McHugh Rivers. 2008. "Children's Health and Health Care." In *Kids Having Kids: Economic Costs and Social Consequences of Teen Pregnancy*, 2nd Edition, edited by Saul D. Hoffman and Rebecca A. Maynard, 221–56. Washington, DC: Urban Institute Press.

Yang, Zjhou, and Laura M. Gaydos. 2010. "Reasons for and Challenges of Recent Increases in Teen Birth Rates: A Study of Family Planning Service Policies and Demographic Changes at the State Level." *Journal of Adolescent Health*, 46: 517–24.

Chapter 24

What Happened to Cash Assistance for Needy Families?

David C. Ribar and Carolyn M. Wolff

GOALS OF SOCIAL ASSISTANCE

Controversy has surrounded the federally supported cash assistance program for poor families with children since its inception in the Social Security Act of 1935.[1] Originally called the Aid to Dependent Children program, it was rechristened the Aid to Families with Dependent Children (AFDC) program following reforms in 1962 and later the Temporary Assistance for Needy Families (TANF) program following reforms in 1996. Part of the controversy likely stems from the program's costs; empirical studies have found that taxpayer support for transfers falls when the cost of assistance increases (Gramlich 1982; Moffitt 1990; Orr 1976; Ribar and Wilhelm 1999). However, more controversy seems to center on the ways that means-tested programs work at cross-purposes, alleviating the immediate condition of poverty while at the same time encouraging behaviors that can lead families into poverty.

What are the goals of cash assistance programs for poor families with children, and given the attendant costs, why would broad sets of taxpayers ever support them? Rational self-interest might be one motivation—taxpayers might want a safety net in place in case they ever fall on hard times. Though reasonable, selfishness seems like an incomplete explanation because few people would ever have the need for this assistance. Hochman and Rodgers (1969) proposed a more universal motivation, theorizing that taxpayers are partially altruistic and care not only about their own well-being but also about the well-being of others, such as disadvantaged families. Even with this explanation, however, the question remains of how best to improve the well-being of disadvantaged families.

On the one hand, transferring money to people improves their well-being by giving them more resources to use to purchase goods and services. On the other hand, transferring money to a family also changes the incentives for that family to earn income on its own and may even encourage the family to expand its needs.

We can consider some of these incentives for work. The vast majority of people get their incomes through work and earnings. If people value the time they spend away from their jobs (or dislike the time they spend at their jobs), transferring money to them will reduce their incentives to work, lowering their earnings and making them poorer in terms of nontransfer income. Worse from an incentives standpoint, the process of means testing in cash welfare programs causes the eligibility for and amount of assistance to fall as a person's pretransfer income increases. Means testing is intended to limit assistance to those who need it most, but it has the unintended effect of acting as an extra tax on the earnings of program recipients, lowering the rewards associated with work. In some cases, including the TANF programs currently operating in some states today, benefits are docked exactly one dollar for each dollar earned in pretransfer income, completely eliminating the financial incentive to work among people who command low hourly wages or can work only a few hours per week.

In addition to the short-term effects on work, welfare programs may encourage other behaviors that contribute to poverty over the longer term (Murray 1984). Because the AFDC/TANF program is available only for households with children, it may encourage people to have more children than they otherwise would. Rules that have either limited welfare to single parents or have made welfare harder to obtain for married parents have the unintended effect of discouraging marriage. The availability of welfare may also reduce the incentives to complete school or to acquire skills. Moreover, a parent's participation in welfare may also influence the future behavior of her children, leading to an intergenerational dependence on assistance. While all of these longer-term effects raise concerns, most empirical research indicates that these effects are modest or negligible (Blank 2002; Moffitt 1992).

As we discuss in this chapter, the U.S. cash welfare system underwent a number of significant reforms to address the programs' deleterious incentives. The reforms were intended to discourage dependency and promote economic self-sufficiency. Most of these reforms, however, took the form of direct or indirect reductions in assistance to families. Examples of direct reductions include imposing lifetime limits on the receipt of assistance and ending the entitlement to assistance. Indirect reductions include conditioning welfare receipt on work or schooling. These restrictive actions raise the question of whether the other goal of welfare programs—to provide help to the disadvantaged—has been compromised.

In the next section of this chapter, we review the reforms that occurred in the AFDC program, starting in the early 1990s. We also discuss the economic circumstances in which these changes occurred. We follow that discussion with a description of trends in outcomes and well-being measures for at-risk families generally, including trends in employment rates, poverty, single parenthood, and welfare participation. Many of these trends indicate that well-being improved on average, at least in the years initially following the reforms. Finally, we examine the conditions and circumstances of the shrinking number of families that continued to rely on cash assistance. Average well-being for these families appears to have suffered in the wake of reform.

POLICY AND ECONOMIC CHANGES SINCE THE EARLY 1990s

AFDC, the cash welfare program in place at the start of the 1990s, was a federal-state partnership. The states operated and administered the assistance programs under a general set of rules and with financial support from the federal government. Within these rules, each state set its own maximum benefit level and determined the maximum level of income that qualified for assistance. States were also responsible for the day-to-day administration of the program. Financial assistance from the federal government took the form of open-ended matching grants in which a dollar of benefit spending by the states was matched by one to as much as three and a half dollars in federal support, depending on the state's relative economic standing. The rules set by the federal government included the general benefit and eligibility formulas. Following an earlier reform in 1988 (the Family Support Act of 1988), states were required to offer assistance to two-parent families (though under stricter conditions than single-parent families), operate job assistance programs, mandate work among some recipients, offer child care to working recipients, and provide transitional assistance to families who worked their way off the program (Moffitt 1992).

Because of the widespread dissatisfaction with the AFDC program, the federal government began granting states waivers from the program rules, starting in the early 1990s. The waivers were intended to allow states to experiment with different program structures and were generally granted if a state could show that the changes would not cost the federal government more money. Ultimately, 43 states took advantage of this opportunity to reform their own programs and were granted waivers.

The waivers generally included changes in several program elements, with the set of changes being unique to each state. Crouse (1999) categorized the changes into six types: (1) imposition of time limits on the receipt of benefits, (2) changes in the groups covered by mandatory work and training requirements, (3) changes in the amount of time before recipients were required to work, (4) changes in benefit sanctions from not meeting work and program requirements, (5) imposition of "family caps" (families could not collect additional benefits for children born while the family was on assistance), and (6) increases in earnings disregards or decreases in benefit reduction rates. With the exception of the modifications in earnings disregards and benefit formulas, the changes had the effect of reducing the generosity of welfare. Time limits on receipt reduced the duration of benefits and were intended to shift welfare toward being temporary rather than permanent assistance. The changes in work rules made welfare harder to obtain by conditioning receipt on employment or other work activities, including job search, education, training, and community work experience, and were intended to promote employment. The changes in earnings disregards and benefit formulas were also intended to promote employment but through the positive incentive of letting welfare recipients keep more of their welfare benefits as their earnings increased.

In 1996, Congress passed the Personal Responsibility and Work Opportunity Reconciliation Act (PRWORA), which replaced the states' AFDC programs with TANF programs and also reformed other assistance programs. The PRWORA changed the cash assistance system in several fundamental respects. First, it restricted federally supported welfare by limiting lifetime receipt to five years and by imposing new work requirements on recipients. Second, it changed the federal support from an unlimited matching grant to a fixed block grant. The block grant would be conditioned on a proportion of the state's caseload meeting work requirements and on the state expending a portion of its own funds. Third, the PRWORA eliminated the entitlement to assistance—once states had exhausted their annual block grants and met a maintenance-of-effort requirement with their own funds, they were no longer required to pay benefits. Fourth, it removed other restrictions from the states' operation of their programs, allowing them to incorporate their own reforms. Thus the legislation included more restrictions on states in some elements of their assistance programs but more flexibility in other areas.

States had to submit their TANF plans to the Department of Health and Human Services (DHHS) for approval. The first TANF programs were implemented in September 1996, and all of the states had implemented programs by the start of 1998. Where they had the option to do so, some states adopted elements from their AFDC waivers, while others crafted entirely new programs (Crouse 1999).

TANF was initially authorized for five years. When TANF came up for renewal, legislative disagreements over the types of subsequent reforms led to a series of one-year continuations. During this period, the U.S. Government Accountability Office issued a report identifying inconsistent and suspect practices across states in the types of activities that could count toward meeting the federal work requirements and in the internal controls used to verify the accuracy of reported work hours (U.S. Government Accountability Office 2005). For example, the Government Accountability Office found that some states were counting bed rest, exercise, smoking cessation, and massage therapy as "work readiness activities." When TANF was reauthorized as part of the Deficit Reduction Act of 2005, work requirements were strengthened through three main channels: (1) by requiring that families in separate state-funded programs meet the work requirements, (2) by increasing the percentage of recipients required to work in each state, and (3) by standardizing work eligibility and the activities that satisfy the work requirement across states. These changes went into effect on October 1, 2006 (Reauthorization of the Temporary Assistance for Needy Families Program: Interim Final Rule 2006).

The changes in the AFDC and TANF programs were accompanied by changes in other assistance programs. The Earned Income Tax Credit (EITC), a refundable tax credit available to people with low to moderate levels of earned income, was expanded significantly in 1993, when AFDC waivers were becoming more common. The EITC significantly reduced the tax burden of low-income households, thus increasing the incentives to work. The primary welfare reform legislation, the PRWORA, also made changes to other assistance programs. For example, the PRWORA altered the food stamp program to reduce benefits, eliminate eligibility for most immigrants, and impose work requirements and time limits on able-bodied adults without dependents. Later legislation restored eligibility for many immigrants and made food stamps easier to obtain. In 1997, Congress passed State Children's Health Insurance Programs, which expanded Medicaid coverage to children of low-income, working parents. Families who received or had recently transitioned off welfare automatically qualified to receive Medicaid benefits, creating yet another incentive to become eligible for welfare (Yelowitz 1995). The expansion of these benefits to low-income, working families was partly intended to improve the incentives for work. A study by Moffitt and Scholz (2009) found that the constellation of reforms had the effect of shifting the distribution of transfers away from the poorest single- and two-parent households and toward near-poor households and households with disabled members.

The changes in cash assistance also occurred in the context of a growing economy. The AFDC waivers began to be implemented as the United States was emerging from a recession in 1990–91, and the PRWORA was enacted just a few years into what would become the longest economic expansion in U.S. history. The national unemployment rate dropped from a peak of 7.8 percent in July 1992 to 5.1 percent at the time PRWORA was enacted in August 1996. The national unemployment rate continued to fall throughout the late 1990s, reaching a low of 3.8 percent in April 2000. A mild recession in 2001 caused unemployment to rise, but only to a level of 6.3 percent. From the middle of 2005 until the start of the Great Recession at the end of 2007, unemployment remained at or below 5 percent (U.S. Department of Labor 2011). A rising tide might not lift all boats, but the robust job market that characterized most of the 1990s and much of the 2000s undoubtedly made the policy goals of promoting work and economic self-sufficiency among the disadvantaged easier to achieve.

Conversely, with unemployment soaring during the Great Recession, the well-being of disadvantaged families has likely deteriorated.

TRENDS IN GENERAL WELL-BEING OUTCOMES

One measure of the general well-being of at-risk families is the welfare caseload, the number of families receiving welfare benefits. As the caseload decreases, we might believe that the well-being of at-risk families has increased. Prior to the start of the AFDC waiver period in fiscal year (FY) 1990, there were approximately 3.9 million households in the United States receiving cash welfare payments.[2] The initial waivers were requested and granted at a time of expanding caseloads. However, after reaching a peak in FY 1994, the caseload began a 14-year decline. In FY 1995, just one year before PRWORA was enacted, there were roughly 4.8 million households receiving AFDC benefits, and by FY 2008, the caseload had dropped to approximately 1.6 million households.

Of course, if caseload reduction were the foremost goal of assistance policy, we could achieve that goal overnight by eliminating TANF altogether. Instead, welfare assistance focuses on alleviating poverty. The poverty rate among those at risk of becoming dependent on welfare, single mothers with dependent children, has exhibited clear trends over the past 20 years. In 1991, over 47 percent of all single mothers with children under 18 were living in poverty. As economic conditions improved over the 1990s, so did the poverty rate among this group of women, and it reached an all-time low of 33 percent in 2000. However, between 2000 and 2008, conditions worsened for single mothers, and the percentage of those living in poverty grew to just over 37 percent in 2008 (U.S. Census Bureau 2011b).

The employment rate of single mothers is a measure of well-being closely tied to poverty and self-sufficiency. In particular, the earned income from employment may be enough to elevate a woman and her family out of poverty and into self-sufficiency so that she is no longer dependent on welfare assistance. The employment of single mothers improved throughout the 1990s. In 1990, almost 56 percent of single mothers in the United States were working, and by 2000, this figure had reached almost 63 percent. However, by 2003, the employment rate for this group had dipped to approximately 60 percent, and it remained between 60 and 61 percent from 2003 to 2008.[3]

The welfare program primarily benefits single-parent families. Thus a key measure of well-being that puts a woman at risk of becoming dependent on assistance is female headship or the birth of a child out of wedlock. Data from the Centers for Disease Control and Prevention (2011) show that nonmarital births have been generally increasing over the past 20 years. In 1990, 28 percent of all births were to unmarried mothers. By 2000, this figure had surpassed 33 percent. The percentage of nonmarital births continued to rise over the next eight years, reaching just under 41 percent by 2008. The fertility rate of unmarried women has also risen since 1990; however, the increase occurred primarily in more recent years. In 1990, there were fewer than 44 live births to unmarried women age 15–44 per 1,000 such women in the population. Between 1990 and 2004, the rates fluctuated between 43 and 46; however, after 2004, the fertility rate of unmarried women began a marked increase. By 2008, there were almost 53 live births to unmarried women age 15–44 per 1,000 such women in the population.

As the fertility rate of unmarried women increases, so too does the proportion of women at risk of becoming dependent on the welfare system. However, there have been some positive trends. In particular, the fertility rate of unmarried teenage women has been decreasing over the past 20 years. In 1990, there were approximately 30 births to single women age 15–17 per 1,000 single women age 15–17 in the population. Between 1990 and 1995, this figure fluctuated between 30 and 32; however, beginning in 1996 it started to decline. In 2005, the fertility rate of single teens had dropped to just under 20 live births per 1,000 teen women. Although the fertility rate of single teens did increase slightly between 2005 and 2008, it remained below 21 live births per 1,000 teen women during these years (Martin et al. 2010).

Numerous studies have examined the ways in which welfare reform and other policy and economic changes have contributed to these different trends, with the findings from the studies being summarized in several comprehensive reviews by Blank (2002), Grogger and Karoly (2005), and Moffitt (2002). The studies have generally found that welfare reform has played a role in reducing the assistance caseload, increasing employment, and increasing earnings. There is less agreement, however, regarding which specific reform components have been responsible. For example, the Council of Economic Advisors (1997) found that only work sanction waivers had a significant impact in reducing welfare recipiency. However, Moffitt (1999) concluded that work requirements and family caps were important, while Grogger and Karoly (2005) concluded that mandatory work requirements and financial incentives were crucial. In contrast to the research on case-load and economic outcomes associated with welfare reform, the find-ings regarding the associations with demographic outcomes, such as marriage and single-parenthood has been more equivocal.

DATA ON RECIPIENTS

While the economic well-being of families at risk of becoming dependent on welfare did improve between 1990 and 2008, those actually receiving welfare have not experienced the same progress. In order to show that this is the case, we will make use of administrative data from the DHHS on recipients of AFDC and TANF assistance. The DHHS publishes tables and makes available annual, public-use data on a sample of households from the AFDC and TANF programs in each state (U.S. DHHS 2011a, 2011b, 2011d). Information on active AFDC households is available from FY 1967 through FY 1997, while data on both active and closed TANF cases are available from FY 2000 through FY 2008, to date. Data on closed TANF cases are reported for the households' last month of TANF cash receipt. In this chapter, we will focus on AFDC data from fiscal years 1990 and 1995 and TANF data from fiscal years 2000, 2005, and 2008 for all 50 states and the District of Columbia.

The DHHS data encompass a rich set of variables for analysis. For each household in the sample, the data contain information such as household size, assistance received, and financial resources. The data also contain detailed information on both recipient and nonrecipient individuals in each household. The person-level data include relation-ships within the household, demographic information, education level, employment status, citizenship, and disability receipt. The broad range of both household-level and person-level characteristics available in this dataset make it particularly well suited for this chapter. The data on earned and unearned income, education, and employment allow us to study trends in the economic well-being of welfare recipients, while the extensive data on cash and noncash assistance allow us to study trends in recipiency over the past 20 years of welfare reform.

The Rise in Child-Only Cases

One of the most noticeable trends in the cash assistance caseload has been the steady rise in the proportion of cases in which children are the only members of the household receiving assistance—so-called "child-only" cases. The DHHS (2010a) tabulations indicate that in FY 1990, child-only cases comprised just under one-eighth of the welfare caseload. By 1995, just prior to the enactment of the PRWORA, the fraction had increased to slightly more than one-sixth. By FY 2000, the fraction had reached one-third, and by FY 2008, the fraction had climbed to slightly over one-half. The absolute number of child-only cases peaked in FY 1996 at nearly 1 million, fell in the first few years after the PRWORA, but began climbing in FY 1999. In FY 2008, there were slightly more than 800,000 child-only cases (Charlesworth, Hercik, and Kakuska 2011).

Child-only cases arise under a number of circumstances. In about two-thirds of these cases in FY 2008, a parent is present in the household but is not included in the welfare assistance unit (U.S. DHHS 2010b). A parent would not be included in the assistance unit if she was receiving disability on her own, was an immigrant, had been sanctioned for not complying with a work or other requirement, or was excluded for other reasons. In the remaining one-third of child-only cases, the parent is not present in the household, and the children are being cared for by a relative or other caretaker.

There are several policy and well-being concerns surrounding child-only cases. First and foremost, these cases generally receive fewer benefits than they might otherwise because at least one fewer person is included in the assistance unit. In cases in which the parent is present in the household, this will mean fewer resources for the family. In cases where other caretakers are responsible for the children, the hardships can extend to other family members and may discourage some people from caring for relatives. The second concern is that these are cases where there are few options for promoting self-sufficiency. Third, the generally upward trend in the number of child-only cases since 1999 is an indicator of underlying economic needs.

Outcomes for Parent-Headed Cases

We use the administrative micro-data from the DHHS to construct tables describing how assistance, economic outcomes, and other characteristics for more traditional parent-headed cases have changed over time. Statistics for these families are reported in Table 24.1. The figures indicate that the average amount of monthly cash assistance for these households has declined markedly over time from $662 (in constant 2008 dollars) per family in FY 1990 to $413 in FY 2008, a 28 percent

Table 24.1

Characteristics of Active AFDC/TANF Cases with Adult Recipients

	FY 1990	FY 1995	FY 2000	FY 2005	FY 2008
Household Composition					
Number of household members	3.7	3.8	3.2	3.0	3.0
Number of recipients in the household	3.1	3.1	3.1	2.9	2.9
Percent with two or more adult recipients	7.3%	8.5%	6.0%	4.5%	7.3%
Percent headed by teen parents		0.2%	0.5%	0.4%	0.3%
Percent with recipient adults receiving disability benefits	0.9%	1.4%	0.9%	0.7%	0.8%
Percent with recipient children receiving disability benefits	0.1%	1.5%	0.5%	0.6%	0.9%
Household Public Assistance Receipt					
Amount of cash benefits received	$662	$556	$458	$431	$413
Months of cash benefit receipt			23.1	25.6	26.0
Percent receiving food stamps	91.2%	94.4%	89.2%	91.1%	89.4%
Percent receiving medical assistance			99.4%	97.7%	97.5%
Percent living in public housing	9.9%	8.3%	7.1%	5.9%	5.0%
Percent receiving a rent subsidy	15.4%	15.9%	12.7%	13.2%	10.3%
Household Income and Resources					
Percent with earned income	10.6%	13.4%	25.2%	20.5%	24.1%
Earned income amount[a]	$57	$83	$212	$156	$199

(continued)

Table 24.1 (Continued)

	FY 1990	FY 1995	FY 2000	FY 2005	FY 2008
Percent with unearned income	9.6%	13.7%	9.2%	8.5%	9.5%
Unearned income amount[b]	$37	$58	$35	$33	$30
Percent with any income	19.1%	25.5%	32.3%	27.4%	31.5%
Total income amount	$94	$141	$248	$189	$229
Percent with cash resources/liquid assets	14.4%	15.2%	13.0%	13.2%	11.9%
Cash resources/Liquid assets	$33	$36	$43	$28	$22
Characteristics of Heads of Households					
Age	29.9	30.7	31.0	30.4	29.9
White[c]	40.1%	38.1%	32.3%	36.3%	35.8%
Black[c]	40.0%	37.0%	39.2%	40.1%	37.2%
Hispanic[c]	14.5%	18.3%	21.5%	18.8%	21.9%
Other/missing race[c]	4.1%	4.6%	5.9%	4.4%	5.0%
Completed high school	26.8%	34.5%	51.2%	59.3%	56.8%
U.S. citizen	92.9%	87.8%	91.0%	93.4%	93.1%
Number of households (millions)	3.4	3.9	1.5	1.0	0.8

Note: The statistics are authors' calculations from DHHS administrative data from the AFDC and TANF programs. All dollar figures are expressed in constant 2008 amounts deflated using the CPI-U.
[a]In FY 1990–95, earned income is computed for all recipients age 18 and older; in FY 2000–2008, earnings of 18-year-olds enrolled full-time in secondary school are excluded.
[b]In FY 1990–95, unearned income does not include housing assistance; in FY 2000–2008, it does.
[c]The data on race and ethnicity are mutually exclusive in FY 1990–95 but not in FY 2000–2008. For comparability, race was assigned in FY 2000–2008 as Hispanic, non-Hispanic white, non-Hispanic black, and non-Hispanic other.

drop. By way of comparison, the poverty threshold for a family of three in 2008 was $1,467, so average benefits fell from 45 percent of the poverty standard in FY 1990 to just 28 percent of the poverty standard in FY 2008.

However, cash assistance was not the only resource that welfare families could draw on. The reforms to the welfare system were intended to increase work among recipients. These efforts were partially successful. While fewer than one in nine welfare cases with an adult recipient had earned income in FY 1990, approximately one-quarter of such cases had earned income in FY 2008. While the percentage increase in recipients with earnings was sizeable, the percentage was still well short of the 50 percent goal in the PRWORA and DRA.

The increased work effort among recipients led to higher levels of earnings. Average monthly earnings in adult-headed cash assistance households were $57 in FY 1990 but nearly $200 by FY 2008. Over the same period, average monthly unearned income was little changed—$37 in FY 1990 and $30 in FY 2008. Because of the increase in earnings, total monthly pretransfer incomes rose from an average of $94 in FY 1990 to $229 in FY 2008. These increases in pretransfer income offset some but not all of the decrease in assistance benefits. Combining earned income, unearned income, and welfare assistance amounts, total monthly posttransfer incomes decreased from $776 (52% of the poverty threshold) in FY 1990 to $642 (44% of the poverty threshold) in FY 2008. Thus TANF families were working harder after welfare reform but receiving less money overall.

The picture does not change much when other types of assistance are taken into account. The percentage of adult-headed welfare families that also received food stamps fluctuated only a little over the period. However, the value of the food stamps received increased slightly because of the fall in total posttransfer incomes (the means-testing formula for food stamp benefits includes the value of cash assistance) and because of the shift in composition of income toward earnings (the food stamp formula provides an extra deduction for earned income). Welfare families were generally categorically eligible for Medicaid before and after the reform, and thus we do not see much change in the receipt of medical assistance over this period. Conversely, we do observe a decline in the proportion of welfare families receiving housing assistance. Finally, welfare families with earnings benefited from more generous payments from the EITC. For instance, a single-parent household with two children and monthly earnings of $200 (the average earnings for TANF families in 2008) might have qualified for an EITC worth the equivalent of $80 per month in 2008. In 1990, the EITC for the same-size family with $57 in monthly earnings (the average in 1990) would have been just $8.

When we examine the demographic characteristics of adult-headed welfare households, we see that the average number of people in each household shrank from 3.7 in FY 1990 to 3.0 in FY 2008. However, the average number of members of each assistance unit was essentially unchanged at about three in each period. The number of household members would be higher than the number of case members if older relatives or adult children were living with the recipient family.

The average age of household heads also changed little over the period, with the average age being around 30 years old. The proportion of adult heads who were white or black decreased slightly from FY 1990 to FY 2008, while the proportion that was Hispanic increased slightly.

One surprising trend is that among household heads who are welfare recipients, the percentage who have completed high school or an equivalent credential doubled from 27 percent in FY 1990 to 57 percent in FY 2008. The increase was much steeper than the overall rise in educational attainment in the United States (figures from the Census Bureau [2011c] indicate that the proportion of women aged 25 years or older who had completed high school rose from 77% in 1990 to 87% in 2008). We might expect the caseload to have become less skilled over time, as adults with more skills and greater earnings potential left or avoided welfare to pursue other opportunities. However, the statistics indicate that the remaining caseload actually became more highly educated, which suggests that less-skilled adults were disproportionately dropped or diverted from the program. Reduced participation among the least skilled is consistent with evidence from the food stamp program that exceptionally disadvantaged households have more trouble completing applications, keeping up with program paperwork, and complying with other participation requirements (Ribar and Edelhoch 2008; Ribar and Swann 2011). The unsettling implication of these trends is that cash assistance might be bypassing the most disadvantaged and truly needy households.

Additional evidence that selective attrition from the caseload occurred from both the high and low ends of the skill distribution comes from examining the characteristics of closed cases (welfare leavers) in the month before they exited. Characteristics of these cases are reported in Table 24.2. The statistics indicate that cases that were about to close had higher levels of work effort and higher levels of earnings than cases generally. In FY 2008, nearly a third of adult-headed cases that were about to close had earnings, while only a quarter of the general adult caseload had earnings. Average earnings in cases that were about to close were $374 compared to $199 in the general caseload. Though work and earnings for closing cases were higher in a relative sense, it is important to note that two-thirds of the adult cases closed without any earnings. At the same time, education levels for leavers

Table 24.2
Characteristics of Closed TANF Cases with Adult Recipients

	FY 2000	FY 2005	FY 2008
Household Composition			
Number of household members	3.0	2.9	3.0
Number of recipients in the household	2.8	2.8	2.8
Number of recipient children in the household	1.7	1.7	1.7
Household Public Assistance Receipt			
Percent receiving food stamps	69.6%	82.3%	83.5%
Percent receiving medical assistance	94.3%	93.6%	93.6%
Percent living in public housing	9.2%	5.1%	4.8%
Percent receiving a rent subsidy	8.4%	10.1%	9.7%
Percent receiving subsidized child care	17.2%	10.7%	10.4%
Household Income and Resources			
Percent with earned income	39.5%	32.4%	32.0%
Earned income amount[a]	$465	$362	$374
Percent with unearned income	17.3%	19.6%	20.7%
Unearned income amount[b]	$93	$106	$112
Percent with any income	51.2%	46.6%	46.5%
Total income amount	$558	$468	$486
Characteristics of Heads of Households			
Age	30.6	30.3	30.7
White[c]	37.4%	38.6%	38.1%
Black[c]	37.0%	35.0%	34.9%
Hispanic[c]	17.6%	20.5%	21.7%
Other/missing race[c]	7.9%	5.8%	5.4%
Married	24.8%	23.3%	20.8%
Completed high school	51.4%	59.6%	50.8%
US citizen	91.9%	93.7%	93.3%
Number of households (millions)	1.5	1.4	1.3

Note: The statistics are authors' calculations from DHHS administrative data from the TANF program. All dollar figures are expressed in constant 2008 amounts deflated using the CPI-U.
[a]Earnings of 18-year-olds enrolled full-time in secondary school are excluded from household earned income.
[b]Unearned income includes housing assistance.
[c]The data on race and ethnicity are not mutually exclusive. Mutually exclusive race was assigned as Hispanic, non-Hispanic white, non-Hispanic black, and non-Hispanic other.

in FY 2008 were lower than education levels for the general caseload, which may be indicative of selection among less-skilled individuals. Also, the incidence and amount of earnings among cases that were closing were each lower in FY 2008 than in FY 2000.

We can also examine the reasons why cases were closed. The DHHS (2011c) reports that in FY 2008, 15 percent of cases closed because they failed to cooperate with program rules, 13 percent closed because of sanctions, and 2 percent closed because of state or federal time limits. Only 20 percent of cases closed because of increased earnings. Thus the majority of cases closed not because the families achieved self-sufficiency but rather because they failed to meet program requirements.

CONCLUSIONS

Concerns that cash assistance was fostering dependency and eroding responsibility among recipient families led the states and ultimately the federal government to undertake fundamental reforms of the welfare system in the 1990s. The reforms were intended to promote economic self-sufficiency by requiring recipients to work and by placing time limits on assistance. The work rules and some other program requirements were backed up by the possible loss of benefits for those who failed to comply. More generally, disadvantaged families lost their entitlement to assistance. Although some of the reforms adopted by some states included positive incentives for work, such as higher earnings disregards and lower benefit reduction rates in calculating assistance, most of the reforms were punitive, involving a loss of benefits if certain behaviors did not occur. The negative nature of these reforms created countervailing concerns that the assistance function of the cash welfare system would be compromised and that the well-being of many disadvantaged families would suffer.

The evidence presented in this chapter indicates that many disadvantaged families experienced beneficial outcomes following the implementation of the reforms. The most notable beneficial effects were a sharp decrease in the proportion of single-parent households in poverty from just under half prior to the reforms to a third by 2000 and an increase in employment from 54 percent of single mothers prior to the reforms to 63 percent in 2000. Since 2000, poverty has crept back up, while employment has decreased. Even more dramatic has been the sharp fall in the cash assistance caseload from 4.8 million families in 1995 to 1.6 million families in 2008, a two-thirds decrease. Research indicates that the reforms contributed substantially to these outcomes.

However, the reforms have also been associated with deleterious effects. The fall in the caseload has been accompanied by profound changes in its composition. Child-only cases have increased from a small fraction of the caseload prior to welfare reform to half of the caseload in 2008. In most of the current cases where household children qualify for assistance but adults do not, parents have been sanctioned off the program or have been made ineligible for benefits. Thus these families are receiving fewer benefits than they would have prior to the reforms. About a third of the child-only cases, however, represent children who are living with a caregiver other than their parents. In either circumstance, child-only cases represent a growing policy challenge because there are few ways for the welfare system to incentivize the economic self-sufficiency for the family.

Among the more traditional, parent-headed assistance cases, work and earnings have increased, though the incidence of work and the average amount of earnings remain very modest. In 2008, one out of four parent-headed assistance cases received earnings, and the average monthly earnings among those who worked was about $800, far below the poverty threshold for these families. At the same time, average benefits have fallen faster than earnings have grown. The net result is that parent-headed assistance families are working harder than they were before the reforms were enacted but receiving smaller amounts of posttransfer income.

Evidence also suggests that the reductions in the caseload may have occurred disproportionately among households with the least skills. The average level of education among adult heads of assistance cases, while still lower than the population average, has risen substantially since the enactment of welfare reform. Only about 20 percent of families who leave welfare have done so because earnings made them ineligible; a much larger fraction leaves because of sanctions and other program rules. Indeed, two-thirds of families do not have any earnings in the month before they leave the program.

The picture that emerges is of a program that has all but abandoned its assistance mission. The Census Bureau (2011a) estimates that 23.7 million people (including 13.5 million children) were members of families with children that had incomes below the poverty line in 2008. Of these, the TANF program provided cash benefits to 3.7 million people, or fewer than one in six. The cash benefits that were provided were only a fraction of the income needed to reach the poverty level. Food, energy, housing, and medical in-kind assistance programs still assist substantial proportions of disadvantaged families, but the TANF program does not.

NOTES

1. The controversies leading up to the creation of the Aid to Dependent Children program in 1935 are documented in Gordon (1994). Evidence of later controversies can be seen in the major presidential candidates from John Kennedy to George W. Bush calling for major reforms to the program.

2. These and subsequent figures include all 50 states and the District of Columbia but exclude U.S. territories.

3. The employment figures were calculated from the Integrated Public Use Microdata Series of the U.S. Current Population Survey (see King et al. 2010).

BIBLIOGRAPHY

Blank, Rebecca. 2002. "Evaluating Welfare Reform in the United States." *Journal of Economic Literature* 40 (4): 1105–66.

Centers for Disease Control and Prevention, National Center for Health Statistics. 2011. VitalStats. Accessed June 9. http://www.cdc.gov/nchs/vitalstats.htm.

Charlesworth, Leanne, Jeanette Hercik, and Courtney Kakuska. 2011. "TANF Child-Only Cases Trends and Issues." Accessed June 9. http://peerta.acf .hhs.gov/pdf/child_only.pdf.

Council of Economic Advisors. 1997. "Explaining the Decline in Welfare Receipt, 1993–1996." Washington, DC: Council of Economic Advisors.

Crouse, Gil. 1999. "State Implementation of Major Changes to Welfare Policies, 1992–1998." http://aspe.hhs.gov/hsp/waiver-policies99/policy_cea.htm.

Gordon, Linda. 1994. *Pitied but Not Entitled: Single Mothers and the History of Welfare.* New York: Free Press.

Gramlich, Edward. 1982. "An Econometric Examination of the New Federalism." *Brookings Papers on Economic Activity* 1982 (2): 327–60.

Grogger, Jeffrey and Lynn Karoly. 2005. *Welfare Reform: Effects of a Decade of Change.* Cambridge, MA: Harvard University Press.

Hochman, Harold and James Rodgers. 1969. "Pareto Optimal Redistribution." *American Economic Review* 59 (4): 542–57.

King, Miriam, Steven Ruggles, J. Trent Alexander, Sarah Flood, Katie Genadek, Matthew B. Schroeder, Brandon Trampe, and Rebecca Vick. 2010. *Integrated Public Use Microdata Series, Current Population Survey: Version 3.0.* [Machine-readable database]. Minneapolis: University of Minnesota. http://cps .ipums.org/cps/index.shtml.

Martin, Joyce A., Brady E. Hamilton, Paul D. Sutton, Stephanie J. Ventura, T. J. Matthews, and Michelle J. K. Osterman. 2010. "Births: Final Data for 2008." National Vital Statistics Reports 59 (1). Hyattsville, MD: National Center for Health Statistics.

Moffitt, Robert. 1990. "Has State Redistribution Policy Grown More Conservative?" *National Tax Journal* 43 (2): 123–42.

Moffitt, Robert. 1992. "Incentive Effects of the U.S. Welfare System: A Review." *Journal of Economic Literature* 30 (1): 1–61.

Moffitt, Robert. 1999. "The Effect of Pre-PRWORA Waivers on AFDC Caseloads and Female Earnings, Income, and Labor Force Behavior." In *Economic Conditions and Welfare Reform*, edited by Sheldon H. Danziger, 91–118. Kalamazoo, MI: Upjohn Institute.

Moffitt, Robert. 2002. "The Temporary Assistance for Needy Families Program." NBER Working Paper No. w8749, National Bureau of Economic Research, Cambridge, MA.

Moffitt, Robert and John Karl Scholz. 2009. "Trends in the Level and Distribution of Income Support." NBER Working Paper No. w15488, National Bureau of Economic Research, Cambridge, MA.

Murray, Charles. 1984. *Losing Ground: American Social Policy, 1950–1980*. New York: Basic Books.

Orr, Larry. 1976. "Income Transfers as a Public Good: An Application to AFDC." *American Economic Review* 66 (3): 359–71.

Reauthorization of the Temporary Assistance for Needy Families Program: Interim Final Rule. 2006. 71 Federal Register 125: 37454–83.

Ribar, David and Marilyn Edelhoch. 2008. "Earnings Volatility and the Reasons for Leaving the Food Stamp Program." In *Income Volatility and Food Assistance in the United States*, edited by Dean Jolliffe and James Ziliak, 63–102. Kalamazoo, MI: W. E. Upjohn Institute for Employment Research.

Ribar, David and Christopher Swann. 2011. "Applying for and Staying on the Supplemental Nutrition Assistance Program in South Carolina." Contractor and Cooperator Report No. 65, Food Assistance and Nutrition Research Program, U.S. Department of Agriculture, Washington, DC.

Ribar, David and Mark Wilhelm. 1999. "The Demand for Welfare Generosity." *Review of Economics and Statistics* 81 (1): 96–108.

U.S. Census Bureau. 2011a. "Annual Social and Economic Supplement, POV03: People in Families with Related Children Under 18 by Family Structure, Age, and Sex, Iterated by Income-to-Poverty Ratio and Race: 2008." Accessed June 9. http://www.census.gov/hhes/www/cpstables/032009/pov/new03_100_01.htm.

U.S. Census Bureau. 2011b. Current Population Survey, Annual Social and Economic Supplements. Accessed June 8. http://www.census.gov/hhes/www/poverty/data/historical/families.html.

U.S. Census Bureau. 2011c. "Educational Attainment: CPS Historical Time Series." Accessed June 9. http://www.census.gov/hhes/socdemo/education/data/cps/historical/index.html.

U.S. Department of Labor, Bureau of Labor Statistics. 2011. Current Population Survey, Labor Force Statistics, Series ID LNS14000000. Accessed June 7. http://data.bls.gov/timeseries/LNS14000000.

U.S. DHHS, Administration for Children & Families. 2010a. "Characteristics and Financial Circumstances of TANF Recipients, Fiscal Year 2008: Table 5." Last Modified January 17. http://www.acf.hhs.gov/programs/ofa/character/FY2008/tab05.htm.

U.S. DHHS, Administration for Children & Families. 2010b. "Characteristics and Financial Circumstances of TANF Recipients, Fiscal Year 2008: Table 9." Last Modified January 17. http://www.acf.hhs.gov/programs/ofa/character/FY2008/tab09.htm.

U.S. DHHS, Administration for Children & Families. 2011a. "AFDC Data Archive—Download." Accessed June 9. http://aspe.hhs.gov/ftp/hsp/AFDC/AFDCdownload.shtml.

U.S. DHHS, Administration for Children & Families. 2011b. "Characteristics and Financial Circumstances of TANF Recipients." Accessed June 9. http://www.acf.hhs.gov/programs/ofa/character/.

U.S. DHHS, Administration for Children & Families. 2011c. "Characteristics and Financial Circumstances of TANF Recipients, Fiscal Year 2008: Table 46." Accessed June 9. http://www.acf.hhs.gov/programs/ofa/character/FY2008/tab46.htm.

U.S. DHHS, Administration for Children & Families. 2011d. "Temporary Assistance for Needy Families (TANF): Data and Documentation." Accessed June 9. http://aspe.hhs.gov/ftp/hsp/tanf-data/index.shtml.

U.S. Government Accountability Office. 2005. *Welfare Reform: HHS Should Exercise Oversight to Help Ensure TANF Work Participation Is Measured Consistently across States*. GAO-05-821. Washington, DC: General Accountability Office.

Yelowitz, Aaron. 1995. "The Medicaid Notch, Labor Supply, and Welfare Participation." *Quarterly Journal of Economics* 110 (4): 909–39.

Chapter 25

Inequalities across States in a Federally Funded System: The Case of Child Welfare Subsidies

Mary Eschelbach Hansen[1]

Social safety nets are intended to reduce inequality by providing a minimum quantity of resources and minimum quality of life for those people with the worst of luck. In the United States, federal support for unlucky employees who were laid off began with the 1933 Federal Emergency Relief Act. The Unemployment Insurance program became a permanent part of the 1935 Social Security Act along with old-age insurance. Food stamps (1939), Medicaid (1965), and housing vouchers (1974) provide in-kind benefits for those who lack the income to make key purchases. The Social Security Act also included Aid to Dependent Children, which provided resources to support those unlucky children whose parents were without income. Today, nearly 10 of every 1,000 children in the United States have one of the worst kinds of bad luck: they are victims of abuse and neglect perpetrated by their parents or caregivers (U.S. Department of Health and Human Services 2010). The social safety net for them is the child welfare system.

Like most of the social safety nets in the United States, the child welfare system is federally supported but state-run. That is, each state's child welfare system receives a significant share of its monies from the federal government, but, beyond some minimum standards, individual states are free to decide who will be eligible to receive benefits, how large the benefits will be, and how the benefits will be delivered. This chapter describes the substantial differences in the resources provided to abused and neglected children that depend, arbitrarily, on the state in which they came into contact with child welfare services.

The chapter begins with a brief discussion of key features of federally funded social safety net programs in the 20th-century United States. Then the subsidies for foster and adoptive families—key parts of the states' child welfare systems—are described. The third section provides evidence of the significant state-to-state variations in subsidy receipt and in levels of subsidy support. The final section of the chapter argues that the potential benefits of standardizing subsidies outweigh the costs and summarizes the barriers to standardizing the subsidies under current law.

SOCIAL SAFETY NETS IN THE UNITED STATES

In 2010, Congress rejected the idea of a federal health care insurance system. Instead it adopted a system for health insurance reform that relies on states to make key policy choices and to physically deliver the key elements of reform through the creation of state-based insurance exchanges and state-level expansions in Medicaid eligibility. The debate over whether social safety nets should be run on a national basis or run by the states is not a new debate. Except for the disability and old-age pension provisions of the 1935 Social Security Act, Medicare (1965), and some 1960s grants that went directly to localities as part of the War on Poverty, federal supports for the unlucky have been "delivered" through the states and have allowed substantial leeway for states in deciding eligibility criteria and levels of benefits for programs that support the unemployed and the poor.

In general, state administration of government-funded programs is viewed as a way to allow the programs to vary according to local tastes and preferences. For example, agricultural experiment stations (established in 1887), agricultural extension (1914), highway construction (1916), and vocational education (1917) are federal programs in which states receive funds but can decide what research, education, and transportation improvements are most appropriate depending on the resources and needs of the states. It is less clear why the preferences and needs of the states ought to drive the provision of social safety nets. Scholars in several disciplines have concluded that in the 1930s, the decision by Congress to locate control of unemployment insurance and Aid to Dependent Children in the states was made because of a desire for political patronage jobs and the desire of local elites, whether industrial or agricultural, to maintain control of the local economy (Piven and Cloward 1971; Alston and Ferrie 1985).

Among the debates and stop-gap measures of the 1950s and 1960s that eventually led to the formation of the Medicare and Medicaid programs, the 1960 Kerr-Mills Act included a provision that has had lasting impact. Kerr-Mills provided insurance coverage for the "medically indigent" over 65 who were not eligible to receive Social Security benefits. The Kerr-Mills Act created a "federal matching percentage" for each state that defined how much of state expenditure on the program would be reimbursed by the federal government. The matching percentage ranged from 50 to 80 percent, with the highest reimbursements going to the states with the lowest per capita income and the lowest rates going to the states with the highest incomes. That basic formula, now known as the Federal Medical Assistance Percentage, was never applied to Medicare. It was, however, applied to Medicaid when it was created in 1965. It is also the rate at which states are reimbursed for many key child welfare programs, including the critical subsidies that are discussed in the next section.

SUBSIDIES FOR CHILD WELFARE

Child welfare systems in the states support a large number of programs that are intended to provide a minimum level of safety, permanency, and well-being for children who are victims of abuse or neglect. Child welfare agencies in the states have programs that deliver services directly, such as counseling, and programs that transfer resources, such as subsidies paid to foster and adoptive parents. Although these subsidies are paid to adults, they are key elements of the safety net *for children* because the subsides provide incentives for families to take on the responsibilities of caring for abused and neglect children, and because the subsidies provide the resources for adequate maintenance and needed special services to help the children recover from abuse and neglect. Family care is preferred to institutional care because the well-being of children cared for in family settings is superior to the well-being of children cared for in institutions (Hansen 2007).

The first federal grants for child welfare services were part of Title IV of the Social Security Act. In 1958, Congress changed the program to a matching grants program, which was capped at an amount determined in annual federal budget negotiations. In 1961, Congress approved expansion of the federal matching program to include subsidies for foster parents. In 1980, the federal matching program was again expanded to include subsidies for parents who adopted children from foster care. The federal reimbursement for adoption subsidies is capped at the maximum reimbursement for foster care payments that could be made on behalf of the child, although states are free to pay higher subsidies out of their own funds.

States are required to define eligibility for foster care and adoption subsidy according to the characteristics of the child. Means tests of foster or adoptive parents are not allowed. Federal regulations allow states to provide resources that are greater when children's needs or disabilities are greater.

Within these broad guidelines, states enact specific eligibility requirements and payment schedules for the subsidies. The monthly amount of the subsidy is usually calculated from a daily "board rate" that is set at the state level in all but four states. In the other four states the rates are set at a more local level, such as the county level. Child welfare subsidies fall far short of what the average family spends on the average child (see, for example, Laws and O'Hanlon 1999; Children's Rights 2006) even though the cost of caring for a foster or adopted child who has been abused or neglected is likely to exceed the cost of raising a healthy child. Direct outlay for care of the child plus the opportunity cost of lost time at work may be substantial.

States design child welfare subsidy programs differently. Some states and localities set subsidies at a rate high enough to provide general support and some needed special services. Others set subsidies at a rate that supports only basic care for a child, and provide needed special services at the parent's request (Barth et al. 2006). Even keeping these differences in mind, it is clear that child victims of abuse and neglect in different states receive unequal treatment.

VARIATIONS IN SUBSIDIES

Figure 25.1 shows the range of average subsidy amounts paid by states on behalf of children who received subsidies. The statistics are derived from the Adoption and Foster Care Reporting System

Figure 25.1

Top: Variation in Child Welfare Subsidies. Bottom: Variation in Eligibility.

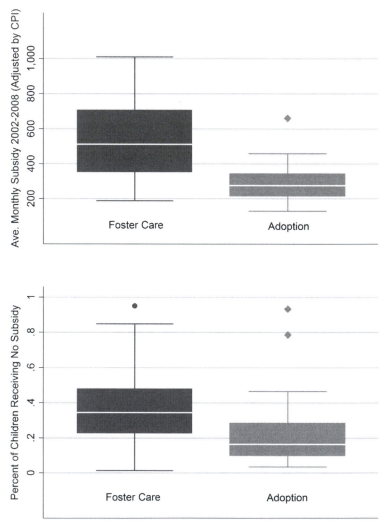

Source: AFCARS Foster Care and Adoption Files 2002–2008.

(AFCARS). AFCARS is a twice yearly census of each child in foster care, including the monthly subsidy paid by the state in support of the child during the month of the census. AFCARS also includes data on each child adopted from foster care, including any cash subsidy paid to support the adoption. To calculate the average state subsidy shown in Figure 25.1, we first calculated the average subsidy paid in each year from federal fiscal years 2002 through 2008 inclusive. Then we averaged across years. All dollar values are expressed in terms of real 2000 dollars (adjustments made using the Consumer Price Index-Urban).

The average state paid a subsidy of $554 per month for children in foster care and $286 per month for adopted children. The range of subsidies was quite large. The lowest state average subsidy for children in foster care was $197, while the highest was just over $1,100. For children in adoption the lowest average subsidy was $153 and the highest was $661.

Looking at average subsidy at the state level could be misleading if the children in foster care or the children adopted from foster care vary widely from state to state. This is because the size of the subsidies depends on the age and needs of the children. However, in several studies of adoption subsidies, geographic differences in adoption assistance between states cannot be explained by differences in the cost of living or child-specific factors (Dalberth, Gibbs, and Berkman 2005; Hansen 2008). For example, in New York State, differences in adoption assistance between counties could not be explained entirely by differences in the cost of living or other factors examined (Avery and Ferraro 1997). Analysis of national data confirms that there are significant differences between and even within states that cannot be explained by differences in prices or in characteristics of children (Hansen and Pollack 2005). It is clear from these studies that the strength of the safety net for children varies widely from place to place.

Similarly, the likelihood that a child receives a subsidy varies widely from state to state. The bottom panel of Figure 25.1 shows the range of the percentage of children who received subsidy in the states, again averaged over federal fiscal years 2002 through 2008. The take-up rate on foster care and adoption subsidies is high, so receipt and eligibility are nearly identical in practice. About 38 percent of children in foster care received no subsidy, while about 19 percent of children adopted from foster care received no subsidy. Nonreceipt of foster care subsidy ranged from 1.4 percent (that is 98.6% of children were eligible and received a subsidy) to 85 percent. Nonreceipt of adoption subsidy ranged from 3.6 percent to 46 percent.

Table 25.1 lists the states with the least generous and most generous subsidies, as well as the states with the lowest and highest proportions of abused and neglected children receiving subsidies. No clear patterns emerge. Some states (such as Missouri) have low subsidies but

Table 25.1

States with Most and Least Generous Child Welfare Subsidies

Lowest Subsidies[a] for		Fewest Subsidies[b] for	
Foster Care	*Adoption*	*Foster Care*	*Adoption*
Alabama	Utah	Mississippi	New York
Nevada	Missouri	Washington	Indiana
Arkansas	Florida	Alaska	Alabama
New Mexico	Indiana	Nevada	North Dakota
Hawaii	Idaho	Virginia	Delaware
Oregon	Oklahoma	Florida	Minnesota
Idaho	North Carolina	Ohio	Georgia
South Dakota	Louisiana	Kansas	Kentucky
Washington	Mississippi	Texas	Connecticut
Alaska	Alabama	Arkansas	Florida
***Highest* Subsidies for**		***Most* Subsidies for**	
Foster Care	*Adoption*	*Foster Care*	*Adoption*
West Virginia	Maine	Idaho	North Carolina
Connecticut	Alaska	Utah	Ohio
Delaware	Vermont	Maine	South Dakota
Tennessee	Connecticut	Connecticut	Illinois
Rhode Island	Iowa	Louisiana	Michigan
Pennsylvania	Washington	Pennsylvania	Oregon
District of Columbia	District of Columbia	Hawaii	Alaska
Minnesota	Wisconsin	New York	Maryland
New York	Nevada	District of Columbia	Missouri
Kansas	New York	Minnesota	Maine

[a]Based on average reported monthly subsidy, federal fiscal years 2002–8, adjusted for inflation.
[b]Percentage of valid observations federal fiscal years 2002–8 with a subsidy of one dollar or less.
Source: Author's calculations from AFCARS data.

offer this meager support to most children. On the other hand, while some states (such as Alabama) have both low subsidies and poor coverage, other states (such as Pennsylvania) have both high subsidies and good coverage rates.

The differences in the social safety net for abused and neglected children between states cannot be easily explained, but the consequences for states that have a weak safety net for these children is clear.

STANDARDIZING SUBSIDIES

The only comprehensive study of the costs and benefits of providing a sturdy safety net for abused and neglected children estimates that every \$1 invested in adoption from foster care yields \$3 in benefits to society (Hansen 2007). Abused and neglected children who do not receive adequate resources through the social safety net are more likely to have poor adult outcomes, including poor educational outcomes and higher rates of incarceration and welfare dependence. For example, the average adopted child is 23 percent more likely to complete high school than the average child who ages out of foster care and more than twice as likely to attend college. The adopted are 24 percent less likely to be unemployed and 32 percent less likely to have been incarcerated as young adults. (Although the impact of placement into foster care may be negative at the margin of placement [Doyle 2007], no study has measured the average treatment effect of placement into foster care.)

This evidence suggests that inadequate safety nets for abused and neglected children results in a larger population of adult dependents of the state. The support of these adult dependents requires higher taxes or lower government expenditures on productive activities, including protection of abused and neglected children, in the future. Thus the consequence of continuing the state-based, unequal system of funding and administering child welfare funding and other social safety nets is likely to be continuing divergence in equality of outcomes across states. On the other hand, providing a sturdy, standardized social safety net for abused and neglected children would contribute to an equalization of outcomes between states in the long run.

There are, however, barriers to standardizing child welfare subsidies. The primary barrier is the argument that having diverse, state-determined social safety nets gives people choices. According to this argument, differences across states in the social safety net are not worrisome because people can choose their state residence. Adults who prefer a more generous social safety net are free to move to obtain it. However persuasive this argument may be for policies relating to social safety nets for adults, it simply cannot be argued that children are free to move to states that afford them better protections.

Alternatively, it may be that the attachment to the status quo is rooted in midcentury history. In the 1950s and 1960s, demands for state control of federally funded social safety nets aimed at the underprivileged and unlucky were driven by a desire among some states for autonomy regarding decisions of how to address "the Negro question" (Smith and Moore 2008). Today there is a larger percentage of African American families in poverty than there is in the population (for example, Anderson 2011); similarly, African American children are overrepresented among those who come into contact with the child welfare system (Lu et al. 2004).

Even if Congress does not act, what keeps courts from mandating that child welfare subsidies be standardized? In spite of the historical tie between state control of welfare and preferences for racial discrimination across states, U.S. courts have found that the holes in states' social safety nets are unconstitutional only in cases in which the holes impinged on a "fundamental right" (including implied rights such as the right to privacy or to interstate travel) or affected a "suspect class" (such as a racial minorities) *within* states (Harvith 1967; Neuman 1987; Gellhorn 1994). The ability of states to create holes in the social safety net has been upheld, time and time again, as a legitimate and reasonable method through which state legislatures may allocate their scarce resources. To escape this precedent, legal scholars have advanced the argument that social safety nets could fall under the umbrella of human rights law (for example, Park 1987). This argument has not gained traction on policy issues relating to adults. It is unlikely that it will gain traction on children's policy, given that the United States is not a signatory to the UN Convention on the Rights of the Child.

As noted by Lauren Damme (2010), "A system that increases inequality will have negative repercussions for all Americans." Decisive congressional action is needed to prevent the lack of standardization in our system of social safety nets for children from continuing to exacerbate inequalities in outcomes.

NOTE

1.   The data used here were made available by the National Data Archive on Child Abuse and Neglect, Cornell University, Ithaca, New York, and have been used with permission. Data from the AFCARS were collected by the Children's Bureau. Funding for AFCARS was provided by the Children's Bureau, Administration on Children, Youth and Families, Administration for Children and Families, U.S. Dept. of Health and Human Services. The collector of the original data, the funder, the Archive, Cornell University, and their agents or employees bear no responsibility for the analysis or interpretation presented here. Research assistance was provided by Philip Gautier.

BIBLIOGRAPHY

Alston, Lee J., and Joseph P. Ferrie. 1985. "Labor Costs, Paternalism, and Loyalty in Southern Agriculture: A Constraint on the Growth of the Welfare State." *The Journal of Economic History* 45: 95–117.

Anderson, Robin J. 2011. "Dynamics of Economic Well-Being: Poverty, 2004–2006." Bureau of the Census. Accessed October 9, 2011. http://www.census.gov/hhes/www/poverty/publications/dynamics04/P70-123.pdf.

Avery, Rosemary J., and Rosellina Ferraro. 1997. "Unequal Treatment: Adoption Subsidy Support in New York State." *Adoption Quarterly* 1(2): 59–85.

Barth, Richard P., C. K. Lee, Judith Wildfire, and S. Guo, S. 2006. "A Comparison of the Governmental Costs of Long-Term Foster Care and Adoption." *Social Service Review* 80(1): 127–58.

Children's Rights. 2006. "Ending the Foster Care Life Sentence: The Critical Need for Adoption Subsidies." Accessed August 20, 2006. htp://www.childrensrights.org/pdfs/FINAL%20ADOPTION%20SUBSIDY%20DATA%20REPORT.doc.pdf.

Dalberth, Barbara, Deborah Gibbs, and Nancy Berkman. 2005. "Understanding Adoption Subsidies: An Analysis of AFCARS Data. Final Report." Office of the Assistant Secretary for Planning and Evaluation, U.S. Department of Health and Human Services. Accessed September 30, 2006. http://aspe.hhs.gov/hsp/05/adoption-subsidies/index.htm.

Damme, Lauren. 2010. "Problems with a State-Based Social Welfare System." New America Foundation. Accessed January 5, 2011. http://growth.newamerica.net/sites/newamerica.net/files/policydocs/Damme%20-%204%20of%206%20-%20Problems%20with%20state-based%20social%20welfare%20system.pdf.

Doyle, Joseph J. 2007. "Child Welfare and Child Outcomes." *The American Economic Review* 97(5): 1583–1610.

Gellhorn, Gay. 1994. "Justice Thurgood Marshall's Jurisprudence of Equal Protection of the Laws and the Poor." *Arizona Law Review* 26: 429–60.

Hansen, Mary E. 2007. "The Value of Adoption." *Adoption Quarterly* 10(2): 65–87.

Hansen, Mary E. 2008. "The Distribution of a Federal Entitlement: The Case of Adoption Assistance." *Journal of Socio-Economics* 37(6): 2427–42.

Hansen, Mary E., and Daniel Pollack. 2005. "Unintended Consequences of Bargaining for Adoption Assistance Payments." *Family Court Review* 43(3): 495–511.

Harvith, Bernard Evans. 1967. "Federal Equal Protection and Welfare Assistance." *Albany Law Review* 34: 210–49.

Laws, Rita, and Timothy O'Hanlon. 1999. *Adoption and Financial Assistance: Tools for Navigating the Bureaucracy.* Westport, CT: Bergin & Garvey.

Lu, Y. E., J. Landsverk, E. Ellis-Macleod, R. Newton, W. Ganger, and I. Johnson. 2004. "Race, Ethnicity, and Case Outcomes in Child Protective Services." *Children and Youth Services Review* 26: 447–61.

Neuman, Gerald. 1987. "Territorial Discrimination, Equal Protection, and Self-Determination." *University of Pennsylvania Law Review* 135: 261–382.

Park, Ann I. 1987. "Human Rights and Basic Needs: Using International Human Rights Norms to Inform Constitutional Interpretation."*UCLA Law Review* 34: 1195–1264.

Piven, Frances F., and Richard A. Cloward. 1971. *Regulating the Poor: The Functions of Public Welfare.* New York: Pantheon.

Smith, David G., and Judith D. Moore. 2008. *Medicaid Politics and Policy: 1965–2007.* New Brunswick and London: Transaction Publishers.

U.S. Department of Health and Human Services, Administration for Children and Families, Administration on Children, Youth and Families, Children's Bureau. 2010. Child Maltreatment 2009. Accessed October 10, 2011. http://www.acf.hhs.gov/programs/cb/stats_research/index.htm#can.

Wallace, John Joseph, and Wallace E. Oates. 1998. "The Impact of the New Deal on American Federalism." In *The Defining Moment: The Great Depression and the American Economy in the Twentieth Century,* edited by Michael Bordo, Claudia Goldin, and Eugene White, 155–80. Chicago: Univ. of Chicago Press.

Chapter 26

The Impact of Health Care Reform on Vulnerable Populations

Lynn Paringer

INTRODUCTION

More than 50 million Americans lack health insurance coverage in the United States. Declining incomes and high unemployment have contributed to the recent loss in coverage. During the 2007–9 recession more than 5 million individuals lost employment-based coverage (Holahan 2011). More than one-fifth of the adult population under the age of 65 are uninsured. Underinsurance in the United States is also a problem. Data from the Commonwealth Fund Biennial Health Insurance Survey for 2007 estimated that 14 percent of all nonelderly adults were underinsured in 2007 (Schoen et al. 2008).

Lack of health insurance or inadequate coverage can have devastating effects on the individuals affected and their families. The uninsured are more likely to go without needed care, more likely to skip filling prescriptions due to lack of resources, less likely to have a usual source of care, and less likely to have chronic health conditions diagnosed in a timely manner than their insured counterparts. To the extent that the uninsured may exhaust their resources and eventually fall onto the rolls of the taxpaying public, the costs can be staggering. It is estimated that more than 60 percent of all bankruptcies that occurred in 2007 were medical related. More than 90 percent of medical debtors had medical debts above $5,000 or 10 percent of pretax income (Himmelstein et al. 2009). The full costs resulting from lack of insurance or underinsurance derive not just from the inability to pay medical bills but also from the cost to society in lost productivity resulting from ill health.

The Patient Protection and Affordable Care Act (ACA) was signed into law in March 2010 and is designed to ensure that everyone, regardless of health status or income, has access to affordable health insurance. Full implementation of the ACA will have a dramatic impact on health insurance coverage among the U.S. population (Table 26.1). The number of uninsured nonelderly in the United States is expected to fall from 50 million to less than 30 million after implementation of the health reform bill. An estimated 23 million individuals are expected to receive coverage through the nongroup exchanges that will be established under the ACA, and Medicaid/Children's Health Insurance Program enrollment is expected to increase by more than 10 million. It is expected that some employers who are currently offering employment-sponsored insurance (ESI) will drop such coverage, and others will elect to purchase coverage through the exchanges.

Table 26.1

Estimated Health Insurance Coverage of the Non-elderly Pre- and Post–Health Reform

Coverage in Millions	Prereform		Postreform	
	N	Percent	N	Percent
Insured	218.0	81.3	245.9	91.8
Employer (nonexchange)	151.6	56.6	130.4	48.7
Employer (exchange)	0.0	0.0	20.7	7.7
Non-group (nonexchange)	14.8	5.5	3.3	1.2
Non-group (exchange)	0.0	0.0	23.1	8.7
Medicaid/CHIP	42.9	16.0	59.7	22.3
Other	8.7	3.2	8.7	3.2
Uninsured	49.9	18.6	22.1	8.3
Total	268.0	100.0	268.0	100.0

Source: Matthew Buettgens, Bowen Garrett, and John Holahan, "America under the Affordable Care Act," Urban Institute, December 2010.

The overall rate of uninsurance among the nonelderly is expected to fall from 18.7 percent to 8.2 percent. Many of the remaining uninsured will be immigrants whose citizenship status precludes them from gaining coverage through Medicaid or through the exchanges.

This chapter reviews the insurance situation of the most vulnerable groups in society. It describes the characteristics of the ACA and examines how the ACA will impact insurance coverage and access to care among vulnerable groups including the poor and near-poor young adults, the near-elderly, and immigrants.

THE AFFORDABLE CARE ACT

The primary means by which the ACA will increase insurance coverage is through the expansion of Medicaid income eligibility and the creation of health insurance exchanges through which individuals and families can purchase coverage with premium and cost-sharing credits available to those with incomes between 133 percent and 400 percent of the FPL. Employer exchanges will also be developed to help employers access coverage on behalf of their workers. These expansions will be fully operational by January 1, 2014. Table 26.2 shows the FPL in 2011 for individuals and families of various sizes.

The ACA as enacted into law requires U.S. citizens and legal residents to have health insurance or pay a penalty. The ACA specifies a range of services that must be included in any benefits package and requires that preventive services be covered without any cost sharing. Beyond these constraints, the different levels of coverage under the ACA are not defined in terms of specific deductibles, copayments, or coinsurance. They are specified in terms of their "actuarial value." Four different plans will be offered by the insurance exchanges

Table 26.2
2011 Federal Poverty Level Guidelines

Percent of FPL	Individual	Family of Two	Family of Four	Family of Six
100%	$10,890.00	$14,710.00	$22,350.00	$29,990.00
133%	$14,483.70	$19,564.30	$29,725.50	$39,886.70
200%	$21,780.00	$29,420.00	$44,700.00	$59,980.00
400%	$43,560.00	$58,840.00	$89,400.00	$119,960.00

Source: *Federal Register*, Vol. 76, No.13, January 20, 2011, pp. 3637–38.

developed under the ACA: bronze, silver, gold, and platinum. The bronze plan is to be set up with an actuarial value of 60 percent, meaning that 60 percent of the cost of services provided to the average enrollee is to be covered by the premiums with the enrollee expected to pay the remaining 40 percent through a combination of deductibles and copayments or coinsurance. The silver plan will have an actuarial value of 70 percent, the gold 80 percent, and the platinum 90 percent (Levitt and Claxton 2011).

The ACA also requires that plans cap the maximum out-of-pocket costs based on the out-of-pocket limits for enrollees in high-deductible plans that can be paired with a Health Savings Account. The limit for 2014 will be $5,950 for an individual and $11,900 for a family and will be adjusted over time. The ACA reduces the out-of-pocket maximum for those enrollees in families with incomes less than 400 percent of FPL. The caps in out-of-pocket expenditures by income are shown in Table 26.3. Out-of-pocket spending is capped at $1,983 for individuals with incomes up to 149 percent of FPL and increases to the $5,950 Health Savings Account maximum for those with incomes at 300 percent or more of the FPL.

Because plans will be defined in terms of their actuarial value, the cost-sharing structure can vary from plan to plan. Copayments, coinsurance rates, and deductibles can vary and the services to which

Table 26.3
Contribution to Premiums, Maximum Out-of-Pocket Spending, and Plan Actuarial Value by Household Income Level under the Affordable Care Act

Income Level (% FPL)	Maximum % of Income Allocated to Premiums	Actuarial Value of Plan	Out-of-Pocket Maximum
<133% (Medicaid Eligible)	0	100%	0
<133% (Not Medicaid Eligible)	2.0%	94%	$1,983
133%–149%	3%–4%	87%	$1,983
150%–199%	4%–6.03%	73%	$2,975
200%–249%	6.03%–8.05%	70%	$2,975
250%–299%	8.05%–9.5%	70%	$3,967
300%–399%	9.5%	60%	$5,950

Source: Jonathon Gruber and Ian Perry, "Realizing Health Reform's Potential: Will the Affordable Care Act Make Health Insurance Affordable?," Commonwealth Fund, Publication #1493, Vol. 2, April 2011.

they are applied can also vary. One plan with an actuarial value of 70 percent might have a $25 copayment for physician visits and a $1,500 deductible, while another might have a $15 copayment and a $2,100 deductible.

Premium subsidies to individuals will be based on the silver plan. For example, assume that the premium for single coverage in a silver plan is $3,000 per year for an individual age 30 and that the individual has an income of $21,780 (200% of the FPL). Based on Table 26.3, the individual is required to spend 6.03 percent of his or her income on the premium, or $1,313.33. He or she would then receive a premium subsidy of $1.686.66. The maximum out-of-pocket expenditure on deductibles, copayments, and coinsurance that the individual would be liable for is $2,875.00. If the individual wanted to enroll in a gold plan that had a premium of $3,500, the individual's contribution to the premium would be $1,313.33 + $500.00 = $1,813.33. In other words, individuals who elect to enroll in a plan with a higher actuarial value than the silver plan will be required to pay the difference.

Plans will not be allowed to underwrite policies on the basis of any characteristics other than the age of the enrollee and his or her smoking status. Prior conditions, health status, obesity, and chronic conditions will not affect the premiums. Furthermore, there is a restriction on age banding such that the oldest age category cannot experience premiums that are more than three times that of the youngest age category. Using our example, if the premium for the 30-year-old is $3,000 per year in a silver plan, the premium for a 64-year-old cannot exceed $9,000. The banding on smoking is 1.5:1 so that a smoker cannot be charged more than 1.5 times the premium of a nonsmoker in the same age category. The actual expenditures by age category are such that the near-elderly (ages 50–64) incur more than four times the cost of the youngest age. Because age-banding limits the relative premiums to 3:1, it will result in cross-subsidization from the young to the old (Blumberg, Buettgens, and Garrett 2009, 2010; America's Health Insurance Plans 2009).

Income used to determine premium subsidies will be based on Modified Adjusted Gross Income. The use of Modified Adjusted Gross Income represents a new methodology for determining eligibility for Medicaid as well as eligibility for premium subsidies in the exchanges. Family size will be determined based on the number of personal exemptions claimed on a tax return. The household income will be the Modified Adjusted Gross Income of the taxpayer, the spouse, and any child or person who must report his or her income on a separate return but is still claimed as a dependent by the taxpayer. Assets will not be counted in determining eligibility for Medicaid or the exchanges (Kaiser Commission on Medicaid and the Uninsured 2011).

Individuals who are offered ESI through their employer must avail themselves of the ESI unless the amount they would need to contribute to the premiums exceeds 9.5 percent of their income. In that case, the household may elect to use the insurance exchange.

One of the difficulties in implementing the ACA has to do with the calculation of income and the fact that incomes can fluctuate significantly over the course of the year. The income that will be used is what is reported on the tax return unless another verifiable income source is available. Since many people receiving subsidies do not have the cash to pay the entire premium and then receive reimbursement, the federal government will advance the premium credits to the health insurer directly. The premium subsidies will be based on the tax return, which may or may not be an accurate reflection of current income. As a result, there will be a need to reconcile the amount of the subsidy received against actual income. It is likely that not only will a considerable number of individuals and families receive a subsidy that is too high based on current income; they will also not be in a financial position to return the excess subsidy received to the federal government. As a result, the federal government caps the amount of repayment that must occur for everyone except those above 500 percent of FPL (Kaiser Family Foundation 2011a).

Small businesses will have their own set of health exchanges known as Small Business Health Options Program through which individuals and small businesses with up to 100 employees can purchase coverage for their employees. States may allow larger employers to purchase coverage through the exchanges beginning in 2017. Small employers with no more than 25 employees and average annual wages of less than $50,000 can receive a tax credit. For tax years 2010 through 2013, a tax credit of up to 35 percent of the employer's contribution toward the employee's health insurance premium may be paid if the employer contributes at least 50 percent of the premium or 50 percent of a benchmark premium. The full credit will be available to employers with 10 or fewer employees and average wages of less than $25,000. The credit phases out as firm size and wage rates increase. For tax years 2014 and later, small businesses that purchase health insurance through the exchanges will be eligible for a tax credit of up to 50 percent of the employer's contribution to the employee's health insurance premium if the employer contributes at least 50 percent toward the premium. This credit will be available for two years. The full credit will be available to firms with 10 or fewer employees and average annual wages of less than $25,000.

The Kaiser Family Foundation expects that under the ACA, up to 16 million individuals who receive insurance through the exchanges would have been uninsured otherwise. The Congressional Budget Office estimates that 81 percent of individuals who purchase health insurance through the exchanges in 2019 will receive subsidies and that 65 percent of those getting coverage on the exchanges will be transitioning from being uninsured. More than one-third of those moving to the exchanges will have gone for more than one year without receiving a checkup, and more than 4 in 10 did not have a usual source of care. The adults enrolling in the exchanges are predicted to be in worse health and to have fewer diagnosed chronic conditions than currently privately insured patients. Use of services on the part of exchange enrollees is expected to be similar to that of those currently enrolled in ESI plans (Kaiser Family Foundation 2011b).

In the remainder of this chapter we examine how various population groups are predicted to fare under the new ACA, how the program is being financed, and what the distributional impact of the program is expected to be. We will focus analysis on six population groups: the poor, near-poor, young adults, the near-elderly, the elderly, and immigrants.

THE POOR

The group that will gain the most from implementation of the ACA is low-income adults. Recent expansions in the income eligibility criteria under Medicaid and the Children's Health Insurance Program have dramatically improved the safety net for children, resulting in an increase in insurance coverage among this age group during the past decade. The ACA, as originally signed into law, mandated that the states expand Medicaid eligibility to cover persons with incomes below 133 percent of the Federal Poverty Level. However, in a Supreme Court decision rendered on June 28, 2012, states were permitted to choose whether or not to expand income eligibility for Medicaid coverage to the extent specified in the law (Congressional Budget Office, 2012). Because the Federal government will pick up more than 90 percent of the costs of expansion under the first several years of the program, it is expected that most states will expand coverage. However, some states may expand coverage at a later date than the January 1, 2012 start date and some states may expand eligibility to a level that is less than the 133 percent of the Federal Poverty Level or may decline to cover selected population groups. The Congressional Budget Office (2012) estimates that between 10 and 17 million additional individuals will be eligible for Medicaid depending on the extent to which the individual states expand their income eligibility requirements. Nearly half of uninsured young adults who are legal residents live in families with incomes of less than 133 percent of FPL and most of them are expected to transition to Medicaid. Up to 3.3 million of the uninsured aged 50–64 live in households with an income less than 133 percent FPL, and they are also expected to transition to Medicaid.

THE NEAR-POOR

The ACA calls for the creation of health insurance exchanges in all states by January 1, 2014. For those individuals who are not eligible for Medicaid and who have incomes below 400 percent of FPL, the exchanges will be the primary source of coverage for the currently uninsured. In addition, workers whose employer plan does not have an actuarial value of at least 60 percent or, where the employee share of premium exceeds 9.5 percent of income, may participate in the exchanges. The Urban Institute estimates that 23.1 million nonelderly Americans will be enrolled in the exchanges (Buettgens, Garrett, and Holahan 2010b).

There is wide variation in health insurance premiums by age and geographic area in the United States as well as by type of insurer and class of policy. The average annual premium for ESI in 2011 was more than $15,000 for family coverage of which the worker paid about 30 percent. The average premium for single coverage in the individual market varied from $1,429 for individuals 18–24 years of age to $5,755 for those 60–64. About 10 percent of individuals 18–24 were denied health insurance coverage in the individual market compared to 29.2 percent in the population age 60–64 (America's Health Insurance Plans 2009). One of the real concerns with respect to the exchanges is the extent to which there will be adverse selection among applicants. The possibility of adverse selection was a prime motivator for the coverage mandate in the law. Given the high cost of premiums and the fact that a large share of the premium cost is borne by workers, it is not surprising that many workers fail to take up coverage when offered and that many others choose to go without. The first year in which the percentage of individuals under age 65 with employer-sponsored insurance (ESI) fell below 60 percent was 2009 (Fronstin 2011). This decline in coverage was limited to workers with low average annual earnings (below $40,000), and to those with a high school education or less. In addition, between 2008 and 2009 the distribution of workers by annual earnings shifted from middle income to lower income, suggesting that workers who managed to keep their jobs were even less able financially to pay the premiums on employer-sponsored health insurance. During the 2007–9 recession, an increasing percentage of uninsured workers indicated that they did not have coverage because of the cost, even though fewer workers said their employer did not offer coverage.

The shift in the earnings distribution in the United States has also impacted the level of health insurance coverage. Between 2000 and 2009, the number of people with incomes below 200 percent of the FPL increased by 25 percent (Holahan 2011). During the 2007–9 recession people who managed to hold on to their jobs also managed to hold on to their health insurance. The percentage of families with one or two full-time workers that experienced a decrease in coverage between 2007 and 2009 was small. All of the decrease in employment-based insurance coverage occurred in families where there was just a part-time worker or no worker. One effect of the recession was that there was a reduction of 9 million of the number of people in families that had at least one or two full-time workers. In addition there was an increase of 12.3 million in the number of people in families with only a part-time worker or with no worker.

Hopefully, the ACA will provide sufficient premium subsidy that individuals with incomes less than 400 percent of FPL will be able to access health insurance through the exchanges at affordable rates. Gruber and Perry (2011) studied the "affordability" of premiums under the ACA and found that fewer than 10 percent of families above the FPL "do not have the resources to pay for premiums and typical out-of-pocket costs even with the subsidies put in place by the health reform law."

YOUNG ADULTS

Young adults represent the population most at risk for going without insurance. Nearly one-third of the population aged 19–29 was uninsured in 2009. Adults aged 19–34 experienced the biggest decline in employment-based insurance coverage and experienced the biggest increases in Medicaid coverage during the 2007–9 recession of any age group. However, the increase in public coverage was not enough to offset the decrease in private sector coverage.

In a 2010 survey, Commonwealth Fund found that 45 percent of young adults reported delaying needed care because of costs. Nearly 40 percent reported that they had problems paying medical bills. Of those struggling to pay medical bills, one-third had depleted their savings to pay the bills, and nearly one in five took on credit card debt. Nearly half of young adults that are legal residents are in families with incomes of less than 133 percent of FPL, and an additional 4.9 million have incomes from 133 to 399 percent of FPL (Collins, Garber, and Robertson 2011).

Part of the reason for the high rates of uninsurance among young adults was due to the fact that they were excluded from their parents' policies when they graduated from high school or college. The Commonwealth Fund Survey of Young Adults found that in 2009, 42 percent of young adults graduating from high school who were covered on their parents' plans through high school either lost or switched coverage after graduating.

Under the ACA, beginning in 2010 young adults up to age 26 are permitted to stay on their parents' health plans if those plans include dependent coverage. The law applies to all adult children, regardless of living situation, marital status, student status, or degree of financial independence.

In 2012, the ACA requires college health plans to meet new insurance standards for their students. Beginning on January 1, 2012, student health plans are required to follow the same requirements as those that apply to other individual market policies, including the ban on lifetime limits. Until September 2011, annual limits could be no less than $750,000, rising to $1.25 million until September 2012, and $2 million until January 2014, at which time they will be banned completely.

Among the provisions in the ACA, expansions in Medicaid coverage are likely to have the biggest impact on uninsured young adults. It is expected that, starting in 2014, of the 14.8 million adults aged 19–29 who are uninsured, an estimated 12.1 million could gain subsidized coverage once all the provisions of the ACA go into effect. As many as 7.2 million may gain coverage under Medicaid. Approximately 1 million uninsured young adults with incomes of less than 133 percent of FPL are undocumented and will not be eligible for Medicaid coverage.

Under the ACA, a catastrophic plan will be available to adults up to age 30 who are not eligible for subsidized coverage and to those who are exempt from the mandate to purchase coverage. The coverage level will be set at the current HSA level except that prevention benefits and coverage for three primary care visits would be exempt from the deductible. People over age 30 who could not find a plan with a premium that is less than 8 percent of their income can also purchase the young adult plan. This plan will be available only in the individual market.

THE NEAR-ELDERLY

Of the 8.6 million Americans aged 50–64 who were uninsured in 2009, an estimated 6.8 million may gain subsidized health insurance through Medicaid and the insurance exchanges, and 1.4 million are expected to have access to comprehensive plans with new consumer protections. Currently, an estimated 9.7 million adults in this age group with health insurance have such high out-of-pocket costs relative to their incomes that they are effectively underinsured. In 2007, nearly two-thirds of this population (about 35 million) had at least one chronic condition. Of those who tried to buy health insurance in the individual market, 45 percent found it difficult or impossible, and 39 percent were turned down. Seventy-five percent of uninsured adults 50–64 reported not getting needed care because of costs. Because the high cost of health care results in delays in accessing care by the near-elderly, there is pent-up demand for health services once these individuals turn 65 and enter the Medicare program. Michael McWilliams and colleagues (2009) found that, among adults with chronic health conditions, previously uninsured adults who acquired Medicare at 65 had significantly more doctor visits, more hospital episodes, and greater medical costs than did previously insured adults and that this cost difference persisted until age 72.

Going without health insurance can also lead to medical debt and an impaired ability to save for retirement. A 2007 Commonwealth Fund survey found that more than 50 percent of uninsured older adults and more than 75 percent of underinsured older adults spent 10 percent or more of their income on premiums and out-of-pocket costs compared to 20 percent who were insured all year with adequate coverage. Seven out of 10 baby boomers who are uninsured or underinsured reported problems paying medical bills or said that they were paying off medical debt over time compared to 23 percent of adults with adequate coverage.

The ACA will provide specific benefits to this group by: providing new plans for people with preexisting conditions, banning lifetime limits on insurance policies, requiring plans to insure all who apply for a policy, preventing plans from charging a higher premium to sicker people, limiting how much premiums can rise by age, requiring that certain preventive care be offered without cost sharing, helping to preserve ESI for adults retiring between 55 and 65, and expanding Medicaid eligibility.

Under the ACA the premiums that can be charged to the near-elderly cannot be more than three times the premiums charged to any other age group. Since actual average health care spending by the elderly is about five times the amount it is for younger ages, this stipulation results in a cross-subsidy going from the younger age groups to the near-elderly. The amount of the cross-subsidy levied on the youngest age group is somewhat mitigated by the ability of young adults to stay on their parents' plans until age 26 and their ability to enroll in catastrophic coverage policies. However, the population group aged 30 to 54 will incur higher premiums in order to keep the premiums of the near-elderly to the 3:1 ratio.

The near-elderly will see the biggest gains in their well-being come through the coverage bought through the insurance exchanges as there is considerably more variability in service coverage and in underwriting than goes on in the current individual market. Because many near-elderly have more chronic conditions, the requirement that exchange plans cannot charge higher premiums to those with higher expected costs will result in the chronically ill having improved access to health insurance coverage once the exchanges are set up and operational.

IMMIGRANTS

The U.S. Census Bureau estimates that there were about 40 million foreign-born persons in the United States in 2010, representing 13 percent of the population (Greico et al.). Of these, about 17 million were naturalized citizens and about 23 million were estimated to be noncitizens. The number of unauthorized immigrants living in the United States in 2010 was estimated by Homeland Security to be about 11 million (Homeland Security, 2011). Aliens who are legally present in the

United States are subject to the health reform law and are eligible, if otherwise qualified, to participate in the high-risk pools and the exchanges, and they are eligible for premium credits and cost-sharing subsidies. Until the exchanges are in operation, it not known what the shortest period of enrollment will be and whether or not certain immigrants in the United States for limited periods of time would be covered by the mandate. The ACA specifically exempts unauthorized aliens from the mandate to have health insurance coverage and bars them from the exchanges. These individuals may not participate in the exchanges even if they choose to use all of their own resources to purchase health insurance. Instead, they must purchase health insurance outside the exchanges and will not get the protections and the competitive prices of products sold within the exchanges (Ponce, Lavarredda, and Cabezas 2011).

The ACA will not change noncitizens' eligibility for Medicaid. Consequently, some permanent legal residents who are below 133 percent of FPL will be ineligible for Medicaid. Under the Personal Responsibility and Work Opportunity Reconciliation Act of 1996, noncitizens' eligibility for Medicaid depends on their immigration status, whether they arrived in the United States before August 22, 1996, and how long they have lived and worked in the United States. Most legal permanent residents entering the United States after August 22, 1996, are barred from Medicaid for five years, after which they are eligible at the state's option. States may, however, choose to use Medicaid funds to cover pregnant women and children who are lawfully residing in the United States and can also use state funds to provide medical coverage for other legal permanent residents within five years of arrival to the United States so long as they do not use federal funds to do so.

FINANCING THE AFFORDABLE CARE ACT

A variety of different taxes, program participation fees, and cost limitation strategies will be imposed to help finance the ACA. For example, there will be an expanded use of income-related premiums for Medicare Part B at 2010 levels ($85,000 for an individual and $170,000 for a couple) through 2019, and a new income-related premium for Part D coverage will be implemented. In addition, the payroll tax on earnings for higher-income taxpayers (those individuals earning more than $200,000 and couples earning more than $250,000) will increase by 0.9 percent, from the current 1.45 percent of earnings to 2.35 percent beginning in 2013.

In addition to changes in the payroll tax for high-income earners, there will also be a special income tax surcharge on high-income earners. This surcharge will consist of a special 3.8 percent tax on unearned income (income from rent, dividends, interest, etc.) for taxpayers with incomes exceeding $200,000 for the individual and $250,000 for a couple (thresholds not indexed for inflation). This represents the first time that tax filing status will be used to figure out each person's Medicare tax liability and the first time the tax will apply not just to earnings but to investment income as well. In its first year of operation, the tax is expected to hit the top 2 percent of families. However, this percentage is expected to grow over time since the income thresholds are not indexed for inflation. Current estimates are that ACA will take an additional $52,000 from families in the top 1 percent of the income distribution.

The threshold for the itemized deduction for unreimbursed medical expense will increase from 7.5 percent of adjusted gross income to 10 percent of adjusted gross income (the increase will be waived for taxpayers 65 and over in tax years 2013 through 2016). The contributions to flexible spending accounts will be lowered to $2,500 per year and the tax on distributions from a Health Savings Account or an Archer Medical Savings Account that are not used to pay medical expenses will increase to 20 percent beginning January 2011 (was 10% and 15%).

Employers with 50 or more full-time employees that do not offer coverage and have at least one full-time employee who receives a premium tax credit will pay a fee of $2,000 per full-time employee excluding the first 30 employees. Employers with at least 50 full-time employees that do offer coverage but have at least one full-time employee who receives a premium tax credit will pay the lesser of $3,000 for each employee receiving a premium credit or $2,000 per each full-time employee, excluding the first 30 employees from the assessment. Employers with up to 50 employees will be exempted from any penalties. These penalties become effective on January 1, 2014.

An excise tax will be imposed on insurers of employer-sponsored plans with aggregate values that exceed $10,200 for individual coverage and $27,500 for family coverage (thresholds to be indexed by the Consumer Price Index-Urban). These threshold levels will be increased for retired individual aged 55 or older who are not eligible for Medicare and for employees in high-risk professions by $1,650 for individual coverage and $3,450 for family coverage.

REDISTRIBUTION OF INCOME UNDER
THE AFFORDABLE CARE ACT

The obvious question is whether or not ACA will make health insurance affordable for the majority of Americans that are uninsured or underinsured under the current system. Related to this is how the ACA will redistribute income.

On the issue of affordability, as stated earlier Gruber and Perry (2011, 1) found that fewer than 10 percent of families above the FPL "do not have the resources to pay for premiums and typical out-of-pocket costs even with the subsidies put in place by the health reform law." Using the Consumer Expenditure Survey, the authors examined how much "room" people had in their budgets to pay for health care after they had taken care of other necessities. They estimated premiums for a typical exchange plan at each actuarial. They also simulated out-of-pocket costs using data from the Medical Expenditure Panel Survey.

Families with the most difficulty paying for care under the ACA were those with incomes between 201 and 300 percent of the FPL. About 25 percent of this population group with high out-of-pocket spending was deemed unable to be able to afford the costs of health care. Those living in high-cost states were less able to afford health care under the ACA than those living in low-cost states. The primary risk to affordability under the ACA comes not from the premiums and the subsidies but from exposure to high out-of-pocket costs. Those with high out-of-pocket costs are more likely to have chronic health problems compared to those with lower out-of-pocket costs.

Peterson and Gabe (2010) estimated health insurance premiums under the ACA and calculated premiums as a percentage of income for different age categories in both high- and low-cost areas and for individuals and families. Premiums ranged from a low of 4.8 percent of income for adults aged 20 in low-cost areas to over 25 percent of income for a family of four in a high-cost area with adults age 60 in the household. These results suggest that even under the ACA, the premiums are likely to be out of reach for older families living in high-cost areas who are not receiving subsidies and must purchase health insurance in the individual market (Table 26.4).

Because the primary beneficiaries of the new ACA will be individuals of low and moderate incomes, and much of the revenue used to fund the program will come from new taxes placed on high earners, penalties imposed on "Cadillac" health plans, and limitations in

Table 26.4
Illustrative Health Insurance Premiums and Premiums as a Percent of Income

Age	Individual Low-Cost Premium	Individual High-Cost Premium	Family of Four Low-Cost Premium	Family of Four High-Cost Premium
20	$2,110	$3,165	$5,687	$8,530
30	$2,141	$3,211	$6,290	$9,435
40	$2,800	$4,200	$7,548	$11,321
50	$4,342	$6,513	$10,489	$15,734
60	$6,329	$9,494	$14,960	$22,440
Premium as % of Income at 400% of FPL in 2011				
20	4.8	7.3	6.4	9.5
30	4.9	7.4	7.0	10.6
40	6.4	9.6	8.4	12.7
50	10.0	15.0	11.7	17.6
60	14.5	21.8	16.7	25.1

Source: Premium estimates are from: Chris Peterson and Thomas Gabe, "Health Insurance Premiums Credits under PPACA (P.L.111-148)," Congressional Research Service, 7-5700, http://www.crs.gov, R41137, April 6, 2010 (author-calculated percentages based on 2011 FPL).

payments to providers under Medicare, the implementation of the ACA will likely lead to some redistribution of income. Fleenor and Prante (2010) estimated the redistributional impact of the ACA. They found that overall the ACA will redistribute income from high-income to lower-income families. The increase in Medicare taxes on high-income earners and the new Medicare tax on unearned income of those with high incomes also contribute to the redistribution. The primary beneficiaries of the program are expected to be the lower-middle-income groups. The lowest income group is not expected to benefit greatly because many already are eligible for Medicaid or have family members (children) eligible for Medicaid or the Children's Health Insurance Program.

In conclusion, the new ACA will extend health insurance coverage to about 60 percent of those who are currently uninsured at costs that most will be able to afford. The expansions in coverage should lead to improved access to health care and, hopefully, to improved health status among some of the most vulnerable population groups.

BIBLIOGRAPHY

America's Health Insurance Plans, Center for Policy and Research. "Individual Health Insurance, 2009: A Comprehensive Survey of Premiums, Availability, and Benefits," October 2009.

Blumberg, Linda, Matthew Buettgens and Bowen Garrett. "Age Rating under Comprehensive Health Reform: Implications for Coverage, Costs, and Household Financial Burdens," Timely Analysis of Immediate Health Policy Issues, Urban Institute, October 2009.

Blumberg, Linda, Matthew Buettgens and Bowen Garrett. "Update: Age Rating under Comprehensive Health Care Reform," AARP Public Policy Institute, Insight on the Issues, undated.

Buettgens, Matthew, Bowen Garrett and John Holahan. "America under the Affordable Care Act," Urban Institute, December 2010a.

Buettgens, Matthew, Bowen Garrett and John Holahan. "Why the Individual Mandate Matters: Timely Analysis of Immediate Health Policy Issues," Urban Institute, December 2010b.

Collins, Sara, Michelle Doty and Tracy Garber. "Realizing Health Reform's Potential: Adults Ages 50–64 and the Affordable Care Act of 2010," Commonwealth Fund, Publication #1460, Vol. 2, December 2010.

Collins, Sara, Tracy Garber and Ruth Robertson. "Realizing Health Reform's Potential: How the Affordable Care Act Is Helping Young Adults Stay Covered," Commonwealth Fund, Publication #1508, Vol. 5, May 2011.

Congressional Budget Office, 2012. "Estimates for the Insurance Coverage Provisions of the Affordable Care Act Updated for the Recent Supreme Court Decision," July 2012.

Fleenor, Patrick and Gerald Prante. "Health Reform: How Much Does It Redistribute Income?," Fiscal Fact, Tax Foundation, No. 222, April 2011.

Fronstin, Paul. "The Impact of the 2007–2009 Recession on Workers' Health Coverage," Issue Brief No. 356, Employee Benefit Research Institute, April 2011.

Grieco, Elizabeth, et al. "The Foreign-Born Population in the United States: 2010," *American Community Survey Reports*, U.S. Department of Commerce, May 2012.

Gruber, Jonathan and Ian Perry. "Realizing Health Reform's Potential: Will the Affordable Care Act Make Health Insurance Affordable?," Commonwealth Fund, Publication #1493, Vol. 2, April 2011.

Himmelstein, David, Deborah Thorne, Elizabeth Warren and Steffie Woolhandler. "Medical Bankruptcy in the United States, 2007: Results of a National Study," *The American Journal of Medicine,* Vol. 122, No. 8, August 2009.

Holahan, John. "The 2007–2009 Recession and Health Insurance Coverage," *Health Affairs Web First,* Vol. 30, No. 1, pp. 145–52, January 2011.

Homeland Security. "Estimates of the Unauthorized Immigrant Population Residing in the United States: January 2010," Population Estimates, Office of Immigration Statistics, February 2011.

Kaiser Commission on Medicaid and the Uninsured. "Explaining Health Reform: The New Rules for Determining Income under Medicaid in 2014," Kaiser Family Foundation, http://www.kff.org/kcmu, June 2011.

Kaiser Family Foundation. "Focus on Health Reform: Summary of Key Changes to Medicare in 2010 Health Reform Law," Publication # 7948-02, http://www.kff.org, undated.

Kaiser Family Foundation. "Focus on Health Reform: Reconciliation of Advance Payments for Health Insurance Subsidies," Publication #8154, http://www.kff.org, February 2011a.

Kaiser Family Foundation." Focus on Health Reform: A Profile of Health Insurance Exchange Enrollees," Publication #8147, http://www.kff.org, March 2011b.

Kaiser Family Foundation. "Focus on Health Reform: Summary of New Health Reform Law," Publication #8061, http://www.kff.org, last modified April 11, 2011c.

Kaiser Family Foundation. "Focus on Health Reform: Affordable Care Act Provisions Relating to the Care of Dually Eligible Medicare and Medicaid Beneficiaries," Publication #8192, http://www.kff.org, May 2011d.

Kaiser Family Foundation. "Survey of People Who Purchase Their Own Insurance," Survey Report, June 2010.

Kenney, Genevieve, Jennifer Pelletier and Linda Blumberg. "How Will the Patient Protection and Affordable Care Act of 2010 Affect Young Adults?," Timely Analysis of Immediate Health Policy Issues, Urban Institute, July 2010.

Levitt, Larry and Claxton, Gary for the Kaiser Family Foundation. "What the Actuarial Values in the Affordable Care Act Mean," Publication #8177, http://www.kff.org, April 2011.

McWilliams, J. Michael, Ellen Meara, Alan Zaslavsky and John Ayanian. "Medicare Spending for Previously Uninsured Adults," *Annals of Internal Medicine*, Vol. 151, No. 11, pp. 757–66, December 2009.

Merlis, Mark. "Medigap Reforms: Potential Effects of Benefit Restrictions on Medicare Spending and Beneficiary Costs," Program on Medicare Policy, Kaiser Family Foundation, July 2011.

Mulvey, Janemarie and Kirsten Colello. "Community Living Assistance Services and Supports (CLASS) Provisions in the Patient Protection and Affordable Care Act (PPACA)," Congressional Research Services, 7-5700 R40842, http://www.crs.gov, January 5, 2011.

Munnell, Alicia, Maurice Soto, Anthony Webb, Francesca Golub-Sass and Dan Muldon. "Health Care Costs Drive Up the National Retirement Risk Index," Center for Retirement Research at Boston College, Number 8-3, February 2008.

Peterson, Chris and Thomas Gabe. "Health Insurance Premium Credits under PPACA (P.L.111-148)," Congressional Research Service, 7-5700, http://www.crs.gov, R41137, April 6, 2010.

Pew Hispanic Center. "U.S. Foreign-Born Population: How Much Change from 2009 to 2010?" Pew Research Center, January 9, 2012.

Ponce, Ninez, Alex Lavarreda and Livier Cabezas. "The Impact of Health Care Reform on California's Children in Immigrant Families," Health Policy Brief, UCLA Center for Health Policy Research, PB-2011-8, June 2011.

Schoen, Cathy, Sara Collins, Jennifer Kriss and Michelle Doty. "How Many Are Underinsured? Trends among U.S. Adults, 2003 and 2007," In the Literature, Commonwealth Publication #1144, June 2008.

Siskin, Alison. "Treatment of Noncitizens under the Patient Protection and Affordable Care Act," Congressional Research Service, R41714, March 22, 2011.

Towers, Watson. "Shaping Health Care Strategy in a Post-reform Environment," 16th Annual Towers Watson/National Business Group on Health Employer Survey on Purchasing Value in Health Care, 2011.

Chapter 27

Do Labor Unions Have a Future in the United States?

Richard B. Freeman and Kelsey Hilbrich

In summer 2011, a labor dispute between National Football League owners and players threatened to derail the 2011 NFL season. The collective bargaining agreement between owners and the NFL players union had run out. To force players to take a smaller share of football's $9 billion of annual revenue and to accept an increased number of games in a season—which risked the health and safety of players and the length of their careers—the owners closed the workplace and stopped paying salaries. A similar dispute in the National Basketball Association led NBA owners to lock out workers, remove information about them from team web pages, and stop paying their salaries. In most disputes between management and labor, workers strike until they and their employer reach agreement over pay and the terms of work. But sometimes, as in the NFL and NBA disputes, owners lock out workers to pressure the workers to accept what the owners want (*Washington Post* 2011).

Not so long ago, unions and collective bargaining touched the lives of virtually all Americans. Unions negotiated with management the wages and working conditions of a large proportion of the U.S. workforce and influenced the wages and conditions of many nonunion workers and firms as well. In 1955 when the two major U.S. labor federations, the American Federation of Labor (AFL) and Congress of Industrial Organizations (CIO), merged to form a single federation, the AFL-CIO, about 38 percent of workers in the private sector were covered by collective contracts. If you were not a union member, someone in your family or someone on the street where you lived was a member. If you managed a large firm, some part of your firm dealt with unionized workers. If your firm was nonunion and wished to remain so, you paid close attention to collective agreements between unions and other firms. Matching negotiated improvements in wages and benefits could keep your employees happy and nonunion.

The labor scene in 2011 was markedly different than in the 1950s and 1960s. Unions and collective bargaining covered a small and declining share of private sector workers. In 2011 just 6.9 percent of private sector workers were in unions, the smallest percentage since 1900. In some parts of the country, such as North Carolina, Tennessee, or South Dakota, the proportion of private sector workers unionized was 3 percent or less and falling.[1] With so few unionized workers in the private sector, the only connection many people had to unions was through the products made by union workers: as sports fans during the NFL or NBA disputes, or as fans of weekly TV series delayed during the 2007–8 season, when film, television, and radio writers struck to gain a bigger share of compensation from new media forms (Wikipedia 2011a).

In 2011 workers in the public sector, virtually none of whom were organized in the 1950s, made up the majority of union members. Local, state, and federal government workers unionized rapidly in the 1970s and 1980s so that 37 percent were union members in 2011, a proportion over five times that in the private sector. The typical union member was a teacher, police officer, firefighter, or other city or state employee rather than an automobile worker, steelworker, or construction worker (Bureau of Labor Statistics 2011).

The laws that regulate unions and collective bargaining differ between the private sector and the public sector. National law in the form of the National Labor Relations Act (NLRA) governs private sector labor management relations. State law, which differs by state, governs labor-management relations for the state and local employees who make up most public sector workers.[2] Hawaii, New York,

California, Massachusetts, and many other states have laws favorable to public sector collective bargaining, with the result that most of their public sector workers have union contracts. Other states such as Alabama, Virginia, Texas, and South Carolina discourage public sector collective bargaining so that few if any of their public sector workers have collective agreements with their employers. Among teachers, for instance, collective bargaining determines the pay and working conditions of 95 percent of elementary and secondary school teachers in New York and 98 percent in Massachusetts, while it determines pay and conditions for only 2 percent of the teachers in Alabama and 0 percent in Texas (Moe 2011, Table 2-2).[3]

Following a conservative tide in the 2010 elections, public sector unions and collective bargaining came under attack. The 2008–9 recession and weak recovery had reduced state and local revenues throughout the country and squeezed government budgets. Arguing that public sector collective bargaining was part of the problem and that unions hampered state efforts to balance budgets, the newly ascendant conservatives sought to dislodge unions from their one remaining stronghold. The efforts of Wisconsin governor Scott Walker and the state legislature gained even more attention than the NFL and NBA lockouts. Democratic legislators opposed to Walker's bill left the state to prevent the legislature having the quorum necessary to enact the law. Union supporters demonstrated in the state capitol against the bill. The legislation eventually passed at a midnight meeting. Ohio enacted a similar law, and conservative Republicans in many states introduced comparable bills to weaken public sector collective bargaining. Democrats opposed the legislation, which created the greatest partisan division over unions and bargaining in U.S. history.

The precipitous drop in private sector union density and the effort to eliminate public sector collective bargaining raise the title question of this chapter. Extrapolating the decline of private sector unions, many labor and management experts believe that unions have little or no future. Extrapolating the effort to weaken public sector collective bargaining, many analysts wonder whether public sector unions can survive in an era of weak private sector unions, political polarization, and fiscal austerity.

But extrapolating trends is not a reliable way to answer our title question. In 1932 in the midst of the Great Depression, the president of the American Economic Association, one of the country's top experts in unionism, predicted that unionism, which had been losing membership throughout the roaring 1920s, could not possibly expand in the depressed 1930s (Barnett 1933). This was just before unions had their greatest growth of membership in U.S. history. In 1955 the president of the AFL-CIO, the top union leader in the country, dismissed unionization in the public sector on the grounds that "it is impossible to bargain collectively with the government" (Meany 1955). A decade later unions began their growth spurt in the public sector.

To answer our title question we must look beyond extrapolations to the reasons why workers form unions, the way workers who want unions gain recognition from employers and collective bargaining contracts, and the attitudes of workers and business toward unions.

Why do workers form a union? The main reason workers form unions is that they have interests in common that a union can help advance. These interests range from the physical conditions at the workplace to company-wide policies regarding wages and benefits ranging from family leave to vacation time to health care insurance and company pensions. By conveying their collective concerns to employers, unions influence the terms and conditions at work. This is the collective voice channel of unionism—voice referring to the channel of communication and discussion on issues where management would otherwise make unilateral decisions; collective referring to the fact that the mechanism is through the elected union officials who represent workers as a group (Freeman and Medoff 1984).

The second reason for forming a union is that bargaining as a group gives workers greater clout with an employer than bargaining individually. When workers are organized at a workplace, the union has some monopoly power with which to bargain for workers' interests against management, which invariably holds the upper hand in the firm. Negotiating with management as a group puts greater pressure on the employer than do individual workers bringing up an issue by themselves.

The history of unions in the United States is a story of workers' struggle to organize unions and convince or force employers to recognize them for bargaining. From the early days of the republic through enactment of the NLRA, the way workers got management to recognize and negotiate with a union was through economic force. This often led to violent battles between the two sides. Firms would hire security guards and call in strikebreakers. If a dispute got particularly violent, the police, the National Guard, or even federal troops would intervene, almost always to support the employer. According to historians Philip Taft and Philip Ross (1969), "the United States has experienced more frequent and bloody labor violence than any other industrial nation" with the "most virulent form of industrial violence [occurring] in situations in which efforts were made to destroy a functioning union or to deny a union recognition."

The Depression sparked an upsurge of worker desires for unions. It may seem odd that workers would seek to unionize in a period of high joblessness when most efforts to unionize in better economic times had failed. But the Depression destroyed faith in business leadership and convinced many workers that unions offered the only way to improve their standard of life. Leaders of the AFL, the sole labor federation at the time, argued over how best to help workers organize. Most believed that only skilled craft workers had the economic muscle to win battles against management and shied away from organizing less skilled workers into unions based on the industry that employed them. Arguing for industrial unionism at the 1935 AFL Convention, United Mine Workers president John L. Lewis punched Carpenters Union president Bill Hutcheson (Wikipedia 2011b), then led the unions favoring industrial unionism out of the convention to form a new federation, the Congress of Industrial Organizations. Organizing in the United States thus involved battles not only between workers and firms but between rival union groups.

The ensuing effort to organize industrial workers fits with the violent history of organizing in earlier periods. In one famous incident the United Auto Workers initiated a sit-down strike against General Motors, in which workers occupied their workplace rather than leaving it. The company called on the police and National Guard to remove the workers, which produced a 40-day "Battle of the Running Bulls" in Flint, Michigan (http://apps.detnews.com/apps/history/index.php?id=115). The Roosevelt administration proposed and Congress enacted the NLRA in 1935 to shift organizing from the streets to the ballot box. The act established the National Labor Relations Board (NLRB) to organize government-sponsored secret ballot elections at workplaces so workers could vote for or against having a union. The Supreme Court declared the act constitutional in 1937.

From the late 1930s to the mid-1950s, unions won the vast majority of NLRB elections, greatly increasing the proportion of workers who were union members. During the Cold War the United States had the strongest labor movement in the free world—a fiercely anti-Communist movement that sought to convince workers worldwide to choose independent unions favorable to market economies rather than Communist-controlled unions in state-run economies. Most U.S. employers accepted unions as a fixed part of the economic system and sought good relationships with them.

The NLRA, amended in various ways,[4] remains the law governing unionization today. The act seeks "laboratory condition" elections to ascertain the desire of workers to unionize or not—elections that are not tainted by undue pressure or blatantly dishonest statements from management or unions. The law makes it illegal for the employer to threaten to close the workplace if the workers choose the union or to fire or otherwise discriminate against workers for favoring the union, and places some restrictions on union campaigning as well.

NLRB elections are far from laboratory conditions. Employers usually campaign vigorously to convince workers that they would do better to trust management to remedy problems than to have a union represent them. As part of management's campaign, employers can order workers to assemble during the work day to hear antiunion speeches or to watch antiunion videos, and to meet separately with supervisors who try to convince them to vote against the union. Many employers bring in union prevention firms (colloquially known as union busters) who specialize in turning a union majority into a minority through hard-nosed tactics. The elections substitute political battles within a company over unionization for physical battles in the streets and in workplaces.

The unionization of Harvard University's technical and clerical workers in the 1980s shows how workers come together as a group and unionize under U.S. labor law. In 1973 some technicians went to their supervisor to ask for changes in their workplace (Hoerr 1997; Hurd 1993). The supervisor said that management could not change practices in response to the desires of a few, but that if the workers formed a union to represent everyone, management would pay attention. The technicians organized the majority of workers at the workplace, but the university insisted that the majority cover not only those workers but the thousands of clerical and technical workers in the entire university—most of whom had never thought about unionizing. It took 15 years and substantial support from the American Federation of State, County, and Municipal Employees union, with whom the Harvard workers affiliated, and the AFL-CIO before the prounion workers convinced a majority to vote for the Harvard Union of Clerical and Technical Workers (2005). The university and union have negotiated contracts amicably ever since.

The Harvard example is unique in some respects. The union campaigned on making Harvard a better place for all rather than on attacking management, as is common in many union-organizing campaigns. The union slogan for higher wages and benefits fit the prestigious university: "We can't eat prestige." But the Harvard experience is also representative of organizing efforts under the NLRA. When a majority of workers vote for the union to represent them, the NLRA requires that management and the union meet and bargain "in good faith" over key wage and working conditions. But the law does not require that they reach agreement. The union can demand large wage gains. The employer can demand large wage cuts. If the two sides do not modify their demands and agree, the employer can unilaterally set conditions. The workers can strike. If they strike, the firm can hire new workers to replace the strikers. Or the firms can lock out workers to pressure them to agree to its terms.

What do workers gain from unionizing? When unions seek to convince workers to vote union they invariably tout the gains that unions bring in wages, benefits, and workplace conditions—what analysts call the union premium. One way to estimate the size of the union premium is to compare the pay of workers who are union with the pay of nonunion workers with the same measured characteristics—workers with the same age, gender, education, ethnicity, in the same industry, occupation, and region, and so on. Such comparisons find that unionized workers earn on average 15 percent or more than their nonunion counterpart (Blanchflower and Bryson 2007). But this comparison may overstate the union impact on pay, since a firm that offers higher wages will attract a large queue of job applicants from which to choose. If the firms identify better workers from this queue on the basis of attributes that are not measured, comparisons of union and nonunion workers with the same measured characteristics will overstate the effect of unions on the pay of workers with "truly identical" skills. It is also possible, however, that the union wage gains cause nonunion firms to raise their pay to compete for the best workers, which makes the premium underestimate the increase in wages due to unions.

To deal with these problems and identify the impact of unions on workers with truly identical skills, analysts compare the pay of the same worker in a nonunion job with their pay on a union job. Such comparisons find a smaller but still substantial union wage effect on the order of 5 to 10 percent. Analysts also estimate the size of the union premium by comparing wages at a firm before and after the workers gain a collective bargaining contract. Estimated wage gains are often small because unions generally seek health insurance, pensions, non-wage benefits, and union security clauses on a first contract and push more on wages in later negotiations. Comparisons of unionized and nonunion workers and firms before and after unionization find that the effects of unions on pensions, health insurance, vacation time, and other benefits are larger than on wages.[5]

Going beyond pecuniary benefits, unions also provide a means for workers to discuss and negotiate with employers how management runs the workplace. Virtually every union contract establishes a grievance and arbitration system that allows workers due process to redress individual workplace problems. Management and the union will investigate jointly the problem and either come to a decision or hire an outside arbitrator to resolve the issue.

What about the dues that workers pay to unions? Dues vary among unions, generally being higher for highly skilled workers and lower for less skilled workers but average around 2 percent of earnings. Increases in pay and benefits on the order of 5 to 10 percent and costs of 2 percent or so make unionization profitable to workers.

So why are most workers nonunion? One reason is that there are large costs and risks to an organizing drive when the employer opposes it. The NLRA makes it illegal for management to fire or discriminate against union supporters, but the penalties for breaking the law are small. Enough managements break the law that union activists risk their job and future with a firm by seeking to organize. Another reason is that many organizing campaigns resemble marital disputes, which create unpleasant conditions long after the campaign has ended. Finally, even if unions win an NLRB representation election, they may not be able to gain a contract. On the order of one-third of union victories in the elections do not produce a contract.

Some may wonder whether workers need unions to help them in a free market. If the market functioned perfectly, a worker could always take the "exit option" of quitting when he or she is unhappy about the firm and find comparable work elsewhere. Since it is expensive for firms to recruit and train workers for most jobs, high quit rates pressure management to take account of workers' concerns in their decisions. But by itself exit is often an inefficient way to improve situations. Workers build up skills that are specific to a given workplace, making quitting costly to the worker as well as the firm. In periods of high unemployment, workers are unlikely to risk leaving their job to find another one. Workers who do quit have no incentive to tell the firm about the workplace problems that led them to leave, so management will not learn about what it might do better. Workers who stay at the firm may be unwilling to speak up individually for fear of being blamed as the bearer of ill tidings. Unions provide a mechanism for workers as a group to raise difficult issues with the firm.

Why do most firms oppose unions organizing their workers? The economics answer is simple. The higher wages and benefits and better working conditions shift profits from owners to workers. Management will try to raise productivity to offset the higher cost of labor but usually cannot do so fully. Communication with a union may provide a better flow of information about worker attitudes than an employee opinion survey and can promote compromises or concessions when the firm faces genuine problems. The higher wages and benefits and the union-initiated grievance system lowers quit rates, which reduces labor costs. But the cost-increasing effects of unions almost always exceed the cost-reducing effects, giving most managements a monetary incentive to keep their firm nonunion.

In addition, unions reduce the power of management to control workplaces. Management must negotiate changes through collective bargaining or grievance procedures. When most firms engaged in collective bargaining, many managers took courses in negotiations and learned how to deal with unions. With collective bargaining becoming less frequent, business schools have replaced labor relations courses with human resource management or personnel courses that teach future managers to make decisions without bargaining with employees.

The incentive for management to oppose unionism differs in European Union (EU) countries from that in the United States. In most EU countries collective bargaining agreements are largely between employer federations and unions of workers in an entire sector or region. The employer group—say, the federation of electrical machinery firms—will sign an agreement with the union that covers the sector. The agreement becomes legally binding on all firms and workers in the sector, whether they are members of the federation of firms or of the union or nonunion. Since every firm pays essentially the same negotiated wages and benefits, management has little incentive to campaign against workers joining a union. Managements compete on the basis of better productivity, innovations, or service—not on the basis of lower labor costs. At the same time workers who can free ride on the collective bargaining agreement have less incentive to form or join a union at their workplace than in the United States.

This produces what seems paradoxical from an American perspective: huge proportions of workers covered by collective contracts coincident with modest proportions of workers who join unions. The exemplar is France, whose unionization rate is in the single digits yet where collective bargaining sets wages for some 90 percent of the workforce. Collective bargaining coverage also greatly exceeds union density in the Netherlands, Austria, and several other EU countries, where contracts are extended to cover all firms and workers.

Why has unionism declined consistently in the U.S. private sector? To get a better sense of the possible future of unions in the United States, it is important to understand what set them along the path of continuous decline in density. Two factors that often receive attention are the shift in employment from blue-collar industry jobs to white-collar service sector jobs and President Ronald Reagan breaking the Professional Air Traffic Controllers' strike in 1981 (McCartin 2011). Neither of these factors stands up to scrutiny as drivers of the decline in union density.

The composition of jobs in the United States has shifted from manufacturing and related industries where union density has historically been high to white-collar and service jobs where union density has historically been low. But this has contributed little to the downward trend in unionization. The best way to demonstrate that the changing composition of jobs is not a major factor is to look at the union density *within* sectors that have been hotbeds of union strength. If density fell largely within heavily unionized sectors, something more than shifts in the composition of jobs must be at work. This is what the data show. From 1983 to 2010, the percentage of workers in unions dropped in motor vehicles production from 58.5 percent to 20.3 percent, in transportation and warehousing from 49.4 percent to 30.5 percent, and in construction from 28.0 percent to 14.6 percent (Unionstats.com 2011). These declines exceed the drop in union density in the country over the same period!

In a dynamic market economy, moreover, the mix of jobs always changes. A healthy union movement would adjust to changes in the mix of jobs by organizing workers in emerging sectors, as unions did for industrial workers in the 1930s and 1940s and for public sector workers in the 1970s. During the period of declining density, with the exception of the health care sector, unions failed to organize workers in the expanding traditionally nonunion industries.

In 1981 the Professional Air Traffic Controllers, one of the few unions that supported President Reagan in the 1980 presidential election, called an illegal strike to force the president and Congress to agree to its bargaining demands. The president fired the strikers and kept air traffic going by using military air traffic controllers. The federal government decertified the Professional Air Traffic Controllers as the representative of workers. But Reagan did not attack private sector unions or legal strikes or the right of air traffic controllers to organize a union that operated within the law. When the air traffic controllers chose a new union to represent them in 1987, the Reagan administration bargained with it (Wikipedia 2011c). For all the attention given to the Professional Air Traffic Controllers strike, it had no noticeable effect on union density. From the mid-1950s through 2010, the percentage of private sector workers in unions fell under Republican and Democratic administrations alike; in boom times and in recessions; under NLRBs favorable to unions and NLRBs favorable to business.

An explanation for the trend lies in fundamental changes in the economy in which U.S. business and labor operated and in the incentives affecting business and labor toward unionism and their power to act on those incentives.

From the end of World War II through the 1960s, U.S. firms had a virtual monopoly of modern technology and production. Europe and Japan were recovering from the destruction of the war. China was a Communist-run economy experiencing episodes of political instability and the inefficiencies of centralized planning. The Soviet Union produced missiles and bombs and little else of commercial value. India and most developing countries had barely entered the industrial era. As a result U.S. firms dominated production in most products and services, making the United States the world's leading export nation. Unions derive power from the economic strength of the companies and industries they organize. When unionized firms have market power and/or high profitability, unions are better able to shift profits to workers.

Then the economic world changed. Europe recovered and began to close the economic gap with the United States. Japan developed so rapidly that Professor Ezra Vogel of Harvard published a book in 1979 entitled *Japan as Number One*. Then Korea developed rapidly and moved from producing cheap clothes to manufacturing to high tech. The United States shifted from being a substantial exporter in global markets to running huge trade deficits year after year. In the 1990s U.S. firms began outsourcing many jobs to low-wage countries that joined the global economy, notably China and India. Firms stiffened their opposition to union organizing.

The problems that hit the automobile industry and United Automobile Workers were archetypical. Dominated by General Motors, Ford, and Chrysler, the three big Detroit-based firms faced little international competition in the 1950s and 1960s and had the profitability to agree to union demands for sizable wages and benefits, which brought many workers into the middle class. But then European firms, particularly Volkswagen, then Japanese firms such as Toyota, and finally Korean firms entered the automobile market, with imports and manufacturing in nonunion plants in the United States. In 2009 both General Motors and Chrysler needed government bailout moneys to survive. The United Automobile Workers negotiated wage concessions, took responsibility for health care plans, and otherwise gave up much of what it had negotiated for workers in better times.

Over the same period, many leading U.S. firms empowered workers to make more decisions at workplaces through employee involvement committees and sought to incentivize their workers with profit sharing and employee share ownership (Bartel et al. 2009). Workers in nonunion firms with greater firm organized employee participation are less likely to vote union in an NLRB election than workers in firms without such programs (Freeman and Rogers 2006). Honda kept its assembly line workers nonunion by its human resource practices despite high levels of unionization in the automobile industry (Fiorito 2001).

But not all firms practice positive labor relations. Surveys show that large numbers of nonunion workers—from one-third to one-half, depending on the year and survey design—say they would vote for a union at their workplace if an election were held immediately. Many nonunion workers also say, however, that they would prefer a joint management and labor committee that meets and discusses workplace matters rather than to negotiate a collective contract (Freeman and Rogers 2006). Firms cannot utilize this mode of worker representation because the NLRA, in an effort to prevent Depression-era firms from setting up sham "company unions," made it illegal for management to initiate organizations to represent workers on labor issues.

The United States is not alone in experiencing a drop in union density and influence in the private sector of the economy, though it has experienced the longest and steadiest downward trend. In the 1970s union density increased in many advanced countries (but not in the United States) as workers flocked to unions to negotiate wage increases to match inflationary prices. But from 1980 to the 2000s, the unionized share of the workforce fell in nearly all advanced countries: from 39.7 percent to 26.3 percent in the EU, from 31.1 percent to 19.7 percent in Japan, and from 49.5 percent to 22.9 percent in Australia (Visser 2006, Table 4). In contrast to the United States where the percentage of workers covered by collective contracts fell as union density fell, however, the rate of collective bargaining coverage remained high in EU countries.[6] The reason is the extension of collective bargaining contracts to all workers in the relevant sectors noted earlier.

The United States is distinct from other advanced countries not so much in its declining proportion of workers in unions as in the declining proportion of wages and conditions set by collective bargaining and by greater employer opposition to unions.

CONCLUSION

So, do labor unions have a future in the United States?

Most analysts answer no. The downward trend in private sector union density shows no sign of abating, much less of turning around. Unions have failed to get the Congress to enact labor law reforms that would make organizing easier. Union leaders have put organizing at the top of the union agenda, but without any notable organizing successes. Public sector unions face attacks on collective bargaining amid fiscal austerity that threatens their ability to function.

But workplaces invariably create collective interests, and collective interests invariably produce collective actions. In years past unions have arisen from the grave, confounding expert analysts and surprising their own leaders as well as corporations and government. Unions grow in sudden sharp spurts in economic crises where workers see them as the only viable voice defending worker interests (Freeman 1998).

Could the crisis created by the 2008 financial disaster and the ensuing jobless recovery and fiscal deficit problems change the union situation as the Great Depression did in the past? It is possible, and not just in the sense that "anything that is not ruled out by the laws of science is possible." The 2010–11 attack on public sector collective bargaining galvanized union activists and their allies to an extent the United States had not seen since the Depression era. It produced mass demonstrations in Wisconsin, a landslide vote in Ohio to repeal legislation restricting collective bargaining in that state, and an effort to remove the governor and several legislators in Wisconsin. The Wisconsin demonstrations arguably set the stage for the Occupy Wall Street protests in the fall of 2011 that made income inequality and the well-being of the middle class a national issue.

What we know from past union growth spurts is that to meet the needs of workers in a crisis unions have to reinvent their structures, strategies, and tactics. If unions have a future in the United States, they will not be your parents' or grandparents' union movement but one that fits today's Internet-based society, global economy, and financial world.

Unions are searching for new forms to carry out their historic function of representing the interests of workers. If they find one that succeeds, they have the potential to rebuild themselves as a vibrant social force. If they fail, employees outside of the union movement, social entrepreneurs, or even managers concerned about worker well-being may find a way to rebuild labor's voice in the U.S. economy.

How might such a future employee organization/union movement differ from the unions of today? One possibility is that it would rely less on collective bargaining and more on social movement pressures to represent workers. In the 2000s the AFL-CIO's Working America signed up 3 million members by canvassing workers door to door and enrolling members over the Internet to join a community coalition to represent workers outside of collective bargaining. In 2010 the United Food and Commercial Workers Union formed an organization to represent Wal-mart workers absent a collective contract. In 2011 customers upset over Bank of America charging people for using debit cards used Internet-based social media to protest and forced the company to back down. Will unions or some innovative worker or social entrepreneur find a way to turn the Internet-based social media into a force that represents workers with little link to traditional union structures?

In a period of economic distress, it would be foolish to count unions or other employee-based organizations out as analysts did in the Depression era.

NOTES

1. The Bureau of Labor Statistics reports annually on union membership and collective bargaining http://www.bls.gov/news.release/pdf/union2.pdf; http://www.unionstats.com/ provides union data for the United States and by state, industry, and occupation, based on the U.S. Census Department's monthly Current Population Survey.

2.   In 1962 President John F. Kennedy issued Executive Order 10988 that recognized unions of federal employees for collective bargaining over the terms of work but not over wages or benefits. In 2011 the Bureau of Labor Statistics estimated that 28.1 percent of federal employees were union members.

3.   The data from National Center for Education Statistics, Schools and Staffing, where values average statistics in 2003–4 and 2007–8.

4.   The Taft-Hartley Act limited what unions can do to pressure firms to agree to a contract, disallows supervisors from unionizing, and allows states to make it illegal for firms to agree to contracts that required workers to join a union or pay dues. The Landrum-Griffin Act further restricted union activity and added protections for union democracy. The 1974 amendments extended the act to the nonprofit health sector.

5.   Bennett and Kauffman (2007) have the best review of quantitative studies of unions in these and other areas.

6.   Fulton (2011) estimates that about two-thirds of EU workers remained covered by collective contracts in the 2000s.

BIBLIOGRAPHY

Barnett, George E. 1933. "American Unionism and Social Insurance," *American Economic Review*, 23 (1): 1–15.

Bartel, Ann, Casey Ichniowski, Kathryn L. Shaw, Ricardo Correa. 2009. "International Differences in the Adoption and Impact of New Information Technologies and New HR Practices: The Valve-Making Industry in the United States and United Kingdom," in *International Differences in the Business Practices and Productivity of Firms*, edited by Richard B. Freeman and Kathryn L. Shaw, 55–78. Chicago: University of Chicago Press.

Bennett, James T. and Bruce E. Kaufman, Editors. 2007. *What Do Unions Do?: A Twenty-Year Perspective*. New Brunswick, NJ, and London: Transaction Publishers.

Blanchflower, David G. and Alex Bryson. 2007. "What Effect Do Unions Have on Wages Now and Would Freeman and Medoff Be Surprised," in *What Do Unions Do?*, edited by James T. Bennett and Bruce E. Kaufman, 79–113. New York: Basic Books.

Bureau of Labor Statistics. 2011. "Table B-1. Employees on nonfarm payrolls by industry sector and selected industry detail." Last modified August 5. http://www.bls.gov/news.release/empsit.t17.htm.

Fiorito, Jack. 2001. "Human Resource Management Practices and Worker Desires for Union Representation," *Journal of Labor Research*, 22 (2): 335–54. Accessed August 11, 2011. http://vwilkins.myweb.uga.edu/Summer07/Fiorito_article.pdf.

Freeman, Richard B. 1998. "Spurts in Union Growth: Defining Moments and Social Processes," in *The Defining Moment: The Great Depression and the American Economy in the Twentieth Century*, edited by Michael D. Bordo, Claudia Goldin, and Eugene N. White, 265–95. Chicago: University of Chicago Press for NBER.

Freeman, Richard B. and James L. Medoff. 1984. *What Do Unions Do?* New York: Basic Books.

Freeman, Richard B. and Joel Rogers. 2006. *What Workers Want*. Ithaca, NY: ILR Press for Russell Sage Foundation.

Fulton, Lionel. 2011. "Worker Representation in Europe," Labour Research Department and ETUI (online publication). Accessed August 11, 2011. http://www.worker-participation.eu/National-Industrial-Relations/Across-Europe/Collective-Bargaining2.

Harvard Union of Clerical and Technical Workers. 2005. "FAQ." Accessed August 11, 2011. http://www.huctw.org/basics/faq.htm.

Hoerr, John. 1997. *We Can't Eat Prestige: The Women Who Organized Harvard.* Philadelphia: Temple University Press.

Hurd, Richard W. 1993. "Organizing and Representing Clerical Workers: The Harvard Model" [Electronic version]. In *Women and Unions: Forging a Partnership*, edited by D. S. Cobble, 316–36. Ithaca, NY: ILR Press. Accessed August 10, 2011. http://digitalcommons.ilr.cornell.edu/articles/319/.

McCartin, Joseph. 2011. "The Strike That Busted Unions," *New York Times*, August 3. Accessed August 11, 2011. http://www.nytimes.com/2011/08/03/opinion/reagan-vs-patco-the-strike-that-busted-unions.html?_r=1&ref=todayspaper.

Meany, George. 1955. "Meany Looks into Labor's Future," *The New York Times*, December 4. Accessed August 10, 2011. http://query.nytimes.com/mem/archive/pdf?res=F50C14FD3C55107A93C6A91789D95F418585F9.

Moe, Terry M. 2011. *Special Interest: Teachers Unions and America's Public Schools.* Washington, DC: Brookings Institution Press.

Taft, Philip and Philip Ross. 1969. "American Labor Violence: Its Causes, Character, and Outcome," in *The History of Violence in America: A Report to the National Commission on the Causes and Prevention of Violence*, edited by Hugh Davis Graham and Ted Robert Gurr. New York: F. A. Praeger. Accessed August 10, 2011. http://www.ditext.com/taft/violence1.html#n.

Unionstats.com. 2011. "Union Membership and Coverage Database from the CPS (Documentation)." Accessed August 10, 2011. http://www.unionstats.gsu.edu/.

Visser, Jelle. 2006. "Union Membership Statistics in 24 Countries," *Monthly Labor Review*, January: 38–49. Accessed August 11, 2011. http://www.bls.gov/opub/mlr/2006/01/art3full.pdf.

Vogel, Ezra. 1979. *Japan as Number One.* Cambridge, MA: Harvard University Press.

Washington Post. 2011. "NFL News Feed: Players' Union Dues Go to Lockout Fund." Accessed August 11, 2011. http://views.washingtonpost.com/theleague/nflnewsfeed/2009/09/players-union-dues-go-to-lockout-fund.html.

Wikipedia contributors. 2011a. "2007–2008 Writers Guild of America Strike," *Wikipedia, The Free Encyclopedia.* Accessed August 10, 2011. http://en.wikipedia.org/w/index.php?title=2007%E2%80%932008_Writers_Guild_of_America_strike&oldid=442637735.

Wikipedia contributors. 2011b. "Craft Unionism," *Wikipedia, The Free Encyclopedia.* Accessed August 11, 2011. http://en.wikipedia.org/w/index.php?title=Craft_unionism&oldid=420698810.

Wikipedia contributors. 2011c. "Professional Air Traffic Controllers Organization," *Wikipedia, The Free Encyclopedia.* Accessed August 11, 2011. http://en.wikipedia.org/wiki/Professional_Air_Traffic_Controllers_Organization_(1968).

Chapter 28

Employment Discrimination Law

Kimberley Kinsley

INTRODUCTION

Comprehensive laws prohibit adverse discrimination in hiring, promoting, training, disciplining, awarding benefits, and employment termination. Federal and state lawmakers enact the legal framework for preventing illegal discrimination in the labor market. In 1964, Congress created the Equal Employment Opportunity Commission (EEOC) to enforce key federal laws that target discrimination and related harassment.

Courts interpret the law and adjudicate the legal rights and duties of parties involved in employment discrimination actions. A rational firm will seek to avoid costly lawsuits and the ill effects of a negative business reputation when these unpredictable outcomes can be mitigated by designing and self-enforcing lawful employment policies and procedures. Employers can study the court's interpretation of legislation for guidance in implementing human resource practices, and the EEOC offers preventative resources, an administrative process, and statutory remedies for employment discrimination. Congress can amend the law if it disagrees with the court's interpretation of legislation. States enact antidiscrimination laws that may parallel federal legislation, and in some cases state laws are stricter.

OVERVIEW OF EMPLOYMENT ANTIDISCRIMINATION LAWS AND EXECUTIVE ORDERS

Employment relationships are traditionally governed by the law of torts, contracts, and agency, and the common law doctrine of *at will*[1] employment. While these legal theories still dominate employment law, federal laws have been enacted since the 1960s to prohibit harmful discrimination in the workplace. Earlier state and federal actions were instrumental in leading to the passage of landmark legislation. In 1945, New York became the first state to pass a fair employment practice law. New Jersey followed, and by 1951 many states had enacted employment legislation to prohibit discrimination based on race, color, creed, or national origin (Berger 1951). More than half of the states had passed legislation requiring fair employment practices before Title VII (U.S. Code 1964) was signed into law on July 2, 1964, by President Lyndon B. Johnson (Perritt 1998, 426).

Title VII is the landmark legislation that protects applicants and employees from discrimination based on the protected class traits of race, color, sex, national origin, and religion. Title VII was amended by the Equal Employment Opportunity Act of 1972 and by the Pregnancy Discrimination Act of 1978. Subsequent amendments enhanced employee rights and provided clarity in the wake of conflicting judicial opinions.

Additional federal nondiscrimination workplace legislation includes, but is not limited to, the following:

- Equal Pay Act (EPA; U.S. Code 1963)
- Age Discrimination and Employment Act (ADEA; U.S. Code 1967)
- Americans with Disabilities Act (ADA; U.S. Code 1990, as amended by the ADA Amendments Act 2008)

It is impossible to remove all discrimination from the labor force. Employment law is complex, discrimination has become subtle, and litigation is highly specialized, expensive, and stressful for the parties. Furthermore, many forms of selectivity are legal and ethical. Therefore it is critical to distinguish lawful selectivity from prohibited discrimination. An employer will prefer to hire a job applicant with 10 years of relevant experience and excellent references over an inexperienced applicant with poor references. This form of employee preference is rational and lawful. A medical firm that specializes in evaluating and treating brain tumors will require its surgeons to have advanced medical degrees from accredited medical schools. This specific degree requirement overtly discriminates against those applicants without a degree in specialized medicine. There is no statutory federal class protection for education levels,[2] specific college majors, socioeconomic standing, tardiness, a sense of humor, or attractiveness. Conversely, if a seemingly harmless employer screening device, also known as a facially neutral employment practice, proves deleterious for a protected class, then the employee, if a member of the protected class, may have a viable disparate-impact discrimination case.

The nuances and complexities of employment discrimination law represent the culmination of congressional intent, judicial decisions, and congressional amendments to codify, or overturn, court opinions. In addition to disparate-impact claims, other legal theories in employment discrimination cases include disparate treatment, mixed-motive cases, harassment, retaliation, and failure to accommodate.

APPLICATION OF ANTIDISCRIMINATION LAWS

The EEOC is the main federal enforcement agency for Title VII. EEOC regulations are located in the *Code of Federal Regulations*. The aggrieved applicant, or employee, must exhaust the EEOC's administrative remedies prior to filing a lawsuit. Administrative remedies include investigating and mediating the dispute. If mediation is unsuccessful, the EEOC may file a lawsuit on behalf of a complaining party, or a *Notice-of-Right-to-Sue* letter will be issued and the applicant, or employee, may file her own lawsuit in federal court.

There are exceptions to Title VII, and it applies only to employers with 15 or more employees.

Title VII Litigation

Title VII cases may be filed by an individual party, or a plaintiff may form a class of other similarly situated employees, or applicants, if the employer allegedly discriminated against a larger group of protected class members. Once a lawsuit it filed, the claimant becomes a plaintiff. Many technical rules are associated with litigating under Title VII. For example, the employee must file the lawsuit in the court with proper jurisdiction, the case must be filed within the statutory time limit permitted for bringing a complaint, and if the plaintiff is filing a class action lawsuit, the class must be certified by the court. Additionally, the plaintiff has the initial legal burden of going forward and making a *prima facie* (on the face) case in a disparate-treatment cause of action, and satisfying burdens associated with the disparate-impact cause of action. A successful plaintiff may be awarded back pay. Punitive and compensatory damages are permitted, but are subject to cap ranges from $50,000 to $300,000 per individual depending on the size of the employer.

Disparate Impact

Disparate-impact analysis is invoked when a facially neutral employment practice has a disproportionate negative impact on members of a protected class. Disparate impact may result as the unintended consequence of a firm trying to be profitable. For example, a construction company may prefer that all employees be at least 5'10" and have the baseline ability to toss around 75-pound objects for hours on end. Yet if the firm makes this a mandatory job requirement, it may find itself embroiled in a disparate-impact lawsuit because fewer female applicants will be able to satisfy these requirements than male applicants. The employer can offer a business necessity defense to rebut the employee's prima facie disparate-impact case, but the employee may still challenge the practice on the basis that a less discriminatory alternative is available.

Employer screening devices that have triggered disparate-impact litigation include height or weight requirements, written tests, and educational requirements.

To establish a prima facie case of adverse impact the plaintiff must show that an identifiable, facially neutral employment policy or practice has a disparate effect on members of a protected class, and that a causal *nexus* exists between the policy and the adverse impact. For example, if a company requires all employees to be at least 5'10", this facially neutral policy will have a disparate effect on female applicants but not male applicants. Furthermore, the disparity in outcomes between the groups is unlikely to have occurred by chance.

The disparate-impact theory was established in 1971 by the U.S Supreme Court in *Griggs et al. v. Duke Power Co.* (1971) (U.S. Supreme Court 1971). Chief Justice Burger wrote, "Good intent or absence of discriminatory intent does not redeem employment procedures or testing mechanisms that operate as 'built-in headwinds' for minority groups and are unrelated to measuring job capability" (U.S. Supreme Court 1971, 432). *Griggs* involved a high school education requirement and two written aptitude tests used as facially neutral thresholds for employment and advancement at Duke Power Company in North Carolina. Prior to *Griggs*, the judiciary interpreted Title VII as requiring some element of disparate treatment or discriminatory intent as a basis for recovery. The *Griggs* Court conceded that there was no showing of discriminatory motive in the case. The facts in *Griggs*, however, presented the Court with the opportunity to examine the underlying purpose of Title VII. The Court found that prior to Title VII blacks were routinely locked into the lowest-paying jobs at Duke Power in North Carolina. The Court reasoned that the intent of Title VII is to achieve equal opportunity in employment, and therefore the act must also prevent unintentional discrimination: "Under the Act, practices, procedures, or tests neutral on their face, and even neutral in terms of intent, cannot be maintained if they operate to 'freeze' the status quo of prior discriminatory employment practices" (U.S. Supreme Court 1971, 430). The Court's holding broadened Title VII coverage to include the adverse effects of employment practices as a separate cause of action notwithstanding discriminatory motive. The *Griggs* Court did not demand statistical precision in its adverse impact analysis, but found that the requirements of a high school diploma and written aptitude tests disqualified blacks (pre-1971) at a substantially higher rate than white applicants. Furthermore, the Court was unable to find a demonstrable connection between a high school diploma or a given score on the aptitude test and job performance at Duke Power. The Court's analysis indicated that the legality of employment practices that have a demonstrated discriminatory impact, but lack discriminatory intent, can turn on the ability of the employer to show that the test genuinely measures a legitimate business necessity (U.S. Supreme Court 1971, 432). The *Griggs* case carved out a new legal basis for recovery—disparate impact—and it provided the employer with the affirmative defense of business necessity.

The method to determine whether the employer's selection process disadvantages a protected class can be complex and potentially lead to inconsistent legal holdings. Generally, the courts apply judicial discretion, the EEOC's four-fifths rule (also known as the 80% rule), statistical evidence, or a combination thereof. The objective is to compare the scores, or acceptance rates, of protected class applicants and employees with the rates of successful applicants or promoted employees. The usefulness of statistics will depend on the facts and circumstances surrounding a case (U.S. Court of Appeals 2007). The controversy includes which pool to consider as the comparative group. The group of successful applicants is obviously one pool, but the comparative pool may contain actual members of a protected class who unsuccessfully applied for a position, or a broader external pool. The external pool may include eligible candidates in a given state, or other geographic locality, whether or not these eligible candidates applied for the position. The facts of each case will determine the court's decision to rely on the actual labor pool or to extend the comparative pool to a broader eligible labor population.

The *Griggs* analysis relied on judicial discretion to determine the strength of the statistical disparity in accessing the relevant employment restrictions. Other courts use the EEOC's Uniform Guidelines on Employee Selection Procedures to determine adverse impact, which is described in 29 C.F.R. § 1607.4 (D) of the *Code of Federal Regulations* as "[a] selection rate for any race, sex, or ethnic group which is less than four-fifths (4/5) (or eighty percent) of the rate for the group with the highest rate will generally be regarded by the Federal enforcement agencies as evidence of adverse impact" (U.S. National Archives and Records Administration 2010). For example, if 60 percent of male officers who take a promotion exam pass, then 48 percent of the female officers must pass. Courts are not required to invoke the four-fifths rule, but may consider it in appropriate situations. Some courts have used multiple regression analysis and other forms of statistical significance tests. The four-fifths rule and statistical significance tests can lead to different results mainly due to variances in magnitude and sample sizes. These methods have not been uniformly adopted as a perfect indicator of adverse impact, and some legal scholars suggest less reliance on statistics in court because statistical analysis may downplay chance as a cause of disparities (Browne 1993).

Disparate Treatment

Most employment discrimination cases fall under the disparate-treatment theory of recovery. To prove motive the plaintiff may assert direct evidence of intentional discrimination, pursue a pretext theory, or pursue a mixed-motive theory. The analysis employed and the availability of defenses will depend on the nature of the alleged discrimination and on the composition of the protected class.

The plaintiff has the initial burden to establish a prima facie case of intentional discrimination, but this threshold is generally not as complex as the requirements for a disparate-impact case. The prima facie case here requires a showing that plaintiff belongs to a protected class, is qualified to perform the job in question, suffered an adverse employment action, and was treated less favorably than employees, or applicants, belonging to a different group. If the plaintiff succeeds, the burden shifts to the employer to articulate a nondiscriminatory reason for the adverse employment action. This stage of the proceeding includes an analysis of *causation*, which is a necessary element in proving disparate treatment. A firm may argue that although Jane is a female, she was not fired because of her protected class status, but because she was the only member of the office to have stolen large quantities of money from the cash register. The employee has an opportunity to rebut the employer's claim of a lawful motive by persuading the court that the employer's motive was in fact discriminatory, or in a mixed-motive case, that a motivating factor in the decision was based on an unlawful motive. The employee must show, by preponderance of the evidence, that the employer's asserted reason was actually a pretext to mask underlying discrimination, or in a mixed-motive case that one of the reasons for the adverse employment action was based on discriminatory intent. This burden-shifting procedure for pretext cases was established by the Court in *McDonnell Douglas Corp. v. Green* (1973) (U.S. Supreme Court 1973). In 1983, the Court added the mixed-motive analysis in its plurality opinion in *Price Waterhouse v. Hopkins* (1989) (U.S. Supreme Court 1989a). The *Price Waterhouse* Court held that a plaintiff may satisfy causation if a discriminatory motive is shown to be a motivating factor for the adverse employment action. The mixed-motive theory of causation was codified by the Civil Rights Act of 1991 (U.S. Code 1991).

A limited right to discriminate is permitted under the bona fide occupational qualification (BFOQ) defense in disparate-treatment cases involving gender, religion, and national origin complaints, but is not available in race or color complaints. An employer may assert a BFOQ defense in disparate-treatment cases where a preference for one class characteristic is "reasonably necessary" in furtherance of normal business operations. BFOQ defenses have been upheld in cases involving rehabilitation facilities, authenticity requirements, and safety, but the defense generally fails if employers intentionally discriminate to satisfy consumer preferences.

Reverse Discrimination

In *Ricci v. DeStefano* (U.S. Supreme Court 2009a), the Court reconciled the disparate-treatment and disparate-impact provisions of Title VII. The tension between these provisions is at the center of reverse-discrimination cases. *Ricci*, an important reverse-discrimination case, was brought by 1 Hispanic firefighter and 17 white firefighters who passed qualifying examinations for promotion in the New Haven, Connecticut, fire department. Many firefighters prepared for months at "considerable personal and financial cost" (U.S. Supreme Court 2009a, 2664) to take the examinations for the opportunity to advance to the ranks of lieutenant or captain. White candidates outperformed minorities on the examinations, and no blacks were eligible for immediate promotion based on the test results (U.S. Supreme Court 2009a, 2678). The New Haven Civil Service Board recognized that if the test was certified, then black candidates would arguably suffer a disparate impact based on the statistical racial disparity in the examination results. To avoid disparate-impact liability the Civil Service Board refused to certify the results. Consequently, the plaintiffs sued under Title VII's disparate-treatment provision claiming that they were denied promotion because the Civil Service Board refused to certify the examination. The Court held that the Civil Service Board's refusal to certify the exam, even if the decision was based on the concern that the test results had a disparate impact against some minorities, was motivated by race, and therefore violated Title VII. The Court held that a threshold showing of a significant statistical racial disparity, without more, does not justify disparate treatment of another class. The Court adopted its *strong-basis-in-evidence* standard in *Ricci* to resolve conflicts that arise between disparate-treatment and disparate-impact provisions of Title VII. The doctrine essentially prevented the city from discarding the test results unless it showed that the examination did not validly measure performance, did not have a business necessity, or that other less-discriminatory alternatives were available.

Retaliation

A retaliation complaint is similar to disparate treatment; however, the distinction lies in the employee's exercise of a protected activity versus membership in a protected class. The protected action can include the employee's participation in a lawful activity, or the employee's *opposition* to the employer's unlawful treatment of a protected class. Filing an EEOC complaint is a lawful activity (U.S. Supreme Court 2006), and white police officers satisfied the opposition clause when they objected to a supervisor's racist remarks about black officers (U.S. Court of Appeals 2006).

The plaintiff establishes a prima facie case of retaliation by showing participation in a protected activity (or, opposition to employer's unlawful action) that is causally linked to a challenged retaliatory action that is *materially adverse* to the plaintiff. If the plaintiff proves a prima facie case of retaliation, the burden shifts to the defendant to produce a nonretaliatory reason for the adverse employment decision (U.S. Court of Appeals 2009a). The plaintiff may demonstrate that the employer's stated reason is a pretext for retaliation (U.S. Court of Appeals 2009b) or a mixed-motive theory may be pursued (U.S. Court of Appeals 2010a).

Significant harm, such as a suspension in pay or reassignment to a less desirable job, must be suffered by the employee to establish the materially adverse element in a retaliation case. Trivial harm is not actionable as there is no code of civility for the workplace, and the law does not prohibit occasional teasing or petty annoyances. For example, "a supervisor's refusal to invite an employee to lunch is normally trivial, a non-actionable petty slight" (U.S. Supreme Court 2006, 2416).

Color and National Origin Discrimination

Discrimination based on color, including intragroup color discrimination, is prohibited by Title VII. For example, it is illegal for a lighter-skinned African American manager to discriminate against a darker-skinned African American employee on the basis of skin tone. An Iranian emigrant established national origin discrimination by showing that he had endured derogatory slurs such as "camel jockey" and "local terrorist" from his supervisors that higher management ignored (U.S. Court of Appeals 1995). The law permits a narrow BFOQ defense in national origin discrimination, but not for color discrimination.

Religion

Employers have a duty to reasonably accommodate an employee's, or applicant's, "sincerely held" religious belief, observance, or practice, but only if the requested accommodation does not present an undue hardship to the business. This balancing of interests creates the conflict in most Title VII religion litigation. The employer can show that the accommodation poses an undue hardship to the business if it is more than "de minimis" in terms of cost or burden. For example, a police department may prohibit officers from wearing religious garb while in uniform.

Title VII expressly allows a religion based BFOQ defense, and certain exemptions for religious organizations are provided. For example, a church that runs a bookstore, or a school, may discriminate against employees who do not affiliate with its religion.

Harassment

Harassment is a form of disparate treatment discrimination and is prohibited by Title VII. This form of discrimination ranges from physical to psychological harm, and it occurs in sex, race, color, national origin, and religion cases. The plaintiff must show that the harassment occurred because of a protected class trait, and that an unwelcome tangible employment action was sufficiently severe or pervasive to create a hostile working environment. The basis for harassment must be attributed to the employer.

Sexual Harassment

Quid pro quo and hostile work environment are the two types of sexual harassment theories recognized under Title VII. The Latin term *quid pro quo* means "this for that" and was first used by a federal court in 1982 (U.S. Court of Appeals 1982). The term was subsequently modified by the Court in *Faragher v. City of Boca Raton* to mean "tangible employment action" (U.S. Supreme Court 1998). This form of harassment is actionable if a supervisor, or other agent of the employer, demands unwelcome sexual favors in exchange for some tangible employment consequence. The employer may invoke an affirmative defense if no adverse employment action was taken, and it can demonstrate that it took reasonable care to prevent and correct the sexual harassment, but the plaintiff failed to follow the employer's procedures (U.S. Supreme Court 1998). The *hostile work environment* theory of harassment does not require plaintiff to suffer a tangible employment action. To determine a hostile work environment, the Court will consider the totality of the circumstances surrounding the case history such as severity and frequency of harassment. Generally, the harassment must be objectively offensive, so that a reasonable person would find it abusive, and the plaintiff must have a subjective belief that the harassment is hostile and abusive (U.S. Supreme Court 1993). For example, a female construction worker may be the target of offensive sexual language and gestures throughout the day as she works with an all-male crew, but if none of the sexual hostility or innuendos bother her, then she lacks a "subjective" belief that the situation is sufficiently hostile for a Title VII recovery. Conversely, suppose Brenda eavesdrops on the conversation of two male colleagues who are having a private discussion during a scheduled lunch break. The males briefly exchange comments about the physical attributes of a female that they both knew from college. While the situation may be "subjectively" offensive to Brenda, she would be unsuccessful in a harassment suit because a reasonable outsider would probably not find that the facts portrayed a hostile work environment. Hostile work environment cases generally require the employer to have some level of knowledge, or acquiescence to, the hostile environment. This element is satisfied if the employer fails to disseminate its sexual harassment policies or guidelines (U.S. Supreme Court 1998, 775).

Racial Harassment

Carol Fuller, an African American plaintiff, worked for Fiber Glass Systems, L.P. from October 2005 through May 2007. The first day that Fuller moved from her initial job as fiberglass pipe checker into the corporate offices, a white coworker told her that she did not like "black people." Fuller's manager told her not to answer phones in the office because customers were not accustomed to a black voice. The hostile work environment included racist remarks, snubbing, and being denied office equipment. Fuller filed a complaint and reported that she was "sick to her stomach" from the emotional distress. The Eighth Circuit found that the jury's award to plaintiff of $65,000, and the court's award of $63,930.94 for attorney's fees were substantial amounts, but that the awards vindicated personal rights and served the public interest (U.S. Court of Appeals 2010b).

Affinity Discrimination

Title VII cases include affinity, or associational discrimination issues. The Second Circuit reviewed a case where a white basketball coach accused Iona College of terminating his employment because he married a black woman. The court held that Title VII applies if an employer discriminates against an employee because of the employee's association with a person of another race (U.S. Court of Appeals for the Second Circuit 2008).

Affirmative Action

Affirmative action is defined by 29 C.F.R. § 1608.1(c) of the *Code of Federal Regulations* as "those actions appropriate to overcome the effects of past or present practices, polices, or other barriers to equal employment opportunity" (U.S. National Archives and Records Administration 2010).

Affirmative action is required in federal government contracts, and many states require affirmative action in government contracts. Conversely, some states have banned preferential hiring in public employment. Title VII does not prohibit or require affirmative action, but an affirmative action decree or remedy may be authorized or imposed by the courts.

Executive Order 11246

E.O. 11246 requires a nondiscrimination clause in federal contracts and subcontracts worth at least $10,000 in a 12-month period. Contractors are required to treat applicants and employees "without regard to race, color, religion, sex, or national origin" (U.S. Department of Labor 2011).

Contractors and subcontractors employing 50 or more employees and with contracts worth at least $50,000 must develop affirmative action plans to be submitted to the Office of Federal Contract Compliance Programs prior to commencing a nonconstruction (supply or services) contract. Federal regulations do not promote quota systems, preferential treatment, or promotions under the pretense of affirmative action numerical goals (U.S. Department of Labor 2011).

Judicial Analysis of Affirmative Action

Courts may impose, or approve, affirmative action where the character of the injury is economic and caused by past discrimination.

The Court in *Johnson v. Transportation Agency, Santa Clara County* (U.S. Supreme Court 1987) upheld an affirmative action plan (AAP) that subsequently led to the hiring of a female road dispatcher over a male dispatcher, even though the male had placed a couple of points higher on an applicant scoring system. The Court held that the AAP was consistent with Title VII because it addressed the underrepresentation of women in the field presented, it permitted the underrepresented gender to be factored in with other desirable traits and criteria for the position, and the AAP did not impose strict quotas.

Conversely, the Court struck a city's minority set-aside program (the Plan) in *City of Richmond v. J. A. Croson Company* (U.S. Supreme Court 1989b). The Court deemed the AAP unconstitutional in the absence of the city's demonstrated compelling interest for preferential hiring. The AAP required nonminority prime contractors to subcontract a minimum of 30 percent of the government contract's dollar amount to at least one minority business. The Court found that the AAP was not narrowly tailored to remedy past discrimination, so because there was "absolutely no evidence of past discrimination against Spanish-speaking, Oriental, Indian, Eskimo, or Aleut persons in any aspect of the city's construction industry, the AAP's random inclusion of those groups strongly impugns the city's claim of remedial motivation" (U.S. Supreme Court 1989b, 506).

The Equal Pay Act of 1963

Congress enacted the EPA, thereby amending the Fair Labor Standards Act of 1938, to address wage differentials between men and women. Employers are required to pay equal wage rates, including allowances, benefits, and expenses, to members of the "opposite sex" performing substantially the same job. EPA plaintiffs, unlike Title VII and ADEA plaintiffs, are not entitled to punitive or compensatory damages. A prima facie EPA case requires the plaintiff to show that the employer pays the opposite sex a different wage for substantially the same work in terms of required skill, effort, working conditions, and responsibility. The plaintiff must identify a "comparator" (an opposite-gender employee) who is employed in a substantially similar position in the same company but is paid at a higher rate.

Once the plaintiff establishes a valid EPA prima facie case, the employer may assert an affirmative statutory defense to show that the disparity in pay is actually based on a seniority system, a merit pay system, a pay system that is based on quality or quantity production, or the catch-all defense, "a differential based on any other factor other than sex" (U.S. Code 1963).

Litigants can hire economists to perform multiple regression analysis to show whether the wage gap is a result of gender discrimination or "other factors." Other factors may include previous experience, specialized training, hours worked, and educational discipline. For example, a wage gap may occur between a female professor and her male comparator in a college. The plaintiff can employ statistical evidence and multiple regression analysis to eliminate the influence of factors, or independent variables, such as "rank, years of service, division, tenure status, and degrees earned" (U.S. Court of Appeals 2001, 478). The employer may also retain economists to conduct a similar analysis or to dispute the statistical significance of the plaintiff's evidence.

The EPA is not a comparable worth statute, although comparable worth proponents argue that the "value" of the employee's worth should be measured in addition to actual job content. Hence, if a female office manager is as valuable to the efficiency of running a business as a male driver, then the female should be compensated at a comparable rate. Federal courts are unwilling to hold employers to this standard given that pay scales are largely based on market factors unrelated to discrimination (U.S. Court of Appeals 1985).

The Americans with Disabilities Act of 1990

The ADA and changes made by the ADA Amendments Act of 2008 (ADAAA) prohibit unlawful discrimination against employees and applicants with a disability, and against those who are "regarded as" having a disability. Civil rights antidiscrimination legislation did not include the disabled as a protected class, but Congress conducted research to substantiate its findings that disabled people, as a group, are subject to severe vocational and economic disadvantages, and that many disabled individuals can be independent and self-sufficient if discriminatory barriers are removed (U.S. Code 1990).

The definition of disability under the amended ADA includes: (1) a physical or mental impairment that substantially limits one or more major life activities, (2) a record of the impairment, or (3) being regarded as having impairment. The ADA provides that employers with 15 or more employees have a duty to provide reasonable accommodation to individuals with disabilities, but only if the accommodation does not result in an undue hardship to the employer. The burden in a religion case is whether the accommodation imposes a "de minimis" cost or burden, but under the ADA the employer must demonstrate that the cost or burden is significant. The plaintiff must establish as part of his prima facie case that he is qualified to perform the essential functions of the job with or without reasonable accommodation.

The "business necessity" defense is available to employers under the ADA. It is also a defense if an employee poses a *direct risk*, defined in §1630.2(r) of the *Code of Federal Regulations* as a "significant risk of a substantial harm" to the employee or to others, and accommodation will not mitigate the risk (U.S. National Archives and Records Administration 2010).

The Court's analysis of legislation can sometimes thwart congressional intent. Congress profoundly disagreed with two separate Court interpretations concerning the ADA of 1990. The Court narrowly interpreted coverage under the ADA in *Sutton v. United Air Lines, Inc.* (U.S. Supreme Court 1999) and in *Toyota Motor Manufacturing, Kentucky, Inc. v. Williams.* (U.S. Supreme Court 2002). Lower courts applied the Court's restricted view and subsequently denied ADA coverage for individuals with substantial impairments. The *Sutton* analysis of the ADA permitted a consideration of mitigating measures before determining whether a disability existed. For example, under *Sutton*'s interpretation of the ADA, a diabetic would not be considered disabled so long as the condition could be controlled with insulin. The Court's opinion in *Toyota Motor Manufacturing, Kentucky, Inc.* required that the disability be "permanent or long term" to be considered substantially limiting under the ADA. Congress amended the ADA in 2008 (ADAAA) to reflect its disagreement with the Court's narrow interpretation of the legislation. The ADAAA specifically expanded disabilities to include illnesses in remission, such as cancer, or conditions that are episodic.

Congress redirected the focus of ADA litigation to be less about analyzing impairments and more about determining whether discrimination occurred. The ADAAA states accordingly "the primary object of attention in cases brought under the ADA should be whether entities covered under the ADA have complied with their obligations, and to convey that the question of whether an individual's impairment is a disability under the ADA should not demand extensive analysis" (ADA Amendments Act of 2008 § 2(b)(5)).

Age Discrimination in Employment Act of 1967

The ADEA of 1967, as amended, prohibits unlawful discrimination against individuals 40 years of age or older and applies if the employer has 20 or more employees. A prima facie case requires the employee to establish membership in the protected class, meet employer's job expectations, and suffer an adverse employment impact while younger employees were treated more favorably.

Employers may show that an alleged adverse employment action was the result of the employee's valid waiver of rights, voluntary early retirement, a seniority system, or an employee benefit plan. The BFOQ defense is available if the age restriction is "reasonably necessary" to usual business operations. This BFOQ is generally valid in jobs where public safety is a critical element, such as in police work, security, and pilot jobs. Individuals over 40 may be terminated for cause.

In 2009, the Court distinguished disparate treatment analysis under the ADEA from Title VII, specifically finding that Title VII's mixed-motive burden shifting procedure does not extend to ADEA cases (U.S. Supreme Court 2009b). Title VII permits a protected class to show that race, color, national origin, religion, or sex is one factor in an adverse employment impact. Conversely, the ADEA plaintiff must show that the adverse employment action was *because* of age, and not merely a motivating factor.

SUMMARY

Congress may enact or amend federal antidiscrimination legislation. The EEOC provides administrative resolution to employment disputes, while the courts interpret legislation to identify, analyze, and assess the rights and duties of litigants. Title VII was passed to subvert discrimination in the workplace when societal wounds from racial prejudice and segregation were fresh. Title VII identifies protected classes that generally have immutable traits such as race, color, national origin, and sex. Religion is also a protected class under Title VII, and employers must provide reasonable accommodation for an individual's sincerely held belief, observance, or practice. The employer can introduce a BFOQ defense in religion, sex, and national origin cases, but never in cases involving race and color. Title VII prohibits intentional discrimination and disparate-impact discrimination, as well as harassment, retaliation, and associational discrimination.

Affirmative action is required under specified federal contracts, and affirmative action remedies may result from judicial proceedings. The EPA requires employers to maintain equity in pay for the same job regardless of gender, but different wages are permitted for reasons other than sex, seniority, or merit pay systems, and quality or quantity production-based pay systems. The ADA and amendments prohibit employers from discriminating against workers with disabilities. Employers must provide reasonable accommodations for those otherwise qualified applicants or employees with disabilities unless the accommodation poses an undue hardship, or the job justifies a business necessity defense. The ADEA carves out a protected class for applicants and employers over 40 years of age. There are exceptions to the prohibition of age discrimination, such as voluntary early retirement, seniority systems, and employee benefit plans. The employer may invoke a BFOQ defense under the ADEA.

Title VII does not currently prohibit employment discrimination based on sexual orientation, socioeconomic class, or physical traits such as attractiveness.

NOTES

1. The *employment-at-will* doctrine permits termination of the employment relationship by either party at any time and for any reason absent a binding contract. There are exceptions to the doctrine; for example, a party may not violate the law or public policy.

2. While there is no statutory prohibition against employers requiring advanced degrees, in *Griggs v. Duke Power Co.* Justice Burger wrote, "The facts of this case demonstrate the inadequacy of broad and general testing devices as well as the infirmity of using diplomas or degrees as fixed measures of capability. History is filled with examples of men and women who rendered highly effective performance without the conventional badges of accomplishment in terms of certificates, diplomas, or degrees. Diplomas and tests are useful servants, but Congress has mandated the commonsense proposition that they are not to become masters of reality" (U.S. Supreme Court 1971, 433).

BIBLIOGRAPHY

Berger, Morroe. "Fair Employment Practices Legislation." *Annals of the American Academy of Political and Social Science* 275 (May 1951): 34–40. doi:10.1177/000271625127500106.

Browne, Kingsley R. "Statistical Proof of Discrimination: Beyond 'Damned Lies.'" *Washington Law Review* 68 (July 1993): 477–558.

Perritt, Henry H., Jr. *Employee Dismissal Law & Practices, 4th Ed., Vol. 2.* New York: John Wiley & Sons, Inc., 1998.

U.S. Code. 1963. The Equal Pay Act of 1963. 29, 206(d). http://www.eeoc.gov/laws/statutes/epa.cfm (accessed July 27, 2011).

U.S. Code. 1964. Title VII of the Civil Rights Act of 1964. 42, 2000e. http://www.eeoc.gov/laws/statutes/titlevii.cfm (accessed July 27, 2011).

U.S. Code. 1967. Age Discrimination in Employment Act of 1967. 29, 621. http://www.eeoc.gov/laws/statutes/adea.cfm (accessed July 27, 2011).

U.S. Code. 1990. The Americans with Disabilities Act of 1990. 42, 12101 (amended by ADA Amendments Act of 2008, Pub. L. No. 110-325, 122 Stat. 3553). http://www.eeoc.gov/laws/statutes/ada.cfm (accessed July 27, 2011).

U.S. Code. 1991.Civil Rights Act of 1991. Pub. L. No. 102-166, 105 Stat. 1071. 42, 2000e-2(m)). http://www.eeoc.gov/policy/docs/disparat.html (accessed August 18, 2011).

U.S. Court of Appeals. 1982. *Henson v. Dundee* 682 F.2d 897 (11th Cir.).

U.S. Court of Appeals. 1985. *AFSCME v. Washington* 770 F.2d 1401 (9th Cir.).

U.S. Court of Appeals. 1995. *Amirmokri v. Baltimore Gas & Electric Co.* 60 F.3d 1126 (4th Cir.).

U.S. Court of Appeals. 2001. *Lavin-McEleney v. Marist College* 239 F.3d 476, 478 (2nd Cir.).

U.S. Court of Appeals. 2006. *Moore v. City of Philadelphia* 461 F.3d 331 (3rd Cir.).

U.S. Court of Appeals. 2007. *Paige v. State of California* 233 Fed. Appx. 646, 2007 U.S. App. LEXIS 12050 (9th Cir.).

U.S. Court of Appeals. 2008. *Holcomb v. Iona College* 521 F.3d 130 (2nd Cir.).

U.S. Court of Appeals. 2009a. *McCullough v. Univ. of Arkansas for Med. Sciences,* 559 F.3d 855 (8th Cir.).

U.S. Court of Appeals. 2009b. *Franklin v. Local 2 of the Sheet Metal Workers Intern. Ass'n.* 565 F.3d 508 (8th Cir.).

U.S. Court of Appeals. 2010a. *Smith v. Xerox Corp.* 602 F.3d 320 (5th Cir.).

U.S. Court of Appeals. 2010b. *Fuller v. Fiber Glass Systems, L.P.* 618 F.3d 858, 869 (8th Cir.).

U.S. Department of Labor. "Office of Federal Contract Compliance Programs." 2011. http://www.dol.gov/ofccp/regs/compliance/faqs/emprfaqs. htm#Q6 (accessed September 30, 2011).

U.S. National Archives and Records Administration. *Code of Federal Regulations.* Title 29. Labor. 2010. http://www.access.gpo.gov/cgi-bin/cfrassemble.cgi? title=201029 (accessed September 8, 2011).

U.S. Supreme Court. 1971. *Griggs et al. v. Duke Power Company* 401 U.S. 424.

U.S. Supreme Court. 1973. *McDonnell Douglas Corp. v. Green* 411 U.S. 792.

U.S. Supreme Court. 1987. *Johnson v. Transportation Agency, Santa Clara County* 480 U.S. 616.

U.S. Supreme Court. 1989a. *Price Waterhouse v. Hopkins* 490 U.S. 228.

U.S. Supreme Court. 1989b. *City of Richmond v. J. A. Croson Company* 488 U.S. 469.

U.S. Supreme Court. 1993. *Harris v. Forklift* 510 U.S. 17.

U.S. Supreme Court. 1998. *Faragher v. City of Boca Raton* 524 U.S. 775.

U.S. Supreme Court. 1999. *Sutton v. United Air Lines, Inc.* 527 U.S. 471.

U.S. Supreme Court. 2002. *Toyota Motor Manufacturing, Kentucky, Inc. v. Williams* 534 U.S. 184.

U.S. Supreme Court. 2006. *Burlington Northern & Santa Fe Railway Company v. White* 548 U.S. 53.

U.S. Supreme Court. 2009a. *Ricci v. DeStefano* 129 S. Ct. 2658.

U.S. Supreme Court. 2009b. *Gross v. FBL Financial Services, Inc.* 129 S. Ct. 2343.

Chapter 29

Affirmative Action: Pro and Con

Barbara R. Bergmann

WHAT AFFIRMATIVE ACTION IS

Affirmative action is planning and acting to end the absence of certain kinds of people—people belonging to groups that have been subordinated or left out—from jobs or schools. It is an insurance company taking steps to break its tradition of putting only white men into jobs leading to executive positions. It is the admissions office at a prestigious university seeking to boost the number of blacks in the freshman class beyond a smattering—looking for black kids who may not have learned to do well on multiple-choice tests, but who are nevertheless very smart. It is a trucking company whose drivers are all white men hiring a black or female driver, and then coping with the anger of the other drivers. It is a big-city police department looking to overcome the obstacles that capable blacks and women had experienced in making sergeant. It is a restaurant whose waiters are all one kind of person, as most such staffs still are today, taking steps to desegregate that staff.

The U.S. government's role in affirmative action programs in employment dates from the days of World War II. Private firms with more than 100 workers that sell to the federal government are required to maintain affirmative action plans with the Office of Federal Contract

Compliance Programs, and they are supposed to be implementing them. However, the budget of Office of Federal Contract Compliance Programs is not large enough to closely monitor compliance; so in effect, the performance of affirmative action in employment has been left to the discretion of individual workplaces, whether private or public. Employers are very seldom called to account for their staffing patterns by Office of Federal Contract Compliance Program, and the continuance of occupational segregation almost never brings serious penalties. Thus, while the government officially promotes affirmative action in employment, it is not an exaggeration to say that its application has been largely voluntary. As a result, desegregation of employment by race and sex has been uneven. Affirmative action by colleges and schools is entirely voluntary.

THE MOTIVES BEHIND AFFIRMATIVE ACTION

We can cite three major motives for affirmative action. First and foremost, it is a way to make systematic efforts to fight against ongoing discrimination in employment against African Americans, Hispanics, and women.

Despite the time that has elapsed since passage of the 1964 Civil Rights Act outlawing discrimination in employment, there are still thousands of American workplaces in which each kind of job seems to be permanently earmarked for a person of a particular race and sex, either for a man or for a woman, either for a person with a light-colored skin or a person with a dark-colored skin (Tomaskovic-Devey 1993; Fix and Struyk 1993). Traditional ideas about what kind of person can be competent in which job are still strong, and still influence selection.

Some opponents of affirmative action deny that there is much if any discrimination and think that the labor market is already quite fair, or would be if we got rid of affirmative action programs (O'Neill and O'Neill 2006; Hymowitz 2011). Their diagnosis of the situation is that women and minority people are not as striving or as capable on average as white men, and so white men win out in the competition for the best jobs because they are the best applicants. They feel that blacks and women are already just about as successful as they deserve to be, perhaps more so, given their talents and the efforts they make.

However, recent data suggest that there is still widespread discrimination going on in the United States, against white women on account of their sex, against African Americans on account of their race, and against Hispanic people on account of their ethnicity. Black and Hispanic women get a double dose (Blau and Kahn 2006; Darity, Guilkey, and Winfrey 1996; Kim 2002; Weinberger and Joy 2009). Data from a 2009 Census survey of wages show that women earn $18,820 less than men of similar education and experience, and blacks earn $7,183 less than similar whites.[1]

Exhortation against discrimination, which can be ignored, will not provide much progress. Nor will expensive lawsuits, which can take decades to work their way through the courts. The U.S. Supreme Court has recently made the remedy for discrimination through the courts much more difficult by rejecting the class action suit of women employees of Walmart.[2]

A second motive for affirmative action is the advantages that integration brings—advantages that come from achieving race and gender diversity in certain activities. Diversity has positive value in many if not all situations, but there are some where its value is crucial. To give an obvious example, a racially diverse community needs a racially diverse police force if the force is to gain the trust of all parts of the community, and if one part of the community is not to feel under the domination of the other part.

Other examples of occupations where diversity is especially important include journalists and media people, physicians, social workers, models in mail-order catalogs, judges (and therefore lawyers), managers and other people in authority, politicians, and government employees. One of the major benefits of diversity is that it provides a visual display that the organization subscribes to the principle that no kind of person is excluded from performing any functions, including responsible, important, and prestigious ones.

Another benefit of diversity is the differing points of view, insights, values, and knowledge of the world that members of various groups bring to their duties. Examples of the harm that lack of diversity causes are easy to find. In the United States, mostly male medical researchers have repeatedly run studies on large groups of subjects consisting entirely of males and had done no corresponding studies on groups of female subjects. The result has been lack of knowledge of the difference in the kinds of treatments that women and men might need. In decades of research on poverty, the white-male-dominated economics profession paid little explicit attention to the concentration of poverty among female single parents and the problems they face with sex discrimination in the labor market, with child care costs, and with child support enforcement. Researchers largely ignored race discrimination as a leading cause of poverty.

While diversity is especially important in certain occupations, it might be argued that there is a positive value attached to having race and sex diversity in any sizeable crew, regardless of its function. Leading a segregated on-the-job life makes workers less fit for life in a community where respect for all groups is the rule. All-male crews sometimes encourage misogynistic attitudes and behavior, and all-white crews sometimes encourage racist attitudes.

A third motive for affirmative action is as a cure for the poverty and low status of certain groups marked out by race or gender. Those who cite this as a good reason for affirmative action are sometimes derided as wanting equality of results, rather than equality of opportunity. The derision seems to imply that the high rate of poverty among blacks or among single mothers with children to support is due to their own bad behavior and is therefore something that they themselves should address by improving their behavior. But discrimination in the job market keeps many black men and many women from access to jobs that would allow them to live at a decent standard. Their inability to keep their children out of poverty is a source of much present suffering. It will ensure much future grief in this country, as today's poor children mature and become one-fifth of the U.S. adult population (Bergmann 1994).

NUMERICAL GOALS AND QUOTAS

Affirmative action plans typically call for efforts to get applications for each kind of job in reasonable numbers from qualified people from previously excluded groups. The office administering the plan will look at the process used to pick those to be hired or promoted, trying to remove any source of bias. It will try to see that people from previously excluded groups are treated fairly and protected from harassment once they are on the job. Under an affirmative action plan an employer might send supervisors—the people who have had a big say in hiring and promotion, and whose past decisions have resulted in sex and race segregation in the firm's occupations—to take training about racism, sexism, and sexual harassment, and the laws and regulations against discrimination.

However, such activities are not all there is to affirmative action. The heart of an affirmative action plan is its numerical hiring goals for each kind of job, based on an assessment of the availability of qualified minority people and women for such jobs. If progress is to be made toward the goals, something different from what was done in the past will generally be required. Those implementing the plan will inevitably have to pay attention to the race and sex of appointees as appointments are made if the goals are to be fulfilled. It is this aspect of affirmative action that draws the accusation that affirmative action involves operating a quota system.

Opponents of affirmative action have been working hard for decades to make "quota" into a word signifying something bad, wrong, and/or indefensible.[3] The measure of their success in demonizing quotas is that many people who favor eliminating occupational segregation feel themselves forced to express assent to that view of quotas. They say that (of course) they too are against quotas, and that affirmative action and quotas are not the same thing.

Advocates of affirmative action have argued that the goals in affirmative action programs are not quotas, because the goals are not hard and fast, but just provisional. The goals can be reduced or abandoned if no suitable male or female African American or white female candidates can be found. This defense does not really address the issue that makes affirmative action goals objectionable to many people. They want a system of awarding jobs that rewards merit and is fair to all candidates. They worry that goals, whether rigid or soft, are incompatible with such a system. They argue that paying attention to a candidate's race and sex is discriminatory, whatever the motive for doing it.

Honest debate over the costs and benefits of affirmative action is probably served if those defending affirmative action acknowledge that such programs do have quota-like aspects. The argument that has to be made to justify affirmative action goals is that under present conditions we cannot achieve diversity without them, and that whatever harm is done by having them is less than the harm of not having them. Of course, that defense is premised on the belief that the absences of certain kinds of people from certain places in our society is not due to lack of potential competence, that such absences are an important source of grief and harm, and that such absences ought to be repaired, if the process of repair is efficacious and tolerable on ethical grounds.

In thinking about goals, we need to ask whether it is possible for a segregated workforce or student body to be desegregated without setting up numerical goals by race and sex. The use of numerical goals to spur action by managers and to direct their behavior has been found useful in all aspects of modern management, and its use in affirmative action follows from the technique's success in other areas. These days a modern business uses numerical goals in managing production, productivity, sales, investment, and costs. The announcement of goals is part of the process of setting up explicit standards for performance. In the absence of numerical goals and of timetables for meeting them, it is difficult to pin down whether anyone has done a good job and to hold anyone responsible for any failures. When people do not think they will be held responsible, significant efforts are less likely to be forthcoming.

Goals are particularly important when the things to be accomplished are difficult and possibly distasteful to those who have to bring them about. In affirmative action, managers are asked to do things that are unfamiliar, that may seem to them risky in terms of productivity, and that they may personally oppose. Ending segregation in a work group by hiring the first woman or the first black may take courage. Managers have to face and brave the resistance that may arise from their peers, from the employees they supervise, and from their customers. They may have to overcome their own biases. In the absence of goals, and a system of rewards for meeting goals, it is natural for managers to let difficult things like that slide and be delayed into the indefinite future.

If a sizeable number of hires or promotions are going to be done all at one time, progress may be made in the absence of formal goals, just on the basis of repeated exhortations to fairness and diversity. These exhortations might lead people to think, "We are going to announce 20 promotions next month. These days, it won't look so good if they are all white males. Maybe the group should have some blacks, some women in it."

Goals, and the enforcement of them, are far more necessary in the usual case where hires and promotions are done one by one. When a single decision is made, the cost of raising a fuss about hiring still another white male is high. The cost of letting one more opportunity to make progress slip by is viewed as small or nonexistent. Moreover, the white or male candidate chosen is sure to be better in at least one characteristic than the black or female candidate not chosen. That provides a handy rationale that can in most cases be offered to justify the hiring of one white male after another, without a break (Clayton and Crosby 1992).

Goals and timetables in a plan in somebody's file cabinet are by themselves not sufficient. Traditional patterns of segregation yield only if managers up and down the organization—all of those in a position of influence in the hiring and promotion process—understand that a judgment of how well they have performed in furthering the integration of the workplace will be an important ingredient in the evaluation of their own job performance and that the success of their own career with the organization will be affected. Indeed, affirmative action plans that lack implicit or explicit rewards and punishments for those with the power to hire and promote are usually dead letters.

AFFIRMATIVE ACTION AND EFFICIENCY

The usual assumption, of both its foes and friends, is that affirmative action does cause some loss of efficiency, because of the relaxation of the practice (supposedly in force in the absence of affirmative action) of picking the "best" candidate for each vacancy. That assumption is not always correct. Affirmative action may lower efficiency in some cases and raise it in others. Where there has been discrimination, and care is taken to find good candidates from previously excluded groups, a properly operated affirmative action program might well result in the appointment of people who do better than those who would otherwise have been chosen. Affirmative action may enlarge the field of candidates and should eliminate selection procedures that screen out candidates for irrelevant reasons.

A favorite tactic of the foes of affirmative action is to ask, "Would you like to be operated on by a surgeon chosen through affirmative action?" Those who ask the question assume that the answer has to be "no." Most surgeons in the United States are white males. The absence of affirmative action in choosing people to be trained as surgeons by no means guarantees that the most meritorious person is always selected. Gross bias against women surgeons has been aimed at even highly placed people. Dr. Frances Conley, professor of surgery at the Stanford Medical School, protested being treated in a biased and disrespectful way (Conley 1991). There is a considerable amount of bad surgery, and some of those currently excluded from training might well do better than some currently included.

Where whole groups are shut out, the highly talented individuals among them are lost. Among monarchs remembered as outstanding in fostering their people's well-being, women figure far out of proportion to the numbers that have been allowed to reign. Queen Elizabeth I of England, Queen Christina of Sweden, and Catherine the Great of Russia are all remembered as more hospitable to modernizing forces and far less wasteful of their country's resources in warfare than their male counterparts. Had rules of monarchial succession not favored males, the history of the human race might well have been a happier one. In more modern times, women heads of government have performed as effectively as their male counterparts.

Sometimes, there will a group of finalists for a previously segregated job, none of whom is head and shoulders above the rest. If some of the finalists are minority males or women, then appointing one of them should not on average lower the quality of appointees. But there will be cases where the abilities of the best of the candidates from previously excluded groups are judged (and let us assume judged honestly and correctly) to be appreciably lower than the best of candidates who are white or male. For such cases, a further search for better candidates may be indicated, or a training program instituted. A decision to allow a seemingly second-rate minority candidate to join the second-rate white males already on the job may work out tolerably, but clearly, the better the minority candidate the less chance for significant trouble. To take on a worker who looks unable to do or learn the job would be a guarantee of trouble down the road. No affirmative action plan requires that this be done.

It is true that in some cases the use of numerical goals may produce a slap-dash attitude toward the quality of the person chosen. "We're under pressure, so let's just find anybody of the right race and sex." Of course, most employers running affirmative action plans cannot afford totally to ignore quality. They have to live at least for a while with the person chosen. Bad appointments can be very costly, whether in the president's cabinet or in the cab of a truck on an interstate highway.

Of course, affirmative action plans will not be operated properly a hundred percent of the time. There is bound to be some misapplication, where atrociously inappropriate people are appointed. With or without affirmative action, picking people for slots is not a well-developed science; incompetents do get hired and promoted, and inadequate students do get admitted. There is no human policy that is immune from misapplication. But those who favor affirmative action have to acknowledge that it may be especially prone to misapplication, and therefore should favor probationary periods and a system where employers can easily fire for cause.

ISSUES OF FAIRNESS

For many who are opposed to affirmative action, fairness is the key issue. They believe that the only fair system is one that puts the candidate judged most meritorious into each vacancy. Under this view, the person who is judged to be the best "deserves" to get the appointment. It is unfair if that person is denied appointment to a particular job or denied a place in the entering class of an elite school under an affirmative action program because that person is white or is male. That is "reverse discrimination," and just as bad as the other kind. The person who gets the slot does not "deserve" it.

Opponents believe we currently have a system of assigning jobs based on merit. There may be occasional lapses, but they see the assignment process as being run fairly in most instances. That system most often awards its prizes, as it should, to the best—to the talented, the hard-working, the well-prepared, the ambitious. They may believe in the theory that discriminating employers are at a competitive disadvantage and tend to fail and disappear from the marketplace (Becker 1957), and that if discrimination ever existed it, is now largely gone. They claim that sticking to a sex-and-race-blind merit system presents our best chance of overcoming any lingering discrimination and getting rid of the influence of race or sex in the selection process (Kahlenberg 1996). They think it is a terrible mistake to compromise the principle of such a system for an increase in racial and sexual diversity in the short term. They see affirmative action leading to the imposition of a hateful Balkanization of the job market, a division of spoils with each distinguishable group raucously demanding its share.

Implementing an affirmative action plan does require in practice excluding candidates who would otherwise have been appointed. Marking off a slot for a woman or a black may be necessary to fend off an otherwise almost-certain male or white appointment. Consider the situation in a company that has always hired only white males for jobs of a certain type, but believes that it has always hired the best candidate for each job. Opponents say that the adoption of affirmative action would mean a shift from "nondiscrimination" to "minority preferences." They are telling us that when affirmative action was adopted we would go from a good and fair system (where only a candidate's merit was considered) to a bad and unfair one (where race or gender was taken into consideration). Earmarking a certain number of job slots for women or for blacks in a previously segregated occupation does show a "preference" for those kinds of persons, although just in the case of those slots. For the remaining slots, the strong preference for white males in such roles would not be interfered with.

A failure to install a "preference" for blacks or women in those slots might well result in a continuation of the past pattern: no women or blacks hired at all. "Nondiscriminatory," "race-blind," and "sex-blind" are possible descriptions of a process that took no special care to get blacks and women included. But "allowing the strong preference for white males to continue unchecked" is a more accurate way to describe it.

Those who advocate nonattention to race and sex as an inviolable principle would enshrine something that is impossible under present labor market conditions, unless employers start hiring people without interviews and were able to ignore the clues to candidates' race and sex in their résumés. The degree of segregation that exists in the labor market shows that sex and race are noticed—to the detriment of women and blacks—when most decisions are made as to who should be hired and into which jobs they should be placed. The idea that we could, starting next week, make people switch off their perception of people's race and sex, and switch off their ideas about who belongs in which job lacks realism. The people who have been noticing sex and race to the detriment of blacks and women will go right on doing so unless a new system is put in place to pay attention to the race and sex of the candidates for the purpose of dismantling the system of segregation.

Opponents of affirmative action say we have to choose between equality of opportunity (without affirmative action) and equality of results (with affirmative action), and they imply that the former is more fair than the latter. But our actual alternatives may be quite different. If there is still extensive discrimination in the system, then equality of opportunity may not be achievable without a stiff dose of affirmative action. If the present capabilities of many women and many African Americans are subpar, then a well-run affirmative action program, which presumably would not put people into roles for which they are unfit, will not produce equality of results anytime soon. The real choice is between a continuation of gross inequality of opportunity (if affirmative action is not pursued) and a slow move toward more equality of both opportunity and result (if affirmative action is kept and strengthened).

One of the curiosities of the debate over affirmative action is that claims of unfairness seldom if ever arise when the principle of "merit" is put aside for purposes other than racial or gender diversity. Geographic balance is routinely sought when political appointments are made, and religious balance is also attended to. When a university gives preference in admission to an applicant who might strengthen the football team, or who is the child of an alumnus, grades and test scores are given less-than-usual weight in the decision. However, little resentment seems to be stirred, even among those directly affected in a negative way (Kahlenberg 2010).

It causes no adverse comment when large and important businesses, such as the New York Times Company, place at their head the son or son-in-law of the majority stockholder or of the previous head. No protest is made that the company is acting unfairly to the better-qualified non-relative who might otherwise have gotten the position. Nor is there any complaint, even from the stockholders, that the company's performance will be degraded by its failure to find the most qualified person. But if the New York Times Company attempts to make sure that it has blacks among reporters and editors, then that does stir resentment. That some departures from choosing "the best" are accepted with no complaint at all, while departures made for the purpose of reducing the exclusion of African Americans or women are so resented and so bitterly complained of, is something that bears thinking about.

COLLEGE ADMISSION

The major justification for affirmative action in the workplace is its use as a systematic method of getting rid of currently occurring discrimination against African Americans and women. The desirability of diversity provides the strongest justification for affirmative action in college admissions. At a university young people are trained for leadership roles in the professions and in public life. If we are anytime soon to erase the deep racial cleavages that currently trouble us, we cannot have campuses in which black or Hispanic young people are rare or absent. We cannot have white leaders who spend their college years in a segregated institution, who have never interacted with African Americans at college or heard their point of view.

Campuses are the places where the training and certification for the most prestigious, conspicuous, interesting, and lucrative careers take place. Obviously, there is a connection between the desegregation of higher education and the desegregation of the workplace, because there are occupations that cannot be entered without a credential from a college or university. Furthermore, there are important niches in certain occupations that those who have not passed through an elite university find much more difficult to enter. So the elite institutions, along with all of the others, cannot be segregated if we are to be able to fully desegregate the country's jobs and to get black and female faces into all ranks, up to the highest.

Affirmative action in higher education admissions speeds the arrival of the day when racial disparities in status and economic success will have been much reduced. It makes allowances for something that admittedly is not black youngsters' fault—their relatively poor preparation on average.

The major argument against affirmative action in higher education admittances is that it is unfair to those candidates with better test scores who are displaced to make room for the African American and Hispanic students. We have already met the assumption behind this argument in the field of employment—that universities (and employers) are obligated to turn themselves into arenas of fair competition among applicants, and that the institution is permitted to allow no consideration other than academic promise to affect the outcome. For those who urge this point of view, the experience of those students who come to the campus and the need of the nation to erase the effects of a shameful caste system are to count for nothing.

WEIGHING THE GOOD AND THE BAD

Deciding whether affirmative action is worthwhile policy involves balancing the good against the bad. We have to weigh the good and the bad results of keeping (or stepping up) affirmative action versus the good and the bad results of abandoning the modest number of vigorous affirmative action plans now in operation. While affirmative action may offer the possibility of important gains, it can have important disadvantages.

Like all "human engineering," affirmative action is difficult to implement effectively. The very fact that so many oppose it so vociferously and feel their interests hurt by it magnifies the difficulty. Unless its management is in skilled and dedicated hands, it is easily bungled or sabotaged. Like painful surgery, affirmative action can legitimately be advocated only as a means of improving a bad situation. We do not want to use surgery if the patient is not really sick, if there is some less radical remedy that will work tolerably, if the pain and disability caused by the operation are likely to be worse than the effects of the disease, or if the operation is likely to be ineffective for the patient's illness.

In the case of surgery, the same person suffers the costs and gets the benefits. However, in the case of affirmative action, the benefits and costs go to different sets of people. If goals and timetables are implemented, some people are denied advantages they might otherwise have had, because others get to share in the advantages previously monopolized by the group they belong to.

Would every gain of blacks and other minorities under affirmative action mean an equal loss for whites? Will men lose to the extent that women gain? If there were a rigidly fixed number of "good" jobs and "bad" jobs, then every time a "good" job was assigned through affirmative action to a black or a woman, a white man would be forced into a "bad" job.

It is not necessarily true that the number of "good" jobs is fixed. The segregation of jobs by race and sex encourages employers to structure jobs earmarked for minority people and women as "bad" jobs. Since such people are not considered promotable, the duties in "their" jobs are restricted to the greatest extent possible to routine tasks. Duties that carry valuable on-the-job training opportunities tend to be kept for jobs earmarked for white males, who are understood to be eligible for higher responsibilities and whose training would be of potential benefit to the employer. A breakdown in job segregation by sex and race would spread interesting duties, opportunities to learn, and opportunities for promotion to the incumbents of many currently "bad" jobs.

Affirmative action is not meant to go on forever. Goals for a group should be ended when that group is well integrated—when there is a good flow of candidates, when discriminatory attitudes have waned, when there is no inhibition to hiring members of that group, and when the group has for some time been represented in the workforce on the appropriate levels in a full range of occupations. We no longer have a "Jewish seat" on the Supreme Court, because that is no longer needed as a way to ensure the access of Jews to appointment to that court. For some time, we may still need black, Hispanic, and female seats on the

Court. But we can certainly look forward to the time when we will not need them, and when we will not need goals for them as police officers, carpenters, machine repairers, or bond salespeople as well.

Finally, if we can reduce discrimination and segregation in the labor market, there will be gains outside of the labor market, as well as in it. All of us will benefit from less dilapidated cities, lower crime rates, and fewer people needing public assistance. All of us will benefit from the chance to live in a country with less injustice.

NOTES

1. These figures are based on the following regression equation computed by the author:

Wage = 10,074 + 11,199 * high school + 21,427 * some college + 43,010 * BA + 73,023 * grad degree + 1,934 * experience − 29 * experience sq − 18,820 * sex − 7,183 * race

R sq = .2021. All coefficients are significant at .0001 level.

2. The Court, by a 5–4 decision, said that the women employees' situation was not sufficiently uniform.

3. Use of the word "quota" in the context of affirmative action suggests an analogy between its goals and the quotas limiting the number of Jews admitted to elite schools prior to World War II. Of course affirmative action brings people in, while the Jewish quotas kept minority people out (Ezorsky 1991).

BIBLIOGRAPHY

Becker, Gary S. 1957. *The Economics of Discrimination.* Chicago: University of Chicago Press.

Bergmann, Barbara R. 1994. "Curing Child Poverty in the United States." *American Economic Review* 84(2), 76–80.

Bergmann, Barbara R. 1996. *In Defense of Affirmative Action.* New York: Basic Books.

Blau, Francine and Laurence Kahn. 2006. "The US Gender Pay Gap in the 1990s: Slowing Convergence." *Industrial and Labor Relations Review* 60(1), 45–66.

Clayton, Susan D. and Faye J. Crosby. 1992. *Justice, Gender, and Affirmative Action.* Anne Arbor: University of Michigan Press.

Conley, Frances K. 1991. "Why I'm Leaving Stanford: I Wanted My Dignity Back." *Los Angeles Times*, June 9, pp. M1, 6.

Darity, William, David Guilkey, and William Winfrey. 1996. "Explaining Differences in Economic Performance among Racial and Ethnic Groups in the USA: The Data Examined." *American Journal of Economics and Sociology* 55(4): 411–25.

Ezorsky, Gertrude. 1991. *Racism and Justice: The Case for Affirmative Action.* Ithaca, NY: Cornell University Press, 38.

Fix, Michael and Raymond J. Struyk, eds. 1993. *Clear and Convincing Evidence: Measurement of Discrimination in America.* Washington, DC: Urban Institute.

Hymowitz, Kay S. 2011. "Why the Gender Gap Won't Go Away, Ever: Women Prefer the Mommy Track." *City Journal* 21(3).

Kahlenberg, Richard G. 1996. *The Remedy: Class, Race and Affirmative Action.* New York: Basic Books.

Kahlenberg, Richard G., ed. 2010. *Affirmative Action for the Rich: Legacy Preferences in College Admissions.* New York: Century Foundation.

Kim, Marlene. 2002. "Has the Race Penalty for Black Women Disappeared in the United States?" *Feminist Economics* 8(2): 115–24.

O'Neill, June and Dave O'Neill. 2006. "What Do Wage Differentials Tell Us about Labor Market Discrimination?" In *The Economics of Immigration and Social Policy,* edited by Soloman Polachek, Carmel Chiswick, and Hillel Rapoport. New York: Elsevier, 293–360.

Tomaskovic-Devey, Donald. 1993. *Gender & Racial Inequality at Work: The Sources and Consequences of Job Segregation.* Ithaca, NY: ILR Press.

Weinberger, Catherine and Lois Joy. 2009. "Relative Earnings of Black College Graduates, 1980–2001." In *Race and Equal Opportunity in the Twenty-First Century,* edited by Marlene Kim. New York: Routledge, 50–72.

Chapter 30

The Role of the Estate and Gift Taxes in Income Redistribution

Sally Wallace

Estate and gift taxes are used worldwide as a means to tax wealth. In the United States a generous estate tax exemption focuses the taxes on estates with large net worth, potentially making them an instrument of redistribution. Estate taxes are typically applied to the value of property at time of death, while a gift tax is a tax on the transfer of property while living (*inter vivos*). The estate and gift tax became a "unified" tax in 1976 to mitigate the erosion in taxable estate value from gifts given during an individual's lifetime. At the same time, the generation-skipping tax was also developed to reduce tax avoidance.[1] This tax will not be the main focus of this chapter.

The estate and gift tax has played a relatively small role as a revenue producer, accounting for an average of 1.14 percent of total federal receipts per year over the last three decades. There have been fluctuations in the relative size of estate and gift tax receipts, but over the last 30 years, the level of revenue has not exceeded 1.52 percent of federal tax receipts (Joulfaian 2011). In 2009, the Internal Revenue Service (IRS) reported total net estate tax receipts of $20.6 billion (IRS 2011).

For comparison purposes, the individual income tax brings in approximately 50 to 60 times more revenue than the estate and gift tax.

While the revenue take of estate and gift taxes is relatively small, the policy debate surrounding the use of estate and gift taxes is lively and there is a substantial amount of research that focuses on the analysis of the impact of estate and gift taxes on wealth accumulation, charitable contributions, and work behavior, among other topics. Arguably, the point of view that estate and gift taxes serve as a necessary redistributive mechanism may be the most contentious view. In addition to the redistributive argument for use of estate and gift taxes, there are other justifications for their use. These include the use of estate and gift taxes as payment for general public goods and services, and as a means to mitigate the revenue impact of loopholes in an income tax system that may benefit the wealthy. One outcome of these debates over the merits of estate and gift taxes was a substantial change to federal estate and gift taxes in 2001. This will be discussed in detail in a later section. The focus of this chapter is to provide insight into the potential for estate and gift taxes to address income equality in the United States.

The remainder of this chapter is structured as follows. The first section provides an overview of the structure of estate and gift taxes in the United States and is followed in the next section by a discussion of income distribution in the United States as it pertains to the analysis of this chapter. In the third section, the "economics" of behavior associated with estate and gift taxes is summarized and the potential impacts on distribution are evaluated.[2] A final section concludes. Throughout this chapter, the central question—does the estate and gift tax affect income distribution—is viewed in the absolute and not by comparing estate and gift taxes with other taxes.

ESTATE AND GIFT TAXES IN THE UNITED STATES

In the United States, estates have been taxed since 1916. Over the decades, federal estate and gift taxes have raised a substantial amount of revenue, but the level pales in comparison with federal revenue sources such as the individual income tax. Over the past decade, the revenue generated by estate and gift taxes has remained very consistent in nominal terms (not adjusted for inflation) at approximately $20 billion per year. In 1999, $22.9 billion of revenue was raised; in 2003, $20.8 billion was raised; and in 2009, $20.6 billion was raised.

The number of taxable estate returns is a small fraction of the number of adult deaths in the United States. In 2000, taxable estate returns were 2.18 percent of adult deaths; in 2009 it was 0.23 percent (Tax Policy Center 2011a). Over the three decades 1975–2005, taxable estate returns as a share of adult deaths peaked in 1976 at 7.65 percent. The reason for the small share of taxable estates is the structure of the estate, generation-skipping transfer, and gift taxes, which provide substantial deductions and exemptions, leaving most estates owing none of these taxes. To understand the role of estate and gift taxes in redistribution, it is important to review the structure of the taxes.

The basic construct of estate and gift taxes is as follows. A decedent's gross estate is defined to include all of the decedent's assets (solely or jointly owned) including cash, property (for example, land, homes, art, cars), and other financial assets such as stocks, bonds, life insurance, and mutual funds. Debts, contributions to charitable organizations, and transfers to a spouse are allowable deductions, which are subtracted from the gross estate to arrive at the net taxable estate value. The estate and gift tax liability is calculated based on the applicable tax rate. An estate tax credit is allowed, which effectively exempts a portion of the estate from tax. A gift tax credit is also allowed. As a result of the deductions and credits, few estates are taxable in the United States.

The applicable estate and gift tax rates and credits have varied over the years. In 2000, the estate tax credit provided an exemption equal to $675,000 of estate tax value. That is, net estate values of less than $675,000 were not subject to the estate tax. In addition, the gift tax exemption was $675,000 in 2000 and the generation-skipping transfer tax was $1,030,000 in 2000. The maximum tax rate for the estate, gift, and generation-skipping transfer tax was 55 percent in 2000.

The federal Economic Growth and Tax Relief Reconciliation Act (EGTRRA) of 2001 altered the effective exemption levels and tax rates for the estate, gift, and generation-skipping transfer tax. The intention of the legislation was to reduce the burden of these taxes and eliminate the estate and generation-skipping transfer tax by 2010. The reductions in tax rates and exemptions under EGTRRA are as follows. The maximum tax rate for the estate and generation-skipping tax was reduced over time from 55 percent in 2000 to 45 percent in 2009 to 0 percent in 2010. The effective exemption for the estate tax was increased over time from $675,000 in 2000 to $3.5 million in 2009, while the effective exemption for the generation-skipping tax increased from $1,030,000 in 2000 to $3.5 million in 2009. In the case of the gift tax, the maximum rate fell from 55 percent (2000) to 35 percent in 2010, and the lifetime exemption increased from $675,000 in 2000 to $1 million in 2010.[3]

Under EGTRRA, these changes to the estate, gift, and generation-skipping transfer tax laws were to "sunset," or disappear, after 2010. That means that without new legislation, the tax structures would be reinstated as they were prior to 2001. In fact, the Tax Relief, Unemployment Insurance Reauthorization, and Job Creation Act of 2010 provided for a short-term fix and imposed a $5 million exemption and a maximum rate of 35 percent for all three taxes for 2011 and 2012. The American Tax Relief Act (ATRA) of 2012 (an intermediate culmination of the fiscal cliff policy debate) raises the rate from 35 to 40 percent but retains the $5 million exemption which is now indexed for inflation. The 2013 exemption level is therefore $5.25 million.

Changes to the effective exemption levels and tax rates have reduced the number of taxable estates and the level of revenue. In 2000, 304,558 estate tax returns were filed, and in 2008 that number had fallen to 252,286 (IRS 2011). The level of revenue from these taxes has remained relatively flat in nominal terms from 2000 to 2008, but in real terms (adjusting for inflation) 2008 revenues were only 77 percent of 2000 revenues.

To better understand the potential impact of estate and gift taxes on income distribution, it is important to be aware of what makes up these estates. The IRS provides detailed information on the composition of estates for which returns are filed. The information on those assets is reported in Table 30.1. As seen there, the IRS tabulates a variety of asset categories, but real property (real estate and personal residences), stocks (closely held and other stock), cash, and annuities account for over 66 percent of reported assets in 2009 and for the majority in all years reported. The changes to the tax system over the period 1995–2009 do not seem to have affected the type of wealth reported in these returns.

The IRS also tabulates deductions reported on taxable estate tax returns. These tabulations are important in that they provide insight regarding what types of wealth transfers are affected by the estate tax. The data in Table 30.2 provide a list of major deductions reported on taxable estate returns and the percentage of each relative to the total amount of deductions presented in the table. The data in Table 30.2 demonstrate that there are two main sources of deductions—bequests to spouses and charitable contributions—which account for over 70 percent of allowable deductions in the case of taxable estate returns.

Table 30.1

Distribution of Assets Reported on All Estate Tax Returns

Type of Asset	1995 Value (millions)	%	2000 Value (millions)	%	2005 Value (millions)	%	2009 Value (millions)	%
Gross estate for tax purpose	117,698	100	217,402	100	184,696	100	194,575	100
Personal residence	8,371	7.1	16,134	7.4	15,694	8.5	14,320	7.4
Real estate	13,854	11.8	21,445	9.9	24,015	13.0	22,378	11.5
Real estate partnerships	1,108	0.9	2,003	0.9	3,114	1.7	5,665	2.9
Closely held stock	7,924	6.7	14,612	6.7	11,768	6.4	14,407	7.4
Other stock	25,953	22.1	68,304	31.4	50,994	27.6	43,224	22.2
State and local bonds	16,812	14.3	21,186	9.7	18,853	10.2	18,860	9.7
Federal savings bonds	632	0.5	925	0.4	427	0.2	283	0.1
Other Federal bonds	4,224	3.6	6,270	2.9	4,813	2.6	3,905	2.0
Corporate and foreign bonds	768	0.7	1,970	0.9	2,371	1.3	2,043	1.1
Bond funds	530	0.5	638	0.3	380	0.2	445	0.2
Unclassifiable mutual funds	1,465	1.2	1,770	0.8	1,059	0.6	1,461	0.8
Cash	10,460	8.9	14,709	6.8	11,035	6.0	21,024	10.8
Cash management	2,908	2.5	8,616	4.0	6,913	3.7	4,396	2.3
Insurance, face value	4,361	3.7	6,170	2.8	3,978	2.2	79	0.0
Insurance, policy loans	122	0.1	190	0.1	87	0.0	7,201	3.7
Farm assets	664	0.6	882	0.4	1,214	0.7	1,564	0.8
Limited partnerships	1,226	1.0	3,243	1.5	4,831	2.6	4,951	2.5

(continued)

Table 30.1 (Continued)

Type of Asset	1995		2000		2005		2009	
	Value (millions)	%	Value (millions)	%	Value (millions)	%	Value (millions)	%
Other noncorporate	2,386	2.0	1,771	0.8	2,810	1.5	3,872	2.0
Mortgages and notes business assets	3,146	2.7	4,168	1.9	3,957	2.1	4,811	2.5
Annuities	6,631	5.6	17,410	8.0	12,209	6.6	13,894	7.1
Depletable/intangibles	573	0.5	561	0.3	547	0.3	683	0.4
Art	412	0.4	1,317	0.6	1,308	0.7	2,845	1.5
Other assets	3,412	2.9	3,497	1.6	2,318	1.3	2,419	1.2

Source: Internal Revenue Service (2011).

Table 30.2
Distribution of Estate Tax Deductions (dollar amounts in millions)

Type of Deduction	1995		2000		2005		2009	
	Level	Percentage	Level	Percentage	Level	Percentage	Level	Percentage
Funeral expenses	197	1.09	353	1.02	175	0.62	158	0.61
Executors' commissions	841	4.63	1,471	4.26	981	3.45	912	3.50
Attorneys' fees	680	3.75	1,091	3.16	711	2.49	689	2.64
Other expenses/losses	563	3.10	985	2.85	910	3.20	907	3.48
Debts and mortgages	2,083	11.47	3,861	11.19	3,233	11.35	3,907	14.97
Bequests to surviving spouse	8,815	48.55	16,984	49.16	8,929	31.35	10,832	41.51
Charitable deduction	4,977	27.41	9,803	28.37	13,544	47.55	8,688	33.29
Total	36,303	100.00	69,422	100.00	57,277	100.00	54,922	100.00

Source: Internal Revenue Service (2011).

Joulfaian (2011) reports characteristics of beneficiaries using data from the IRS, which matches tax returns of decedents and their heirs. Bequests to other than a surviving spouse are not reported as allowable expenses on the decedent's tax return, so these matched data are very valuable to understanding the flow of wealth among generations. According to Joulfaian, the most complete data are for the tax year 1982. The data show that spousal bequests account for about half of distributed assets, bequests to children account for 25 percent of distributed assets, and 11.5 percent of distributed assets are to trusts. In 1982, the total nonspousal bequests amounted to $17.2 billion. The data demonstrate that the children receiving the bequests are wealthy but not as wealthy as their deceased parents. In 1982, the bequests to these children amounted to three times their own income (Joulfaian 2011). This provides evidence of wealth shifting from the decedents to their children and a reduction in the concentration of the parents' wealth.

Few other countries utilize the same type of estate tax as the United States. In most countries, an annual inheritance tax is the norm for taxing wealthy estates. Gale and Slemrod (2001a) provide an overview of taxes on the transfer of wealth in other countries. They report that 21 industrialized countries impose a transfer tax on wealth, but the majority (17) tax wealth via an inheritance tax (Gale and Slemrod 2001a, 16), which is a tax on the recipients of a bequest when it is passed on after death. In comparison, the U.S. federal estate tax is a tax on the estate itself.

INCOME DISTRIBUTION IN THE UNITED STATES

This chapter analyzes the impact of the estate and gift taxes on income redistribution and as such, it is important to provide some detailed information regarding the distribution of income in the United States. There are many different ways to measure both income and equity (or equality in income distribution) as evidenced by some chapters of this volume. The potential of the estate tax to directly redistribute income is partially determined by the relative magnitude of taxable wealth and the overall distribution of wealth (acknowledging that behavioral changes associated with the tax could mitigate or exacerbate the potential impact of estate and gift taxes on income distribution). If wealth is heavily concentrated in the upper end of the distribution, larger taxes may be needed to dislodge the wealth for redistributive purposes.

IRS data on wealth includes only estate wealth for individuals who are required to file an estate tax return, which is a small share of the population. The Federal Reserve Bank's Survey of Consumer Finances (SCF) focuses on wealth and its components for the entire U.S. population. The survey is conducted every three years and provides information on the distribution of wealth in the United States, savings behavior, composition of assets, and other financial information. The SCF net worth measure is an expansive definition of wealth and includes tangible assets (including real estate, vehicles, and art) as well as financial assets (such as life insurance, retirement accounts, and stocks), and it nets out debt (Kennickell 2007). The SCF also provides detailed information on income, which is a less expansive measure than net worth. In the SCF, income consists of liquid financial assets including wages, dividends, and transfer payments. Using data from 1989 to 2007 SCFs, Kennickell (2009) demonstrates that wealth is more unevenly distributed than income over the entire period studied. For example, in 2004 Kennickell (2007) reports that value of wealth in the 90th percentile of wealth was 63 times that of the 25th percentile, while for the income measure, the difference was 6 times (Kennickell 2007, 5).

Based on the 2007 SCF, the total net worth in the United States was $64.6 trillion. The top wealth holders—those at the 90th and above percentile of net worth—held 71.4 percent of total net worth, which amounted to $45.9 trillion. The lowest 50 percent of the population in terms of net worth held 2.5 percent of total net worth ($1.6 trillion). Similar figures for income (based on comparable data for 2006, which is the best year available for comparison) demonstrate less concentration in the top income groups relative to the concentration of wealth. For 2006, the percent of total income held by individuals in the 90th percentile of income and above was 41.3 percent.

Individuals in the top 90th percentile of net worth are not all alike. The mean net worth for that group was $3.3 million in 2007 while the median was $1.1 million. These statistics suggest that there are a relatively small number of very high net worth individuals in this percentile.

The 90th percentile of net worth includes approximately 10.9 million families. Given the mean and median net worth of the families in this stratum of the population, it is reasonable to identify this group as the one most likely to face the estate and gift tax as it is currently structured. So, given the distribution of wealth and size of the net worth base, can a wealth tax such as the estate and gift tax effectively redistribute income in the United States? The simple answer is yes. One could imagine that if such a tax were large enough, it could reduce the net wealth of high-income individuals, which the government could then redistribute to lower-income individuals through increased expenditures targeted at low-income individuals or via reduced income and payroll taxes at the lower end of the income distribution. If all of the estate and gift tax paid was attributed to those in the 90th net worth percentile, the tax paid accounts for 0.045 percent of the net worth of that segment of the population. On the opposite end of the income distribution, the $20 billion of estate and gift revenue collected by the IRS is equivalent to 1.25 percent of the wealth held by the families in the 0 to 50th percentile of net wealth. Is this $20 billion enough redistribution to matter? "Enough" is a relative and somewhat subjective term. At the upper income end, a reduction of 0.045 percent of net worth may not seem to make a difference in the overall distribution of income. However, at the lower end of income, $20 billion of estate and gift tax revenue could completely eliminate federal individual income taxes for taxpayers with income up to $30,000. Without consideration of other potentially mitigating factors (which are discussed later), redistribution is possible through the estate tax and gift taxes under their current structure, although the impact at the top end of the income distribution is relatively small.[4]

Wealth accumulation also has a confounding factor on the long-term concentration of wealth in the upper echelons of income. There appears to be some truth to the adage that the "rich become richer" as bequests are often concentrated among family members. There are most certainly success stories of individuals who begin at low levels of income and through hard work and good investments propel themselves into higher levels of income. But there is also evidence (summarized in Batchelder 2009) that inheritances among family members provide financing for entrepreneurial activities and higher education that can lock a family member into the same high-income group. Economic mobility across generations is thereby potentially hindered by inheritances. If estate and gift taxes reduced wealth accumulation and bequests among generations of families, they may have an impact on intergenerational income distribution.

Given that estate and gift taxes allow for a certain amount of untaxed gifts, the gift tax encourages redistribution during life as well as in death. As noted by Joulfaian (2011), the distributions from parents to children were about three times the level of the children's income before bequests in 1982. The majority of children receiving bequests report levels of income that are substantially less than their parents' net worth. However, the children's income does not report net worth, so their income relative to their parents' estate value is likely to be understated. Still, these data suggest that to the extent that the tax encourages disbursements to children with somewhat lower income through untaxed gifts, there is some potential for income redistribution within families.[5] This is different, however, from large-scale redistribution since children of the wealthy are more heavily concentrated in upper income groups than in the very lowest income groups.

This direct redistribution is just one way that the estate and gift tax could impact the distribution of income in the United States. The story is not that simple, however, and in fact, there are many other avenues for the taxes to impact income distribution. The next section focuses on the other avenues for impacts.

ECONOMICS OF ESTATE AND GIFT TAXES AND IMPLICATIONS FOR REDISTRIBUTION

Based on the previous analysis, the sheer amount of wealth at the upper end of the income distribution might call into question whether a tax on that wealth could make much of a dent in terms of altering the distribution of income. However, the impact of estate and gift taxes on distribution is not a simple matter of taxing one group and giving money (or reducing taxes) for another. It is well known that taxes can change people's behavior as individuals and companies seek to minimize their tax liabilities. It is difficult to know with certainty how people will react to taxes and changes in taxes. What type of behavior do taxes elicit? As an example, a tax on wage income might lead individuals to work less than they would if the tax was quite low. But, at the same time, a high tax rate on wage income may force people to work more so that they can meet their obligations such as paying their mortgage and feeding their family. It is not at all obvious which effect wins out. These responses to tax changes—what economists call elasticities—are quite complicated in the case of the estate tax, and economists disagree on the net impact of these responses. Individuals might react to the estate and gift tax by saving less money, thereby reducing wealth accumulation and the amount of money available for redistribution. However, if savings is reduced, there might also be less money available for charitable contributions and there may also be a reduction in the amount of capital used to expand businesses and create new jobs (which benefit poor and rich).[6] The potential distributional effects of taxing the wealthy may therefore be offset by taxpayer behavior to avoid the tax—or not![7]

There are a variety of behavioral responses to estate and gift taxes that will affect the taxes' impact on the distribution of income. A useful way to work through these alternative avenues is to consider why people save and make bequests, which affects wealth accumulation during life. As previously discussed, there is the direct effect of estate taxes that reduces the net worth of the estate that would be passed on to relatively wealthy heirs. The tax itself may reduce the amount of money available to be distributed to relatives (aside from a spouse), which may reduce the intergenerational growth in wealth among those in the top percentiles of net worth.

Estate and gift taxes effectively increase the cost of making gifts and bequests. Take a simple case in which a donor wants to save enough money to leave her daughter a substantial bequest. An estate tax (or change in estate tax) may reduce the incentive to work to fulfill that bequest motive in the face of substantial estate and gift taxes. The donor may give up and reduce his or her work effort and asset accumulation, being discouraged that the government would be taking a substantial portion of the potential bequest in the form of an estate tax. On the other hand, if the donor has a very specific bequest level in mind, in the presence of an estate tax (or increase in estate tax) he or she has to work and save more in order to achieve his or her bequest goal, net of the tax. The behavior of the donor could therefore increase or decrease wealth accumulation and thereby impact the distribution of income before the tax is levied at death. In the case of accidental bequests, which are not planned, there would be no behavioral impact on savings.

In an influential study, Stiglitz (1978) suggests that if the estate tax does reduce savings, there may be a negative effect on the distribution of income. Specifically, he points out that with reduced savings, there is less capital available for production and labor will not be as productive. Under certain circumstances, this could lead to a reduction in real wages, thus exacerbating inequalities in income distribution.

Since the estate and gift tax may increase or decrease savings (as noted earlier), one needs to look to empirical analysis of the effect of the estate and gift tax on savings to ascertain the real impact. Unfortunately, there is no clear-cut answer in that literature. Some of the more recent studies that focus on the relationship between the estate tax (federal and/or state level) and estate value find relatively small effects. Kopczuk (2010) summarizes these studies and points out that they find results that suggest a 1 percent increase in estate tax reduces the size of the estate by 0.1 to 0.2 percent. Gale and Slemrod (2001b) review similar studies and conclude that the empirical evidence is sketchy and the results are quite fragile.

In addition to the behavioral responses, there are other forms of legal avoidance that can reduce the estate tax and hence the potential for redistribution. Legal avoidance of the tax may not mean less wealth accumulation—it may simply mean using strategies to protect assets from the estate and gift tax. While these strategies are not without cost, there is some evidence that taxpayers use trusts, contributions to charity and family members, and other means to reduce estate and gift tax liabilities. If these strategies reduce net worth (because of the cost of transactions such as putting your money in a trust or due to outright contributions to charities, for example), there is some mitigation of the concentration of net worth among the wealthy. Kopczuk (2010) reviews some empirical work on avoidance strategies and reports that one study finds that one type of avoidance mechanism reduces the gross estate by 10 percent (Johnson, Mikow, and Eller 2001).

With respect to charitable contributions, there is some consensus that a substantial reduction in the estate tax would reduce the level of charitable contributions given during life and death. The main driver in those results is the idea that with estate and gift taxes at rates that are relatively high, the "price" of the contributions is offset by tax savings. A dollar given to charity at death (or during life) is a dollar that is not taxed under the estate (or gift) tax. If the estate tax rate is 55 percent, by giving a dollar to charity, an estate in essence "saves" 55 cents of tax liability so the net cost of the contribution is only 45 cents. Bakija and Gale (2003) estimate that repeal of the estate tax would reduce charitable contributions by approximately $10 billion per year. Joulfaian (2004) estimates a smaller impact. With respect to income distribution, the question that remains is how much of an impact do charitable contributions have on redistribution? Joulfaian (2011) provides data on the type of charitable bequests made by decedents in 2004. By amount, the largest recipients were (in order of size of bequests) philanthropy and voluntarism organizations ($10 billion), educational institutes ($2.6 billion), and religious/spiritual development ($1.1 billion), followed by human service ($0.6 billion), health (general, $0.6 billion), and arts, culture, and humanities ($0.5 billion). As noted earlier in this chapter, assigning the distribution of benefits of contributions to these charities is very difficult and beyond the scope of this chapter. However, it is not unreasonable to assume that some of the charitable bequests are redistributive in nature and thus add to the redistributive impacts of the estate and gift tax.

In the final section these potential impacts of estate and gift taxes on income distribution are summarized and tentative conclusions reached.

CONCLUSION

The current estate and gift tax in the United States taxes the very high value estates. As a result, the potential for the current estate and gift to affect income distribution is smaller than it was in previous decades. However, putting the specifics of the tax such as exemption levels and rates aside, the potential for the taxes to affect income distribution exists and is a function of what happens to the tax that is collected, behavioral responses including the impact on savings, types of bequests and recipients of bequests, and the impact of charitable contributions. To summarize the impact of the estate and gift tax on redistribution, perhaps the best that can be done is to categorize the potential impact of these groups of effects, which is done here:

- *Redistribution of revenue collected from the estate and gift tax.* The base of the tax is affected by behavioral responses, avoidance activities, and net impacts to savings. At the end of the day, however, there is a significant amount of revenue collected. If this revenue is used for propoor spending or tax reductions at the low-income end of the distribution (through lower payroll or income taxes for example), the effect is redistributive and not inconsequential. Reducing the net value of estates through taxation also reduces the level of accumulated wealth that gets passed on to the next generation, thereby increasing to some extent the potential for more intergenerational equity in income distribution.
- *Impact of estate and gift tax on charitable contributions.* Contributions to charity can be deducted from the value of a decedent's estate and thus lower the tax liability. Some of the expenditures of some of the charities that receive bequests may be used in a propoor manner, but it is not plausible that all are used in a propoor manner.

- *The impact of the estate and gift tax on savings and wealth accumulation.* Economic theory suggests that the taxes could reduce or increase savings. Empirical evidence has not been conclusive. If the effect were to reduce savings, there would be less concentration of wealth. However, there could also be a reduction in the level of real wages as capital becomes scarce and the productive capacity of labor falters without sufficient capital to work with.

- *The nature of gifts and bequests and their recipients.* The estate and gift tax encourages gifts to reduce the value of the estate at time of death (within certain parameters). Most gifts accrue to family members. The children who receive these gifts (and bequests) tend to have lower levels of income than their parents, but are generally not poor. The incentive to give gifts may therefore reduce the concentration of wealth but may not lead to substantial shifts in overall income distributions.

In summary, there is room for estate and gift taxes to enhance income equality. However, there are several mitigating factors that may work in the opposite direction. The empirical literature on the subject suggests that the mitigating factors may be relatively small, leaving the direct effect of collecting the tax at the high end of the income distribution and potentially using it to increase after tax income at the low end of the income distribution as the main impact. From this perspective, the relative size of the redistribution is roughly equivalent to the amount of tax collected.

If income distribution is affected by the estate and gift tax, there is potentially more that could be done by reducing the exemption levels, eliminating certain deductions, or raising the tax rate. The reader will recognize that it is difficult to know what would happen to the behavioral and other factors and their impacts on income distribution if the estate and gift tax were reformed.[8] For example, if contributions to charity were no longer deductible, there would likely be a reduction in charitable contributions—and some reduction in the impact on redistribution. However, if elimination of the deduction expanded the estate and gift tax base and therefore revenues, those revenues might be used more (or less) effectively to affect the distribution of income. Higher tax rates may make avoidance behavior more worthwhile. Suffice it to say that the evidence regarding human behavior and taxation is not consistent enough to provide us with exact estimates of the impact of reforms of the tax.

NOTES

1. The generation-skipping tax applies a tax on assets that are transferred in such a way that the tax due under the estate and gift tax is skipped for one generation. A classic example is an estate that when passed from parent to child would be subject to the estate tax is passed instead to the grandchildren. State taxes are also imposed, but they are not the focus of this chapter.

2. Economists typically focus on two types of equity—vertical equity, which refers to how policy affects low-income individuals relative to high-income individuals, and horizontal equity, which refers to how policy treats individuals who are similar in terms of income. The estate and gift tax (like many taxes) may affect both types of equity. The focus in this chapter is on vertical equity. However, given that the estate and gift tax allows deductions including a deduction for qualified family businesses, it is quite likely that two estates that are initially valued at a similar level could end up paying very different amounts in estate tax. These features could have an impact on vertical equity in that the net amount of tax and resulting income could vary.

3. Under previous legislation the lifetime exemption for the gift tax was also $1 million in 2010. EGTRRA increased the threshold beginning in 2002 to accelerate the year the $1 million became effective from 2006 under prior law to 2002 under EGTRRA.

4. The long-term effects of this type of redistribution are difficult to discern since a transfer may be used for consumption or savings and these could have different long-term effects on wealth accumulation.

5. The estate and gift tax may affect only the timing of transfers among family members if the donor planned to make the transfers at some time regardless of the tax.

6. The true distributional impact of charitable contributions lies in the use (expenditures or benefits) of those contributions. Some would argue that gifts to the arts benefit high-income individuals as well as low-income individuals. Measuring the true benefit of charitable contributions is beyond the scope of this chapter. Suffice it to say that charitable contributions may be used in ways that increase income equality.

7. Tax avoidance is the legal means of reducing tax liability. Tax evasion is the illegal means of reducing tax liability and is not specifically considered in this discussion.

8. Some researchers have called for replacing the estate and gift tax with an inheritance tax, which would change the scope of some of the avoidance behavior. Batchelder (2009) provides such an argument.

BIBLIOGRAPHY

Bakija, Jon M. and William G. Gale. 2003. "Effects of Estate Tax Reform on Charitable Giving." *Tax Policy Issues and Options* 6 (July). Washington, DC: Tax Policy Center, Urban Institute-Brookings Institution.

Batchelder, Lily L. 2009. "Estate Tax Reform: Issues and Options." *Tax Notes* February 2: 633–47.

Gale, William G. and Joel Slemrod. 2001a. "Rethinking the Estate and Gift Tax: Overview." National Bureau of Economic Research Working Paper 8205, Cambridge, MA.

Gale, William G. and Joel Slemrod. 2001b. "Rhetoric and Economics in the Estate Tax Debate." Paper prepared for the National Tax Association Symposium, Washington, DC, May 7–8.

Internal Revenue Service. 2011. "Estate Tax Returns, Filing Year by Tax Status and Size of Gross Estate." Accessed on June 21, 2011. http://www.irs.gov/taxstats/indtaxstats/article/0,,id=210646,00.html.

Johnson, Barry W., Jacob M. Mikow and Martha B. Eller. 2001. "Elements of Federal Estate Taxation." In *Rethinking Estate and Gift Taxation*, edited by William G. Gale, James R. Hines, and Joel Slemrod, 65–112. Washington, DC: Brookings Institution.

Joulfaian, David. 2004. "Gift Taxes and Lifetime Transfers: Time Series Evidence." *Journal of Public Economics* 88: 1917–29.

Joulfaian, David. 2011. "The Federal Estate Tax: History, Law and Economics." Social Science Research Network (SSRN) working paper. Accessed on June 23, 2011. http://papers.ssrn.com/sol3/papers.cfm?abstract_id=1579829.

Kennickell, Arthur. 2007. "What's the Difference? Evidence on the Distribution of Wealth, Health, Life Expectancy and Health Insurance Coverage." Federal Reserve Board. Accessed on September 26, 2011. http://www.federalreserve.gov/pubs/oss/oss2/papers/CDC.final.pdf.

Kennickell, Arthur. 2009. "Ponds and Streams: Wealth and Income in the United States 1989 to 2007." Federal Reserve Board. Accessed on September 26, 2011. http://www.federalreserve.gov/pubs/feds/2009/200913/200913pap.pdf.

Kopczuk, Wojciech. 2010. "Economics of Estate Taxation: A Brief Review of Theory and Evidence." National Bureau of Economic Research Working Paper 15741, Cambridge, MA.

Stiglitz, Joseph E. 1978. "Notes on Estate Taxes, Redistribution, and the Concept of Balanced Growth Path Incidence." *Journal of Political Economy* 86 (2):S137–S150.

Tax Policy Center. 2011a. "Historical Returns as a Percentage of Adult Deaths." Accessed on July 15, 2011. http://www.taxpolicycenter.org/taxfacts/displayafact.cfm?Docid=52&Topic2id=60.

Tax Policy Center. 2011b. "Wealth Transfer Taxes." Accessed on July 15, 2011. http://www.taxpolicycenter.org/briefing-book/key-elements/estate/reform.cfm.

Chapter 31

Universal Job Guarantee Program: Toward True Full Employment

Yeva Nersisyan and L. Randall Wray

INTRODUCTION

In a market economy, employment is the main source of income for most of the population. It is through employment that people are able to fully participate in society both because employment itself is a social activity and because the income earned allows one to enjoy the minimum economic and social benefits considered by many to be human rights. Without paying jobs, individuals are unable to partake in a large number of social activities. In capitalist, wage-labor societies therefore joblessness creates a long list of problems—both for the individuals and for society as a whole: self-pity, self-loathing, and rage at society (Harvey 2002); absolute and relative poverty; damage to social status and self-respect; adverse psychological and physical health effects; stress; suicide; and crime and other antisocial behavior. Income inequality is yet another issue closely tied to unemployment.

The most recent data on poverty in the United States shows that about 30 percent of the poor households have no job at all and another 20 percent have members who involuntarily work part-time because they cannot find full-time work (see http://readersupportednews.org/ news-section2/320-80/9563-working-and-poor-in-the-usa). In other words, in half of all households the problem is unemployment and forced part-time work. For those who are lucky enough to have full-time work, the current wage at the low end of the employment ladder is about half of what is necessary to bring an average family out of poverty—in many of those cases the actual wage paid is not even the legal minimum wage.

Even if the Great Recession is officially over, for the 13 million Americans who are still unemployed plus the 8 million or more who cannot get full-time work, it certainly does not feel that way. The U.S. economy has performed especially poorly in terms of job growth even as economic growth has resumed. The current rate of job creation, 120,000 new jobs in November 2011, is not only insufficient to replace the jobs lost during the crisis but can hardly keep up with labor force growth. In reality, the United States will need a minimum of 300,000 new jobs created every month—for years—to solve her unemployment problems. At the same time, income inequality, currently at historical highs, is further exacerbated by the jobless recovery and the nauseatingly outrageous bonuses paid to the top 1 percent—whose income and share of income has exploded over the last few decades.

Surprisingly, however, the persistently high unemployment (8.6% unemployment rate in November 2011) and the even worse underemployment[1] situation as well as inequality have not generated the necessary amount of concern among politicians. The lack of public debate about any serious jobs initiative has been conspicuous. Many commentators have claimed that unemployment is a lagging indicator, and it takes a while for it to catch up to economic growth. The other popular argument is that a large number of people currently unemployed are structurally unemployed; i.e., many jobs lost in the construction sector will not come back even when the economy rebounds, and those workers are likely to remain unemployed for a long time.

The conclusion that follows is that public policy, particularly more government spending, will not help solve the problem of unemployment with some even claiming that it will worsen it. Instead, we are told, we must let the "free market" operate to create new kinds of jobs; at most, government might offer retraining for displaced workers with the wrong skill sets. The problem is not so much one of Keynesian effective demand, but a supply side failure. The more neoliberal response is to increase labor market "flexibility" by removing "barriers to work" such as social safety nets, minimum wage laws, rigid union work rules, and safety regulations.

We start this chapter by a brief discussion of the causes of unemployment, both short term and long term. We argue that the conventional argument that unemployment is a job market issue is misguided and inapplicable to the real world. Rather, the currently high unemployment as well as the long-term unemployment are due to insufficient aggregate spending; i.e., total spending does not create enough jobs for everyone to be able to find employment. The private sector, while usually employing a large portion of the labor force, cannot be entrusted with the task of ensuring full employment. The public sector, on the other hand, can and should assume this role.

But what kind of policy is appropriate to solve not only the short-term unemployment problem but also that of long-term joblessness and the ills of inequality and poverty associated with it? While some have called for increased government spending, we disagree that blind "pump-priming" stimulus is the right solution. Rather, we propose a universal government Job Guarantee program, which will hire anyone who is willing and ready to work. We discuss the design of this program, its implementation and affordability, while answering the usual criticisms charged against such programs.

THE LOST COMMITMENT TO FULL EMPLOYMENT

One of the major deficiencies of market economies is the failure to provide full utilization of resources and particularly full employment of human resources. While the private sector plays an invaluable and dynamic role in providing employment, it cannot ensure enough jobs to keep up with population growth or to speed economic recovery—much less achieve the social goal of full employment for all. Even more importantly, private enterprises do not have employment as their goal: the purpose of private production is not job provision, but obtaining profits. If more profits can be obtained by downsizing employment, firms lay off workers. When sales fall, firms lay off workers. When more efficient production methods are found that permit firms to produce more with fewer workers, they lay off workers. In other words, firms hire more workers only when they have more customers than they can serve with the existing labor force. The fundamental drive is to create profits, not jobs. That should be obvious.

Firms hire the number of workers they think they need to produce the amount of output they think they can profitably sell. There is no reason to believe that there are forces that push the for-profit sector to hire all the available resources, including labor—at any particular point in time, much less on a continuous basis through time. This is especially true in the current climate of financialization of the U.S. economy—in which the system of rewards has changed motivations. The goal of most large corporations is not even to achieve maximum profits but to increase shareholder value, i.e., their stock prices. There are a number of ways to do this, and high employment is certainly not one of them. Quite the contrary, laying off workers is one of the main means to achieve "efficiency" the way the stock market understands it, which then translates into higher stock prices. While we will not go into this topic in further detail, there has been a long-term transformation of developed capitalist economies (especially that of the United States) toward a new version of Hilferding's "finance capitalism," where an ever larger share of corporate profits comes from the realm of finance, which requires very little labor (Hilferding 1910; in recent years the financial sector's share of value added has doubled, to half of GDP, and its share of corporate profits has quadrupled to 40%). As a result, the share of national income going to labor has fallen while even the most venerable industrial powerhouses like General Motors and General Electric seek more profits from their financial divisions and downsize their manufacturing business.

While one would expect that as the private sector has moved further away from attaining full employment, the public sector would have filled the void, the opposite has been true.

In the 1950s and '60s, full or at least high employment was among the primary goals of economic policy: governments across the world tried and achieved relatively high levels of employment through demand management as well as direct hiring and other active labor market policies. It was recognized that social policy is an invaluable instrument for attaining and maintaining full employment. In recent decades, however, full employment has been wrongly dismissed as not only impossible but economically counterproductive. This has been due to a number of factors such as the declining power of labor unions as well as the advent of neoliberal economic thinking. The capture of governments in most of the developed world by proponents of such thinking has pushed employment outside the domain of public policy and subjugated full employment to the whim of free markets.

In the United States, the Employment Act of 1946 committed the federal government to the goal of high employment (it was amended by the 1978 Humphrey-Hawkins Act, which targeted a measured unemployment rate of 3%). And while we rarely achieved that goal—at least for all Americans (we were tolerably close only for the case of white men)—it was an oft-stated goal of policy. Now, however, we act as if full employment would ruin us, destroying the value of our currency through inflation and depreciation, and weakening the labor discipline that high unemployment maintains through enforced destitution. What happened is that rather than viewing low unemployment as a goal of policy, unemployment came to be seen as a *tool* of policy. Indeed, public policy since the late 1970s has been biased against the creation of a sufficient supply of jobs on the belief that full employment is not consistent with price stability. Through the thick and thin of the business cycle, we leave tens of millions of Americans idle in the belief that this makes political, economic, and social sense (Wray 2011).

CYCLICAL, STRUCTURAL, AND "KEYNESIAN" CAUSES OF UNEMPLOYMENT

There is a general consensus among most economists that cyclical or short term, unemployment—i.e., job loss due to the business cycle—is caused by declining aggregate demand. However, not much consensus exists about the kind of public policy that is appropriate to tackle cyclical unemployment. Economists who are characterized as "Keynesians" usually argue for government stimulus spending or tax cuts.

By contrast, those who can be characterized by the general term "neoclassical" argue that unemployment is a labor market problem; i.e., imperfections such as minimum wage legislation, unemployment benefits, and wage contracts make the labor market unable to adjust quickly to resolve recessions, leaving a portion of the labor force unemployed. The logic is that if workers take a pay cut when the economy is slowing down, then "full employment" defined as the lack of involuntary unemployment *at the market clearing wage* will be maintained. The appropriate action then is to make the labor market more flexible. This has been the policy direction in the United States and most developed countries in the last few decades. And while the labor market has become more and more flexible in downturns with employers laying off workers at the slightest sign of slowing business, it has been extremely "inflexible" in the upturn, leaving a large number of the population unemployed during "robust" recoveries and even as labor markets have been made more flexible.

There are a variety of approaches taken to explaining the problem of long-term joblessness, of which the most important views are behavioralist (problems with the individuals who are unemployed), structuralist (for example, skills mismatch), and job shortage (Harvey 1999, 2000). In the United States, the economic theory and the policy based on it emphasize behavioral and structural problems. It is argued that in the long run involuntary unemployment does not exist—the economy operates at what is called the natural rate of unemployment where everyone who is willing to work at the prevailing market wage can find a job. The natural rate of unemployment does not mean zero unemployment as there are always workers between jobs or who have just entered the workforce. Additionally, there are workers whose skills are no longer demanded because the structure of the economy has changed. Employers are looking for a skill set that the unemployed cannot provide. This is the so-called skill mismatch problem, which can be solved by retraining and reeducating the unemployed to fit them to the available vacancies.

However, there is no fine line between short-term and long-term or structural unemployment. In the past 20 years, high unemployment has not been solely a phenomenon of recessions, but even expansions occur without much job creation. Economic growth and employment have seemingly decoupled: the former no longer implies the latter. Jobless recovery is no longer an aberration but has rather become the new normal.

Figure 31.1 depicts the change in employment relative to the prerecession level for 36 months after the official start date of the recession. It is obvious that in the earlier postwar period recessions were shallow (in terms of job losses) and the recoveries were robust. Since 1990 this is no longer true. During the 1990–91 recession it took almost 32 months for employment to reach its prerecession level. In the 2001 recession, even after 36 months the economy had not reached the prerecession level of employment although the decline itself was not extremely steep. The current recession is an aberration from any historical norm both in terms of the speed and steepness of the decline in employment and in terms of how persistent it has been. Even 36 months into the recession, employment has been about 7 percent less than prior to the recession. With the current deficit hysteria and lack of commitment to any meaningful jobs

Figure 31.1

Change in Employment 36 Months after Recession Started (% change from the level prior to the recession).

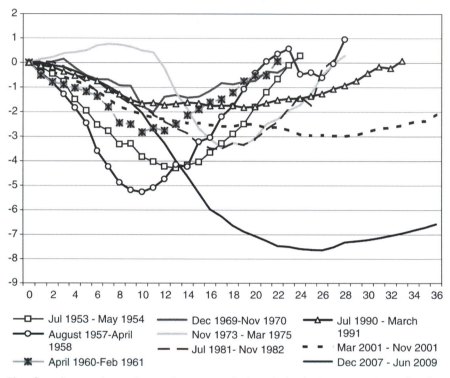

Legend:
—□— Jul 1953 - May 1954
—○— August 1957-April 1958
—✱— April 1960-Feb 1961
——— Dec 1969-Nov 1970
——— Nov 1973 - Mar 1975
— — Jul 1981- Nov 1982
—△— Jul 1990 - March 1991
■ ■ Mar 2001 - Nov 2001
——— Dec 2007 - Jun 2009

Note: Some lines reach zero; i.e., employment goes back to the level prior to recession, earlier than 36 months after the beginning of the recession.
Source: BLS.

program, it is unlikely that the jobs recovery is anywhere near. Indeed, most analysts believe it will be years before the unemployment rate comes down significantly.

The reasons for the phenomenon of "jobless recovery" are numerous and beyond the scope of this chapter. A few of them such as the decline in the manufacturing sector, declining union power, as well as the government inaction in response to unemployment are worth mentioning. Additionally, it is natural to expect that as technology improves, the private sector needs less and less labor to produce the same amount of output, the so-called "machine problem." Companies have used recessions to discard the "unnecessary" labor. While it may be unpopular to lay off a large number of people in good times, during recessions when everyone is laying off workers the firm that is downsizing will not face much opposition.

Furthermore, "jobless recoveries" further exacerbate income inequality. When economic growth resumés, income increases but the unemployed are not getting their share of the increased income. Rather, it is being distributed among fewer people. According to a report by the U.S. Congress Joint Economic Committee (Income Inequality and the Great Recession 2010), during the recovery following the 2001 recession income inequality "skyrocketed," reaching pre–Great Depression levels prior to the Great Recession. This also relates to the often-ignored relationship between income inequality and economic crises. Keynes (1965) pointed this out in *The General Theory*, arguing that while some income inequality is inevitable and even useful for market economies, capitalism tends to generate too much inequality, undermining its own existence. Income is created in the process of producing goods and services. If workers' income is not sufficient to buy the fruits of their own labor, firms will face realization problems and will cut back on production and employment.

Most countries have some public policy in place to counteract the inherent tendency toward inequality to one extent or another. The social safety net, for example, may counterbalance the rising income inequality during jobless recoveries. However, even in the Eurozone countries with relatively generous social benefits, the rise in unemployment due to the global financial crisis has increased inequality by as much as 2 percentage points. The picture is grimmer in the periphery countries where the increase has been as high as 10 percentage points (Morsy 2011). This points to the need for a different type of public policy—one based on providing jobs rather than mere income support.

Still, many have claimed that persistent joblessness is no longer a cyclical issue but rather structural. The structure of the economy, they argue, has changed as the manufacturing sector shrank and other blue-collar jobs disappeared. These jobs will not come back, therefore the workers need to be retrained if they are to find employment. A recent report from the Economic Policy Institute casts doubt on many of the claims that the proponents of the "structural unemployment" argument make. First, if the currently high unemployment was primarily a structural problem, one would expect that it would be concentrated among those with lower educational attainment. The report demonstrates that the composition of unemployment by educational background has remained very stable over the recession with unemployment rates doubling for workers of almost all educational levels (Mishel 2011).

The other argument popular with the "structural unemployment" proponents is that the construction sector has contributed significantly to the high unemployment. Construction jobs that were created during the housing boom are never coming back and those workers are likely to remain unemployed for a long time. Again, the Economic Policy Institute report makes one doubt this claim by showing that the composition of unemployment and long-term unemployment has hardly shifted toward the construction sector. Construction workers made up 10.6 percent of all unemployed and 11 percent of long-term unemployed prior to the recession, with the numbers being 12.4 percent and 12.5 percent respectively as of the second quarter of 2010 (Mishel 2011).

The Economic Policy Institute report provides evidence that dispels the notion that currently high unemployment is a structural issue. Rather it claims that it is the result of lack of demand for workers, which stems from lack of aggregate demand. In fact, in the past two to three decades the U.S. economy has operated with chronically deficient aggregate demand. As the government deficits got smaller and even turned to surpluses under Clinton, withdrawing demand from the economy, first the stock market bubble and later the housing bubble helped maintain the illusion of sustainable growth. Since the collapse of the housing market, however, consumers have cut back on their spending, and businesses facing sluggish sales have laid off workers. This is a vicious cycle of low demand, low spending, and high unemployment that can be stopped only by an entity whose spending does not depend on its income, i.e., the government.

This problem is not restricted to the United States. Before the global financial collapse, the International Labour Office (Global Employment Trends Brief 2007) released a major report on global unemployment. It concluded: "Young people have more difficulties in labour markets than adults; women do not get the same opportunities as men, the lack of decent work is still high; and the potential a population has to offer is not always used because of a lack of human capital development or a mismatch between the supply and the demand side in labour markets." Moreover, the International Labour Office reported that even in 2007, at the peak of the global expansion, 200 million people remained unemployed in spite of strong growth. "Every region has to face major labour market challenges" because growth fuels productivity growth (up 26% in past decade) but does not create many new jobs (up only 16.6%). Again, jobless growth is now the norm in the United States and abroad.

The conclusion that follows is that we need social policy to solve the problem of unemployment, both cyclical and long term. It is too important of an issue for both economic and social reasons to leave it to the private markets. The question then is what kind of economic policy is appropriate to ensure full employment. If the problem is (mostly) a job shortage, which we argue it is, then retraining workers will only redistribute unemployment among the unfortunate, who are blamed for their joblessness. Especially in an expansion, those left behind generally do have characteristics identified with the behavioralist and structuralist arguments, hence concealing the true problem—a chronic job shortage.

PUMP PRIMING VERSUS DIRECT JOB CREATION AS A SOLUTION TO JOB SHORTAGE

Even those who understand that the problem is job shortage or demand shortage usually argue for more stimulus spending (or tax cuts) with little concern for how the stimulus is distributed throughout the economy. There are, however, a number of problems with this approach. First, it is highly possible that government stimulus merely ends up in the pockets of firms as profits and there is no guarantee that those profits spur hiring of more workers. High profits might also be used to engage in mergers and acquisitions and other financial investments rather than in job creation.

The current recession is an example of such a situation, where government spending has improved business profits, and despite sitting on piles of cash (an estimated $2 trillion of it), U.S. corporations are not hiring. This is because they understand that U.S. households are loaded with debt and will not be spending, and in the current political climate there is no expectation that the government will step in to fill this gap. Merger and acquisition activities, on the other hand, have intensified.

Second, the "spend, spend, spend" policy may lead to inflation before full employment is achieved. Inflation hurts those with fixed incomes, such as seniors, as well as creditors; therefore such policies will almost always face resistance from the financial sector. Third, there is the problem of timing. Discretionary stimulus spending has to go through Congress and the whole political theater. Therefore before it is passed and put into action there will be job losses, which is a loss socially and economically. Finally, while stimulus spending may attenuate short-term unemployment, it does nothing to help those who have been displaced from the job market due to structural changes in the economy, or due to perceived "behavioral" problems or insufficient "moral character." There will always be some workers left behind even as fiscal stimulus becomes great enough to generate demand-pull inflation.

For all the aforementioned reasons, we disagree with commentators who are calling for merely more stimulus spending. Instead, we propose a much better alternative, the policy of direct employment creation by the public sector, a Job Guarantee that would offer to provide a job to anyone of legal working age who is ready and willing to work. The program would pay a uniform wage and provide a uniform benefit package. (The legislated minimum wage is meaningless if there are unemployed individuals, because their wage is zero. Only in combination with a job guarantee does a minimum wage become effective.) Hence, the wage paid in the Job Guarantee program would become the effective minimum wage; it would have to be matched by all other employers. Similarly, the package of benefits offered would set a standard that would be matched by other employers.

Workers would do something useful, but with an ultimate goal of preparing them for work in non-Job Guarantee program jobs. Hence, training would be a part of every Job Guarantee job. Job Guarantee must take workers as they are, so there must be a Job Guarantee employment offer for anyone "ready and willing" to work, regardless of level of education, training, or previous work experience. However, the Job Guarantee experience should better equip workers for post–Job Guarantee work.

A key justification for the Job Guarantee is that no capitalist society has ever managed to operate at anything approaching true, full employment on a consistent basis without direct job creation on a large scale by government. Further, the burden of joblessness is borne unequally, always concentrated among groups that already face other disadvantages.

Finally, only the government can offer an infinitely elastic demand for labor (offering to hire all who cannot otherwise find employment) because it does not need to heed narrow market efficiency concerns. Private firms can hire the only quantity of labor needed to produce the level of output expected to be sold at a profitable price. Government can take a broader view to include promotion of the public interest, including the right to work. Through a job guarantee, it will not only provide employment for everyone who wants a job but will also provide goods and services that the society needs but that the private sector will not provide because they do not constitute a profit opportunity. As the Job Guarantee program will not be inflationary, it will allow reaching true full employment and a more equitable distribution of income that will come with it. (This is discussed in more detail later.) Furthermore, giving people jobs that pay a living wage will alleviate poverty. Finally, if health care benefits are a part of the compensation package, the Job Guarantee will also solve the problem of lack of health care that jobless Americans are currently facing. For these reasons, government should and must play a role in providing jobs to achieve social justice.

THE JOB GUARANTEE: PROGRAM DESIGN AND BENEFITS

The benefits of full employment are numerous and include production of goods, services, and income; on-the-job training and skill development; poverty and economic inequality alleviation; amelioration of many social ills associated with chronic unemployment (health problems, spousal abuse and family breakup, drug abuse, crime); community building and social networking; and social, political, and economic stability.

The program has no time limits or restrictions based on income, gender, education, or experience. It operates like a buffer stock: in a boom, employers will recruit workers out of the program; in a slump it will allow those who lost their jobs to preserve good habits, keeping them work-ready. It will also help those unable to obtain work outside the program enhance their employability through training. Unemployment offices will be converted to employment offices, to match workers with jobs that suit them and to help employers recruit staff.

Although the program must be funded by the federal government, its implementation will be decentralized. All state and local governments and registered nonprofit organizations can propose projects; proposals will be submitted to a newly created office within the federal government's Labor Department for final approval and funding. The office will maintain a website providing details on all pending, approved and ongoing projects, and final reports will be published after projects are complete.

Participants will be subject to all federal work rules, and violations will lead to dismissal. Anyone who is dismissed three times in a 12-month period will be ineligible to participate in the program for a year. Workers will be allowed to organize through labor unions.

Workers will not have to leave their communities to seek employment. The program will meet workers where they are and take them as they are: jobs will be available in local communities and will be tailored to suit employees' level of education and experience (though with the goal of improving skills). This will prevent communities and sometimes larger cities from being deserted. Project proposals should include provisions for part-time work and other flexible arrangements for workers who need them, including but not restricted to flexible arrangements for parents of young children.

The program could provide for flexible working conditions such as part-time and seasonal work and other arrangements as desired by the workers. The package of benefits would be subject to congressional approval, but could include health care, child care, payment of Social Security taxes, and usual vacations and sick leave.

The advantage of the uniform basic wage is that it would limit competition with other employers as workers could be attracted out of the Job Guarantee program by paying a wage slightly above the program's wage. Obviously, higher-skilled workers and those with higher educational attainment will be hired first. In an economic boom, employers will lower hiring standards to pull lower-skilled workers out of the program. The residual pool of workers in the program provides a buffer stock of employable labor, helping to reduce pressures on wages—and as wages for high-skilled workers are bid up, the buffer stock becomes ever more desirable as a source of cheaper labor. This is why the program can provide full employment—a job offer to all those willing to work, at the program wage—without pushing wages and prices upward.

All participants will obtain a Social Security number and maintain a bank account in an FDIC-insured bank. Weekly wages will be paid by the federal government directly to participants' accounts. The government will also provide funding for benefits as well as approved expenses up to a maximum of 10 or 25 percent of wages paid for a project (to cover the cost of administrative materials and equipment; the exact percentage would be set centrally, and could vary by type of project). Because the primary purpose of the program is to create jobs, the federal government should cover only a relatively small portion of nonwage costs.

Estimated spending will be 1 to 2 percent of GDP, with economic, social, and political benefits several times larger. Net program costs will be even lower, since with the institution of a Job Guarantee program spending on unemployment compensation and other relief will be reduced—this program will pay people for working, rather than paying them not to work. The promise of increased national productivity and shared prosperity should far outweigh any conventional fears about rising deficits. To fulfill this promise, we need to put Americans back to work.

The Job Guarantee will not only help achieve full employment but will also ensure that all of society's needs are satisfied regardless of whether they constitute profitable business opportunities or not. More generally, it can be used to provide goods and services that are too expensive for low-income households or that markets do not provide. Examples include social services (child and elder care, tutoring, public safety), small-scale public infrastructure provision or repair (clean water and sewage projects, roads), low-income housing and repairs to owner-occupied housing (following the lead of Habitat for Humanity), and food preparation ("soup kitchens," local bakeries). The Job Guarantee will not compete with private businesses and jobs but will rather fill the gaps left by the private sector. Only community needs and imagination would limit the ability to provide adequate and useful jobs. Forstater (1999) has emphasized how Job Guarantee can be used to increase economic flexibility and to enhance the environment by creating green jobs in the framework of the program.

While neoliberals and their ancestors have managed to taint the memory of the New Deal's job creation programs, the truth is that these programs provided lasting benefits. The naysayers actually began to fabricate falsehoods about the program and its participants from the very beginning. With corporate funding and ready access to the media, they painted a picture of lazy tramps leaning on shovels. But the evidence is still plain to see, in the form of public buildings, dams, roads, national parks, and trails that still serve the United States. For example, workers in the WPA (Works Progress Administration)

> shouldered the tasks that began to transform the physical face of America. They built roads and schools and bridges and dams. The Cow Palace in San Francisco, La Guardia Airport in New York City and National (now Reagan) Airport in Washington, D.C., the Timberline Lodge in Oregon, the Outer Drive Bridge

on Chicago's Lake Shore Drive, the River Walk in San Antonio. . . . Its workers sewed clothes and stuffed mattresses and repaired toys; served hot lunches to schoolchildren; ministered to the sick; delivered library books to remote hamlets by horseback; rescued flood victims; painted giant murals on the walls of hospitals, high schools, courthouses, and city halls; performed plays and played music before eager audiences; and wrote guides to the forty-eight states that even today remain models for what such books should be. And when the clouds of an oncoming world loomed over the United States, it was the WPA's workers who modernized the army and air bases and trained in vast numbers to supply the nation's military needs. (Taylor 2008, 2)

The New Deal jobs programs employed 13 million people; the WPA was the biggest program, employing 8.5 million, lasting eight years, and spending about $10.5 billion (Taylor 2008, 3). It took a broken country and in many important respects helped not only to revive it but to bring it into the 20th century. The WPA built 650,000 miles of roads, 78,000 bridges, 125,000 civilian and military buildings, and 700 miles of airport runways; it fed 900 million hot lunches to kids, operated 1,500 nursery schools, gave concerts before audiences of 150 million, and created 475,000 works of art. It transformed and modernized the United States (Taylor 2008, 523–24).

In many important respects, the United States is broken again. Its infrastructure is not worthy of a rich, developed country, as recognized by President Obama in his 2011 State of the Union address when he called for new investments to answer the challenges posed by China. The nation's public buildings, its roads, its bridges, its playgrounds and parks, and many of its schools are in need of repair. We do not want to overemphasize public infrastructure investment, however. The needs are at least as great in the area of public services, including aged care, preschools, playground supervision, cleanup of public lands, retrofitting public and private buildings for energy efficiency, and environmental restoration projections.

A new universal direct job creation program would improve working conditions in the private sector as employees would have the option of moving into the Job Guarantee program. Hence, private sector employers would have to offer a wage and benefit package and working conditions at least as good as those offered by the Job

Guarantee program. The informal sector would shrink as workers become integrated into formal employment, gaining access to protection provided by labor laws. There would be some reduction of racial and gender discrimination because unfairly treated workers would have the Job Guarantee option, although Job Guarantee by itself cannot end discrimination.

Finally, we would also like to emphasize that a Job Guarantee program with a uniform basic wage also helps to promote economic and price stability. The Job Guarantee will act as an automatic stabilizer[2] as employment in the program grows in recession and shrinks in economic expansion, counteracting private sector employment fluctuations. Furthermore, the uniform basic wage will reduce both inflationary pressure in a boom and deflationary pressure in a bust. In recession, workers downsized by private employers can work at the Job Guarantee wage, which puts a floor to how low wages and income can fall.

CONCLUSION

There have been many job creation programs implemented around the world, some of which were narrowly targeted while others were broad based. The American New Deal included several moderately inclusive programs such as the Civilian Conservation Corp and the WPA. Sweden developed broad-based employment programs that virtually guaranteed access to jobs, until government began to retrench in the 1970s (Ginsburg 1983). In the aftermath of its economic crisis that came with the collapse of its currency board, Argentina created *Plan Jefes y Jefas*, which guaranteed a job for poor heads of households (Tcherneva and Wray 2005). The program successfully created 2 million new jobs that not only provided employment and income for poor families but also provided needed services and free goods to poor neighborhoods. More recently, India passed the National Rural Employment Guarantee Act (2005), which commits the government to providing employment in a public works project to any adult living in a rural area.

If the goal of public policy is full employment, the only way it can really be achieved is through direct job creation. A Job Guarantee program will act as stabilizer during recessions, but it can also be designed to tackle the question of structural unemployment by first employing and then training only the long-term unemployed, on the job. This will increase their chance of ever being employed in the private sector again. It will provide every American who wants to work not with just a job but a decent job.

Many of the fears of the critics of Job Guarantee have been shown to be fallacious. Job creation, even on a massive scale and under difficult circumstances, can be successful. Participants welcome the chance to work, viewing participation as empowering. The program can be democratically implemented, increasing participation in the political process, and with relatively few instances of corruption and bureau-cratic waste.

NOTES

1.   We use the Bureau of Labor Statistics' U6 alternative measure of labor under-utilization. It includes the unemployed, people who want a full-time job but had to settle for a part-time one, and those who are not working or actively looking for a job but are available to work and have looked for work in the past 12 months.

2.   Any component of the government budget that automatically moves to widen the budget deficit in a recession (shrink the deficit or create a surplus in an expansion) is considered an automatic stabilizer.

BIBLIOGRAPHY

Forstater, Mathew. 1999. "Full Employment and Economic Flexibility." *Economic and Labour Relations Review,* Volume 11.

Ginsburg, Helen. 1983. *Full Employment and Public Policy: The United States and Sweden.* Lexington, MA: Lexington Books.

Global Employment Trends Brief. 2007. International Labour Office; results sum-marized in "Global Unemployment Remains at Historic High Despite Strong Economic Growth." January 25.

Harvey, Philip L. 1999. "Liberal Strategies for Combating Joblessness in the Twentieth Century." *Journal of Economic Issues* 33(2): 497–504.

Harvey, Philip L. 2000. "Combating Joblessness: An analysis of the principal strat-egies that have influenced the development of American employment and social welfare law during the 20th century." *Berkeley Journal of Employment and Labor Law* 21(2): 677–758.

Harvey, Philip L. 2002. "Human Rights and Economic Policy Discourse: Taking economic and social rights seriously." *Columbia Human Rights Law Review* 33(2): 364–471.

Hilferding, Rudolph. 1981. *Finance Capital: A Study of the Latest Phase of Capitalist Development* (Ed. Tom Bottomore). London, UK: Routledge & Kegan Paul.

Income Inequality and the Great Recession. 2010. Report by the U.S. Congress Joint Economic Committee. Representative Carolyn B. Maloney, Chair; Senator Charles E. Schumer, Vice Chairman.

Keynes, John M. 1965. *The General Theory of Employment, Interest, and Money.* New York, NY: Harcourt, Brace & World.

Mishel, Lawrence. 2011. "Education Is Not the Cure for High Unemployment or for Income Inequality." EPI Briefing Paper #286, Economic Policy Institute.

Mitchell, William and L. Randall Wray. 2005. "In Defense of Employer of Last Resort: A Response to Malcolm Sawyer." *Journal of Economic Issues* 39(1): 235–44.

Morsy, Hanan. 2011. "Unemployed in Europe." *Finance & Development* 48(3).

Taylor, Nick. 2008. *American-Made: The Enduring Legacy of the WPA: When FDR Put the Nation to Work.* New York, NY: Bantam Books.

Tcherneva, Pavlina and L. Randall Wray. 2005. "Gender and the Job Guarantee: The impact of Argentina's Jefes program on female heads of poor households." Working Paper No. 50. Center for Full Employment and Price Stability.

Wray, L. Randall. 1998. *Understanding Modern Money: The Key to Full Employment and Price Stability.* Cheltenham, UK: Edward Elgar.

Wray, L. Randall. 2011. "The Job Guarantee: A Government Plan for Full Employment." *The Nation,* June 27.

Chapter 32

Is Universal Basic Income Still Worth Talking About?

Karl Widerquist

Universal Basic Income (UBI) is the hugely ambitious policy of granting a small income to every person, unconditionally as a right of citizenship. Usually, a "full" UBI is considered to be enough to meet basic needs, while anything less is a "partial" UBI (USBIG Network 2011). In the post–financial crisis days of austerity, cutbacks, and retrenchment, it might seem that such a policy is too ambitious to be worth discussing in the current political climate, especially in the United States. But this chapter will argue that UBI is (and should be) an important part of the political dialogue today.

The first section defines the concept of UBI more thoroughly and shows how it differs from traditional welfare policies. The second section gives a brief history of the idea right up to the present, showing that UBI is an important part of the current debate in many parts of the world and that increasing evidence in its favor is being found.

Portions of this chapter are adapted from articles in the U.S. Basic Income Guarantee Network Newsletter, available online at http://www.usbig.net/newsletters.php. Used by permission.

The third section discusses the inherent importance of UBI. The final section discusses how ambitious policies such as UBI can overcome the hostility of the current political climate in industrialized countries, focusing on the United States as an example.

WHAT IS UBI, AND WHAT MAKES IT DISTINCT FROM TRADITIONAL WELFARE?

UBI is one of a family of policies designed to ensure that everyone has a small income large enough to meet their most basic needs for any reason. It grants this income to every citizen, and then taxes them on their income or their assets or their purchases. UBI has been widely discussed in academic literature, especially in the fields of philosophy, sociology, economics, and political science. Many philosophers have argued that UBI is an essential tool for building a just society (Van Parijs 1992, 1995, 2001; Reeve and Williams 2003; Standing 2002; Goodin 1985; Atkinson 1995).

Table 32.1 shows how the system works with a UBI of $6,000 per person per year and a tax rate at 33.33 percent (one-third). It shows the relationship between an individual's private and total income at eight selected levels of income, chosen to show the effects of UBI on people at very different levels of income. A person with no private income would receive a grant of $6,000, making their total income $6,000. Someone with a private income of $3,000 would pay $1,000 in taxes and receive the $6,000 grant for a total income of $8,000.

The "break even" level occurs at $18,000 of private income. The individual pays $6,000 in taxes and receives $6,000 in the grant. The two balance each other out, and the person is neither a net recipient nor a net taxpayer. Beyond this level of income, the amount of taxes people pay becomes larger than their grant so they are a net taxpayer. For example, a person with an income of $30,000 of private income pays $10,000 in taxes and receives a $6,000 grant for a total after-tax/after-transfer income of $26,000 per year.

Table 32.1 is written for an individual. Most UBI proposals call for giving the same amount of money to every individual regardless of age or family status. However, it is important to note that it is cheaper for families to live together than it is for single people to live on their own. For this reason, a UBI set at a level that will barely get a single person out of poverty will be very generous to families and therefore very expensive. A UBI set at a level just enough to get a family (of a given

Table 32.1
Private Income, Grant Received, Total Income, Taxes Paid under UBI with a Grant Level of $6,000 and a Tax Rate of 33.33 Percent

1	2	3	4
Private Income	Grant Received	Total Income	Taxes Paid
0	6,000	6,000	0
3,000	6,000	8,000	1,000
6,000	6,000	10,000	2,000
12,000	6,000	14,000	4,000
18,000	6,000	18,000	6,000
30,000	6,000	26,000	10,000
60,000	6,000	46,000	20,000
300,000	6,000	206,000	100,000

size) out of poverty will cost much less, but it will not get all single people (or all smaller families) out of poverty. For this reason, some UBI proposals call for a smaller level of UBI for children (Lerner, Clark, and Needham 1999). This trade-off can be seen in the example I gave previously: $6,000 is very meager for a single person, but if every man, woman, and child were eligible, it would amount to the very substantial sum of $30,000 per year for a family of five. The problem of family size is one of the policy choices society needs to make when implementing UBI.

UBI has a very different approach than any traditional welfare system. Although welfare states in the industrialized world vary significantly in the breadth and depth of their coverage, they all employ some version of the categorical approach to poverty. That is, they have different programs to maintain the income of people who fit into different categories of need. Often they will have one program for the unemployed, one for the short-term disabled, one for the long-term disabled, one for the elderly, one for single parents with children, another for people with low skills, and so on (Widerquist and Lewis 2009).

UBI can replace many or all programs designed to support someone's income with one program ensuring that everyone's income will be sufficient to meet his or her basic needs. UBI does not replace programs designed to meet special needs. It does not replace, for example, a program to give free wheelchairs to people who are unable to walk. Nor does it replace public schools, public health care, public streets, or public garbage removal. But it does get rid of categories to determine whether and how much income assistance a person is eligible for.

The ideal of the categorical welfare system is that, if it could work perfectly, it could eliminate poverty without giving anyone reason to work less. If the state had perfect information, it would separate all those who can and should work from all those who cannot or should not be expected to work. For those who can work, the state would find some way to assure that a sufficient number of good jobs are available and provide a specifically tailored program for everyone who can work: old-age pensions, disability, assistance to needy caregivers, and so on. If all these programs worked perfectly, the state could eliminate poverty without creating any work disincentive. But the practice is far from perfection.

People do not fit neatly into categories. A few people absolutely cannot work; many more sit along a continuum from fully able to mostly unable to work. Many people have permanent but intermittent conditions making them sometimes able and sometimes unable to work. Governments create categories by arbitrarily drawing a line and then spend a great deal of money determining on what side of the line a person falls. Sometimes those who can work only with great difficulty fail to qualify.

Others who qualify for programs fall into the poverty trap. Recipients of categorical programs face a very large effective "marginal tax rate." That is, the amount they lose in benefits for each dollar they earn in private income is very high—sometimes greater than 100 percent. They also risk a permanent loss of eligibility if they are unable to keep the job or if the job turns out not to be worth keeping. The traditional welfare state also has difficulty with the fully employable. No government has yet figured out how to ensure permanent, above-poverty-wage employment for everyone who is willing to work. Some people who cannot find jobs are ineligible for unemployment insurance. Those who are eligible for unemployment insurance often face their own poverty trap, in which it is risky to take a job for fear of losing eligibility.

Categorical welfare systems face a trade-off. The more generous systems accept a significant poverty trap in which a significant portion of the population remains more or less permanently on assistance. The less generous systems accept weak coverage. For example, the United States has tacitly or explicitly accepted that at any given time about 10 percent of its population lives in poverty (U.S. Bureau of the Census 2011).

The structure of the UBI system eliminates the poverty trap. Although anyone can choose to live without working, they have nothing to lose by taking a job. In the example shown in Table 32.1, for every $3 a person earns privately, they keep $2. Consider a person living entirely off the $6,000 per year grant. Suppose they have the opportunity to take a $12,000 per year job. They would see their total income rise by $8,000 to $14,000 per year, a very substantial increase.

Some policies within current welfare systems incorporate elements of UBI model. The food stamp program (now officially called Supplemental Nutrition Assistance Program or SNAP) functions almost like a cash grant (although with a paternalistic twist). Social Security, although contributory, functions somewhat like a UBI for retired persons. The Earned Income Tax Credit, which has existed in the United States since 1974, is in one sense a "negative tax" (in which, like UBI, the government pays the individual instead of the other way around), but it does not give any money to people who have no private income. Thus it is only for people who fit into the category of low-wage worker (Widerquist and Sheahen forthcoming). One problem with the Earned Income Tax Credit is that once employers know that their employees are eligible for it, they may be able to reduce wages (Bouquin 2005). Other refundable tax credits, such as the Additional Child Tax Credit, also have this similarity to UBI.

UBI is very different from another proposal discussed in this book: the guaranteed job or the employer of last resort. Under this proposal the government gives a job at a fixed wage rate to anyone who is able to work but either unable to find or unwilling to take a private sector job. The guaranteed job assures that a job is available for everyone who is willing and able to take one in the public sector. UBI assures that everyone has an income whether or not they are willing and able to take a job in either the private or the public sector. The guaranteed job could only be a part of the categorical system, and the state would still have the problem of separating those who can and cannot be expected to work (Widerquist and Lewis 2009). It would also face a great deal of overhead cost to provide the material and supervision for everyone who signed up for the job guaranteed by the government.

UBI does not force anyone to work. It does not use the threat of economic destitution to get people to accept unappealing jobs. It ensures that everyone has enough to meet their basic needs without judging them or making them satisfy some conditions to prove their worth. But, as I have argued, it still has a great deal of room for work incentives. The very idea of UBI is simply that income does not have to start at zero. People can have a small income sufficient to cover their basic needs, and still have plenty of reasons to take jobs that will give them access to the luxuries that the market system makes available.

THE HISTORY OF AND CURRENT DEBATE OVER UBI

UBI, or something like it, has been discussed for centuries. Thomas Paine (1797) argued for a large onetime grant and a basic pension. Lesser-known figures, such as Thomas Spence and Joseph Charlier, laid out the first proposals that more fully fit the definition of UBI (USBIG Network 2011).

Large numbers of intellectuals began discussing UBI under various names in the 20th century. Under the name of "the guaranteed income," it seemed to appear out of nowhere onto the mainstream political agenda in the United States in the mid-1960s, because it was brought to the mainstream agenda from three different sources. President Johnson had recently declared war on poverty, and many policy makers saw UBI as an important alternative. Welfare activists, including Martin Luther King Jr., were pushing for it. Many prominent economists with left and right political leanings, including F. A. Hayek, Milton Friedman, Herbert Simon, James Tobin, and John Kenneth Galbraith, endorsed either UBI or a very closely related idea called "the negative income tax" (NIT) (Widerquist and Sheahen forthcoming).

The discussion got so strong that in 1972, both major-party presidential candidates endorsed versions of it. In 1971, President Richard Nixon proposed an arguably watered-down version called the Family Assistance Plan, which lost very narrowly in Congress. Between 1968 and 1980 the United States and Canada conducted five negative income tax experiments. Although popular perception of the experiments was largely negative, researchers were pleased to find small, tolerable negative effects on labor market participation, and a great improvement in well-being among recipients (Widerquist and Sheahen forthcoming; Widerquist 2005).

Several important offshoots of UBI were introduced at the time including food stamps and the Earned Income Tax Credit (Widerquist and Sheahen forthcoming). Perhaps the most important offshoot of the guaranteed-income discussion in the United States happened not at the federal but at the state level. The state of Alaska introduced the world's first UBI (if a partial and variable one) in 1982 (Widerquist and Howard 2012a). Since then, every man, woman, and child in Alaska has received a small yearly dividend financed by the returns on the Alaska Permanent Fund, the state's savings account for its oil revenues. This dividend has no conditions except that they maintain residency in the state and reapply each year. It varies each year depending on the returns to the Alaska Permanent Fund. It reached a high of $2,069 in 2008—the same year that the state decided to supplement the dividend with an additional $1,200 from the state's budget surplus, making a total dividend of $3,269, or more than $13,000 for a family of four. More often the dividend has been in the neighborhood of $1,000 to $1,500 per person per year, or about $4,000–$6,000 for a family of four (Widerquist and Howard 2012a).

The dividend has helped Alaska attain the lowest poverty and the lowest economic inequality of all 50 states, and it is enormously popular, receiving 83 percent support in a 1998 referendum. Alaska is the only place in the world with a resource fund and dividend at this time, but the success of the program makes it worthy of imitation. Michael W. Howard and I are coediting two books discussing how to do so (Widerquist and Howard, 2012a and 2012b).

Discussion of UBI dropped off at the federal level in the United States in the late 1970s as the movement to improve the U.S. welfare system was replaced by a movement to reduce or eliminate U.S. welfare programs. But the discussion quickly picked up in other parts of the world. UBI became a major topic of discussion in the academic literature, especially in the fields of philosophy, sociology, and political theory since the 1980s. In 1986, a group of academic researchers founded the Basic Income European Network (http://www.basicincome.org). The Network has held conferences every two years ever since. In 2004 it expanded to become the Basic Income Earth Network (http://www.basicincome.org). It now has 18 affiliates around the world, including one in the United States (http://www.usbig.net).

UBI has made an impact on political agendas in surprising places around the world. It has developed considerable grassroots support in postapartheid South Africa and Namibia. Four of the five major parties in Germany have factions supporting UBI. Pilot projects are taking place in India and Namibia. Iran and Mongolia are beginning to implement Alaska-style UBIs (Basic Income Earth Network 2011).

In the last few years, cash transfers have been put into place in many lesser-developed countries. For example, Brazil's cash transfer program, the Bolsa Familia, was introduced in 2005 with an explicit statement that it was the first step toward phasing in a true UBI (with the next steps to be determined later). Although all of these programs have at least some conditions attached and none is strictly based on UBI, they are providing evidence to support the UBI model. In most cases, it seems to be the cash—not the conditions—that is helping improve the lives of the people affected (Standing 2011; Hanlon, Barrientos, and Hulme 2010).

Another surprising place where UBI has made an appearance is in the debate over global warming. Two popular approaches to global warming (tax-and-dividend and cap-and-dividend) involve a small UBI. The differences between these two approaches are not important for the discussion here. Both involve the principle in which the polluter pays for the right to pollute—to emit carbon—and both redistribute the revenue from the sale of pollution rights as an equal-sized dividend for all citizens (Howard forthcoming; Barnes 2007). Therefore people who pay more in pollution taxes than they receive in the dividend are above-average polluters. People who receive more in the dividend than they pay (directly or indirectly) in pollution taxes are below-average polluters. Their receipt of payment is both a reward for polluting less and compensation for the pollution that everyone else is doing.

WHY UBI IS ALWAYS WORTH TALKING ABOUT

The recent history of UBI, recounted earlier, shows both that there is new evidence in its favor and that it is growing in importance in the world debate over social policy. But in this section, I want to talk about the direct reasons it is relevant, the reasons to support it.

The main reason to support UBI is that it is time to get serious about *the elimination* of poverty. Most, if not all, the countries of the world today have the technical capacity to eliminate poverty and economic destitution. The more industrialized countries of the world have had this capacity for decades, and I believe it is now possible on a worldwide basis. In a world with so much wealth, we must no longer force people to live with so much poverty, fear, and economic uncertainty. We need to reach a state of economic maturity in which any poverty in our midst is unacceptable.

If we are ready to talk about the *elimination* of poverty, UBI is the one policy that can do it best. Because UBI is universal and unconditional, it has no cracks to fall through. It puts a floor beneath everyone's income. If that floor is above the poverty line, poverty is eliminated universally.

UBI is not such a radical move, although it might have radical effects. It streamlines and strengthens the welfare system to make it more effective and more comprehensive. Most nations of the world are already spending a substantial amount of money on poverty relief, but too much of that money is going to overhead costs, supervision of the poor, the creation of hoops for the poor to jump through to prove they are worthy, and so on.

Economic destitution is the biggest threat to freedom in the democratic nations of the world today. To be destitute is to be unfree. Economically destitute people are unfree to sleep undisturbed, unfree to urinate, unfree to wash themselves, and unfree to use the resources of the world to meet their own needs. The destitute are unfree in the most liberal, negative sense of the word (Waldron 1993, 309–38). They are not *unable* to use the resources of the world to meet their needs, they are *unfree* to do so, because our government enforces a property rights regime that ensures someone will interfere with them if they try to do it.

Poverty is not a fact of nature. Poverty is the result of the way our societies have chosen to distribute property rights to natural resources. For hundreds of thousands of years (perhaps for millions of years), no one interfered with our ancestors as they used the resources of the world to meet their needs. No one failed to wash because they were too lazy to find a stream. No one urinated in a common thoroughfare because they were too lazy to find a secluded place to do so. Everyone was free to hunt and gather and make their camp for the night as they pleased. No one had to follow the orders of a boss to earn the right to make their living. Our hunter-gatherer ancestors were not rich, but they were not poor as we know it today (Widerquist 2010b). Our laws today make it illegal for people to satisfy the most natural and simple bodily needs, and our laws make it such a fact of life that we can believably pretend that it is all their own fault. There are billions of people today who are more poorly nourished than their hunter-gatherer ancestors (Widerquist 2010b). It cannot be simply their own fault. Poverty and economic destitution are created by the way in which we have chosen to distribute natural resources; we can just as easily choose to create a system that eliminates poverty.

Another advantage of UBI is that it can be used as a cushion for the increasingly unstable economy. The world economy experiences both financial instability and the instability of a constantly changing manufacturing base. It might be desirable to eliminate financial instability, but we do not seem to be on the verge of figuring how to do so, and we can expect financial instability to be with us for a while. The instability created by a changing manufacturing base is not necessarily something that we should want to eliminate. If the theory of creative destruction has any truth to it, the overall health of the economy requires that new and better industries drive others out of business (Schumpeter 1947; Aghion and Howitt 1992). But the instability of creative destruction has a human cost as people lose their jobs and need to find a place in a new and different economy.

The simplicity of UBI system makes it better able to react to all kinds of economic instability. Unlike the traditional, categorical welfare system, a UBI-based system provides a cushion for everyone no matter what the reason that they might be without income. Under UBI, we do not need to recognize some new category of need that the economic system may have created, because we have ensured people against all forms of economic need.

The previous section demonstrated that UBI has a very good work incentive built into the system, but the most common work-based objection to UBI is not so much about work incentives as it is about a moral obligation to work. The argument I have in mind goes as follows. UBI is something for nothing, which is unacceptable. People have a moral obligation to work. Lazy people who will not work should not be rewarded with anything. Therefore any social benefits should be conditional on at least the willingness to accept employment. Even if UBI has better work incentives than conditional welfare programs, we must reject it because it allows some able people to receive something for nothing and shirk their obligation to work. I believe this is a common argument in everyday political discourse, and versions of it have appeared in the philosophical criticism of UBI (Elster 1986; White 1997, 2000, 2003; Van Donselaar 2008).

This argument has several problems. I will discuss two of them. The first problem with it is that UBI cannot be accurately characterized as something for nothing. All societies impose many rules on every individual. Consider the preceding discussion of homelessness. Why cannot homeless people build their own shelter and their own latrine? Why cannot they drink out of a clean river? Why cannot they hunt, gather, or plant and harvest their own food? They cannot do these things because the state has made rules saying they do not have the right to do these things. The state has imposed rules saying that almost all the resources of the Earth belong to someone else. Those of us who benefit from the rules by which our society distributes ownership of the Earth's natural resource benefit every day from the state's interference with the propertyless, and we pay them no compensation. A state *without* UBI is the state that has something for nothing (Widerquist 1999).

UBI is and should be seen not as something for nothing but as the just compensation for all the rules of property and property regulations society imposes on individuals. Democracies, hopefully, make these rules with the consent of the majority. But even the best democracies cannot obtain everyone's consent. No government can function unless it imposes its rules on the willing and unwilling alike. Governments therefore have a responsibility to make sure that their rules are not an undue burden on anyone.

Governments can live up to this responsibility by applying a simple principle in which each person pays for the parts of the Earth he or she uses and receives a share of the payment for the parts other people use. In a small way this principle is embedded in the Alaska dividend and in the tax-and-dividend approach to global warming. Imagine a tax-and-dividend system being applied not just to greenhouse gas emissions but to all forms of resource use: all pollution, all privately held land, all mining and drilling rights, and so on. Some estimates show that a very large UBI could be financed this way (Flomenhoft forthcoming), but what is important here is the moral impact of UBI financed by this method.

One person's assertion of ownership of some of the Earth's resources necessarily involves interference with anything anyone else might want to do with those resources. Under a resource-tax-financed UBI, those who (directly or indirectly) pay more in resource taxes than they receive in the UBI are paying for the privilege of enjoying more resources than the average person is able. They are paying compensation for the interference they impose on everyone else. Those who receive more in UBI than they pay in resource taxes are being compensated for having less access to the Earth's natural resources than everyone else. UBI is most distinctly *not* something for nothing. Furthermore, those who pay more than they receive do so voluntarily and willingly. They obviously think it is worthwhile to pay what they pay for resources they hold or they would choose to hold fewer resources and become a net recipient.

The second problem with the work-based argument against UBI is that it conflates two different senses of the word "work"—one that means toil and one that means employment. In the first sense "work" simply means to work whether it is for one's own or for someone else's benefit. In the second sense "work" means to *work for* someone else— such as a client or a boss. Anyone with access to resources can meet their needs by working only for themselves or with others of their choosing.

But people without access to resources have no other choice but to work for someone else, and they have to work for at least one member of the group whose control over resources makes it impossible for the propertyless to work only for themselves (Widerquist 2006, 2010a).

Working for someone else entails the acceptance of rules, terms, conditions, and subordination, all of which are things that a reasonable person might object to. There is nothing wrong with working for someone else, as long as one *chooses* to do so. But because we interfere with people by denying them access to resources until they work for someone who has some control over resources, we interfere with their ability to refuse. We force them, not to work, but to *work for* at least one member of a particular group of people (Widerquist 2006, 2010a).

We can create an economy based on truly voluntary trade and voluntary participation by applying the principle described earlier in which each person pays for the parts of the Earth they use and receives a share of the payment for the parts other people use. With a sufficient UBI to draw on, each person has the power to decide for him or herself whether the offers in the job market are good to deserve his or her participation. Nothing protects a person better than the power to refuse. This power will protect not only the poor and marginal but all of us.

UBI AND THE CURRENT POLITICAL CLIMATE

The political climate in many Western industrialized countries, most particularly the United States, has become increasingly hostile to UBI. But it is not only cash assistance to the poor or progressive that appears nonviable in the current U.S. political climate. The U.S. government today lacks the ability to pursue any ambitious strategy.

The United States was once a very ambitious country: the New Deal of the 1930s, the G.I. Bill and the Manhattan Project of the 1940s, the interstate highway system of the 1950s, the space program and the Great Society of 1960s were all hugely ambitious goals pursued with ambitious strategies. More than a century ago, when an earthquake hit San Francisco or a fire hit Chicago, we rebuilt those cities better than ever within a couple years. Today, six years after the engineering failure that caused the flood in New Orleans, large parts of the city lie vacant while the government struggles to get the levees back only to where they were before they failed.

The only goal the U.S. government has pursued with any ambition in the last 30 years has been tax cuts for the most privileged Americans, but doing so has hampered the government's ability to pursue any other goals it has taken on. Under the Bush administration, the U.S. government took on the enormous goals of invading and occupying two foreign nations. But the government has pursued those goals with ambitionless strategy: using long-range missiles in the air and bribes for warlords on the ground, rather than committing resources to stabilize and rebuild those countries. Under the Obama administration, the U.S. government has taken on the ambitious goal of establishing universal health care coverage, but it plans to do so by mandating that individuals buy insurance, often from for-profit companies. Whether these goals are good or bad, the ambitiousness of the strategy does not match the size of the goal. Meanwhile, we do not even have the ambition to properly maintain the public transportation systems, highways, and other infrastructure left to us by earlier generations. Western European countries, while not as obsessed with downsizing government as the United States, are also focusing on austerity and cutbacks.

And in this climate, UBI supporters want to talk about this hugely ambitious strategy to eliminate poverty with an unconditional payment to all citizens. How can this be worth talking about here and now?

One important reason to keep pushing for a big ambitious change is that we must not mistake a current political mood for the permanent political reality. The political mood changes for the better and for the worse, and it can change abruptly and unexpectedly. In the 1850s, no one, not even Abraham Lincoln himself, had a good reason to believe that the United States was within 10 years of outlawing slavery. In the 1920s, no one, not even Franklin Roosevelt himself, had a good reason to believe that the United States was within 10 years of introducing old-age pensions, unemployment insurance, a national minimum wage, and so on.

The political mood is only a mood. It changes abruptly because most people do not hold firm convictions about politics. True believers on all sides of any political issue might dominate the debate, but most people's political positions are tentative and subject to change. I cannot predict when and how the political mood will change, but I know that major change requires people to be ready with well-thought-out ideas to take us in another direction. They have to press for it. They need to talk about UBI now to make it viable later.

The outpouring of enthusiasm for the vague ideas of "change" and "hope" in the 2008 election indicates frustration with the bipartisan lack of ambition that continues to handicap the U.S. government. But so far, people have not seen enough change to give them hope.

I wish I could say with assurance that we are on the verge of a major shift in political mood in the direction of UBI. I cannot say that. I cannot see the future, and neither can those people who confidently pretend they can. But I can point to indicators that things are moving in the direction of UBI and small things we can do here and now to push things in that direction.

As I see it, there are four parts to the UBI model: (1) it is in-cash; (2) it is enough to meet a person's needs; (3) it is universal; and (4) it is understood as a human right or a right of citizenship. Anything that establishes even one element of this model moves in the direction of UBI.

Looked at in this way, the United States is not as far away as it might appear. Some of the most successful and popular elements in U.S. social policy are cash based: refundable tax credits, unemployment insurance, Social Security, Supplemental Nutrition Assistance Program, Supplemental Security Income, and so on. Social Security—as imperfectly as it works—is clearly motivated by the belief that all people ought to have a financially secure retirement. Despite all the shortcomings of the health care reform law, it helps to establish the idea that all people should have access to health care.

The public school system is an enormous in-kind universal benefit that is not even limited to citizens. Although the system has great inequities, the ideal of universal education is strong. A fully market-based educational system would offer no more than the faith that all parents will somehow find a way to purchase adequate education for their children. It is not such a big change in mind-set to go from the realization that we cannot assume every parent can provide an adequate education for their children to the realization that we cannot assume every parent can provide adequate food, shelter, and clothing for their children.

As I have shown herein, looking beyond U.S. federal government policies there is an increasing trend worldwide toward the use of cash benefits. Alaska's Permanent Fund Dividend, Mexico's conditional cash transfer program, Brazil's Bolsa Familia, and South Africa's pension system are just a few examples of how well cash grants can work and how popular they can be.

The current recession has reminded many Americans that they are not so different from people in need. Unemployment did not rise from

3 to 10 percent because people suddenly became lazy; the foreclosure epidemic was not caused by a sudden increase in the number of dead-beats. The government has put most of its effort into bailing out the economy from the top down, but there is growing belief that we should be aiming our policy from the bottom up instead.

Movement of the political climate toward a UBI model requires people on the side of both big, ambitious change and small, incremental changes in the direction of UBI. There are many opportunities to nudge policy in the direction of a universalistic, rights-based, or cash-based strategies to meet human needs. Efforts to expand refundable tax credits and the cap-and-dividend approach to global warming are two small steps in that direction that are under serious consideration in the United States, and a big ambitious move toward a full UBI is under serious discussion in Germany and several other countries.

UBI has come and gone and come again to the political agenda in many countries, but as we see, it continues to gain ground slowly and fitfully around the world. The evidence for its effectiveness is mounting. It is far from the agenda in the countries that are responding to the worldwide recession with new "austerity" programs, but it is not far from the agenda in all countries and it is growing in importance in many countries in both the developed and developing world.

Austerity was how most nations first responded to the Great Depression, and it did not work out well then. Most nations did not get out of the Depression until they got the ambition to spend some money. Some had better ideas of what to spend it on than others. But austerity is not the answer to recession. UBI is emerging as a well-thought-out alternative when nations regain their ambition.

BIBLIOGRAPHY

Aghion, Philippe and Peter Howitt. 1992. "A Model of Growth through Creative Destruction." *Econometrica* 60: 323–51

Atkinson, A. 1995. *Public Economics in Action: The Basic Income/Flat Tax Proposal.* Oxford: Clarendon Press.

Barnes, Peter. 2007. *Carbon Capping: A Citizen's Guide.* Minneapolis: Tomales Bay Institute.

Basic Income Earth Network. 2011. *Basic Income News.* Accessed August 13, 2011.

Bouquin, Stephen. 2005. "Social Minima in Europe: The Risks of Cumulating Income-Sources." In *The Ethics and Economics of the Basic Income Guarantee.* Edited by Karl Widerquist, Michael Anthony Lewis, and Steven Pressman, 212–32. Basingstoke, UK: Ashgate.

Elster, Jan. 1986. "Comment on Van der Veen and Van Parijs." *Theory and Society* 15: 709–21.

Flomenhoft, Gary. Forthcoming. "Applying the Alaska Model in a Resource-Poor State: The Example of Vermont." In *Exporting the Alaska Model: How the Permanent Fund Dividend Can Be Adapted as a Reform Model for the World*. Edited by Karl Widerquist and Michael W. Howard. New York: Palgrave Macmillan.

Goodin, R. E. 1985. *Protecting the Vulnerable*. Chicago: University of Chicago Press.

Hanlon, Joseph, Armando Barrientos, and David Hulme. 2010. *Just Give Money to the Poor: The Development Revolution from the Global South*. Sterling, VA: Kumarian Press.

Howard, Michael W. Forthcoming. "A Cap on Carbon and a Basic Income: A Defensible Combination in the United States?" In *Exporting the Alaska Model: How the Permanent Fund Dividend Can Be Adapted as a Reform Model for the World*. Edited by Karl Widerquist and Michael W. Howard. New York: Palgrave Macmillan.

Lerner, Sally C., Charles Michael Andres Clark, and W. Robert Needham. 1999. *Basic Income: Economic Security for All Canadians*. Toronto: Between the Lines.

Paine, Thomas. 1797. *Agrarian Justice*. Published online by the School of Cooperative Individualism. Accessed August 13, 2011.

Reeve, A. and A. Williams. 2003. *Real Libertarianism Assessed: Political Theory after Van Parijs*. Basingstoke, UK: Palgrave Macmillan.

Russell, Bertrand. 1919. *Proposed Roads to Freedom: Socialism, Anarchism and Syndicalism*. New York: Henry Holt and Company. Reprinted online by Digital Text International, August 13, 2011.

Schumpeter, Joseph A. 1947 [1994]. *Capitalism, Socialism and Democracy*, Fifth Edition. New York: Routledge.

Standing, Guy. 2002. *Beyond the New Paternalism: Basic Security as a Right*. New York: Verso.

Standing, Guy. 2011. "How Cash Transfers Promote Work and Economic Security." In *Poor Poverty: The Impoverishment of Analysis, Measurement and Policies*. Edited by J. K. Sundaram and A. Chowdhury, 197–221. New York: Bloomsbury Academic.

USBIG Network, The. 2011. "What Is the Basic Income Guarantee?" The U.S. Basic Income Guarantee Network Website. Accessed August 13, 2011.

U.S. Bureau of the Census. 2011. "Poverty Status, by Type of Family, Presence of Related Children, Race and Hispanic Origin." *Current Population Survey, Annual Social and Economic Supplements*. Accessed August 13, 2011.

van Donselaar, Gijs. 2008. *The Right to Exploit: Parasitism, Scarcity, Basic Income*. Oxford: Oxford University Press.

van Parijs, Philippe (editor). 1992. *Arguing for Basic Income: Ethical Foundations for a Radical Reform*. New York: Verso.

van Parijs, Philippe. 1995. *Real Freedom for All: What (If Anything) Can Justify Capitalism?* Oxford: Oxford University Press.

van Parijs, Philippe. 2001. *What's Wrong with a Free Lunch?* Boston: Beacon Press.

Waldron, Jeremy. 1993. *Liberal Rights*. Cambridge: Cambridge University Press.

White, Stuart. 1997. "Liberal Equality, Exploitation, and the Case for an Unconditional Basic Income." *Political Studies* 45: 312–26.

White, Stuart. 2000. "Social Rights and the Social Contract: Political Theory and the New Welfare Politics." *British Journal of Political Science* 30: 507–32.

White, Stuart. 2003. *The Civic Minimum*. Oxford: Oxford University Press.

Widerquist, Karl. 1999. "Reciprocity and the Guaranteed Income." *Politics and Society* 33: 386–401.

Widerquist, Karl. 2005. "A Failure to Communicate: What (If Anything) Can We Learn from the Negative Income Tax Experiments?" *The Journal of Socio-Economics* 34: 49–81.

Widerquist, Karl. 2006. Property and the Power to Say No: A Freedom-Based Argument for Basic Income. Doctoral Dissertation. The University of Oxford.

Widerquist, Karl. 2010a. "The Physical Basis of Voluntary Trade." *Human Rights Review* 11: 83–103.

Widerquist, Karl. 2010b. "What Does Prehistoric Anthropology Have to Do with Modern Political Philosophy? Evidence of Five False Claims." USBIG Discussion Paper no. 206.

Widerquist, Karl and Michael W. Howard. 2012a. *Examining the Alaska Model: Is the Permanent Fund Dividend Ready for Export?* New York: Palgrave Macmillan.

Widerquist, Karl and Michael W. Howard. 2012b. *Exporting the Alaska Model: How the Permanent Fund Dividend Can Be Adapted as a Reform Model for the World.* New York: Palgrave Macmillan.

Widerquist, Karl and Michael A. Lewis. 2009. "The Basic Income Guarantee and the Goals of Equality, Efficiency, and Environmentalism." In *Environment and Employment: A Reconciliation*. Edited by Philip Lawn, 163–83. London: Routledge.

Widerquist, Karl and Allan Sheahen. Forthcoming. "The Basic Income Guarantee in the United States: Past Experience, Current Proposals." In *Horizons of Reform: Basic Income Around the World*. Edited by Carole Pateman and Matthew Murray. New York: Palgrave Macmillan.

About the Editor and Contributors

EDITOR

Robert S. Rycroft, PhD, is professor of economics and chair of the Economics Department at the University of Mary Washington in Fredericksburg, Virginia. He received his BA in economics from the College of William and Mary and his PhD in economics from the University of Maryland–College Park. Dr. Rycroft teaches classes in labor economics, the economics of poverty, inequality, mobility and discrimination, and philanthropy and nonprofit organizations. He is the author of *The Economics of Inequality, Discrimination, Poverty and Mobility* (2009).

CONTRIBUTORS

Laura Argys, PhD, is a labor economist and demographer whose research examines the effect of social, education, and health policy on the well-being of children and families. Her published work includes studies of the impact of child support and welfare policies on outcomes for children in nonintact families, the impact of peers and policy on adolescent risky behaviors, and the impact of family structure on health. She is a professor of economics and currently serves as associate dean for research in the College of Liberal Arts and Sciences at the University of Colorado Denver. She is a research fellow at IZA and an IBS affiliate of the Population Center at the University of Colorado Boulder.

Susan Averett, PhD, is the Charles A. Dana professor of economics at Lafayette College. She is the author of dozens of academic articles and book chapters. Her research covers a wide array of topics in both labor and health economics. Current research projects include adolescent risky behavior, the effect of marriage on health, and the causes and consequences of obesity. She is the coauthor with Saul Hoffman of the textbook *Women in the Economy: Family, Work and* Pay, and she is the coeditor with Edward Gamber of the *Eastern Economic Journal*. She serves on the board of the Committee on the Status of Women in the Economics Profession.

Mary Ellen Benedict, PhD, is a distinguished teaching professor at Bowling Green State University. She received her PhD from the Heinz College at Carnegie Mellon University in 1991 and has been with BGSU for the past 20 years. Dr. Benedict has published in the fields of economics education, unionization in higher education, wage differentials, and income inequality. She also has won university and national teaching and advising awards for her work with undergraduate and graduate students and for her research in the labor relations field.

Keith Gunnar Bentele, PhD, is an assistant professor of sociology at the University of Massachusetts in Boston. His dissertation research, completed at the University of Arizona, examines the causes of rising earnings inequality in the United States over the past three decades. In addition to research on inequality, poverty, and social welfare programs, he is interested in the processes influencing legislative outcomes in a variety of policy areas. Such research involves special attention to the impact of partisanship, ideology, and social movements on state policies. Currently, he is working on a project examining the performance of U.S. safety net programs during the 2007–9 recession and the disparate impacts and experiences of the recession along racial lines.

Barbara R. Bergmann (PhD, Harvard) is professor emerita of economics at American University and the University of Maryland. Her special interests include social policy, the economics of race and gender, the computer simulation of economic systems, and the state of economic science. Her books on social issues include *The Economic Emergence of Women*, *In Defense of Affirmative Action*, *Saving Our*

Children from Poverty: What the United States Can Learn from France, Is Social Security Broke?: A Cartoon Guide to the Issues, and *America's Child Care Problem: The Way Out* (with Suzanne Helburn). Her work on computer simulation includes *A Microsimulated Transactions Model of the United States Economy* (with Robert Bennett), and on economic science includes "The State of Economics: Needs Lots of Work," *Annals of the American Academy of Political and Social Science* 600 (July 2005). She has served as president of the American Association of University Professors, the Society for the Advancement of Socio-Economics, the International Association for Feminist Economics, and the Eastern Economic Association.

David T. Burkam, PhD, is a researcher and lecturer at the University of Michigan, based primarily in the Residential College's social theory and practice program. He teaches research methods and design, program evaluation, freshman writing, quantitative reasoning, social science thinking, sociology of education, and a course on love. He is the author of many articles and reports, and his research interests include equity issues in kindergarten and early schooling, gender equity in math and science, high school curriculum structure, and measurement issues in student course taking and achievement. He is the coauthor (with colleague Valerie Lee) of *Inequality at the Starting Gate* (2002), an exploration of social background differences in achievement as children begin school. He earned a BA degree in philosophy and mathematics from Wittenberg University and an MS in mathematics and a PhD in education from the University of Michigan.

Miles Corak, PhD, is a full professor of economics with the Graduate School of Public and International Affairs at the University of Ottawa. His research involves comparisons across countries, and focuses on labor markets and social policy. His publications have addressed child poverty, access to university education, social and economic mobility, and unemployment, and he is currently working on issues dealing with the socioeconomic status of immigrants and children of immigrants. Before joining the University of Ottawa, Dr. Corak was a member of the senior management at Statistics Canada, Canada's national statistical agency. He has also been a visiting researcher with the UNICEF Innocenti Research Centre in Florence, Italy, with the Centre for Longitudinal Studies at the University of London, and with the Office of Population Research at Princeton University.

Sarah Dewees, PhD, is the senior director of research, policy, and asset-building programs at First Nations Development Institute, a national nonprofit organization that works with Indian nations to promote economic development in Indian reservations. She is responsible for the coordination of all research and evaluation activities at First Nations Development Institute in order to further the understanding of asset-based community development in Native communities. Sarah joined the staff in 2002 from a position as a research project manager at the Center for Civil Society Studies at Johns Hopkins University. She worked previously at the Rural Policy Research Institute on issues related to rural development and welfare reform. She has worked in both applied and academic research settings and has conducted research on a range of issues including rural community economic development, rural education, and welfare reform. Her publications have appeared in the *Journal of the Community Development Society, Rural Sociology,* and *Sociological Practice.* Sarah received her PhD in rural sociology from the University of Kentucky in 1998, an MA in sociology from Ohio University in 1992, and a BA in government from Oberlin College in 1990.

Ethan Doetsch is a PhD candidate in the Department of Economics at the University of Utah. His research interests include African American economic history, the labor market outcomes of veterans, labor mobility in the early 20th-century United States, and the effects of early life conditions on economic outcomes. His dissertation, "Essays on Veteran Status, Race, and Labor Mobility," explores racial differences in the effect of World War I military service on occupational and geographic mobility.

Christine Exley, MA, is an economics PhD candidate at Stanford University. She holds a master's in economics from Stanford University and a bachelor's in mathematics and economics from University of Mary Washington. In recent years, she has helped to implement and study development initiatives in Honduras, involving microfinance and indoor air pollution. Currently, she works in both behavioral and development economics, with a focus on prosocial behavior.

Raymond Foxworth is currently a PhD candidate in the Department of Political Science at the University of Colorado at Boulder. Raymond also serves as a research and program officer for First Nations

Development Institute. Raymond is a citizen of the Navajo Nation, originally from Tuba City, Arizona.

Richard B. Freeman holds the Ascherman Chair in Economics at Harvard University and is currently serving as faculty codirector of the Labor and Worklife Program at the Harvard Law School. He directs the Science and Engineering Workforce Project at the National Bureau of Economic Research, and is senior research fellow in labor markets at the London School of Economics Centre for Economic Performance. Freeman received the Mincer Lifetime Achievement Prize from the Society of Labor Economics in 2006, and in 2007 he was awarded the IZA Prize in Labor Economics. In 2011 he was appointed Frances Perkins Fellow of the American Academy of Political and Social Science. Professor Freeman is a fellow of the American Academy of Arts and Science.

Sylvia Fuller is an associate professor in the Department of Sociology at the University of British Columbia. Her research investigates relationships among career dynamics, institutional and regulatory contexts, and patterns of inequality and economic insecurity. She has recently published in *The American Sociological Review, International Migration Research, Research in Social Stratification and Mobility,* and *Social Politics.* In 2009 she was awarded the Aurora Prize, which recognizes an outstanding new researcher in Canada in the Social Sciences or Humanities.

Mary Eschelbach Hansen is an associate professor and director of undergraduate studies in the Economics Department at American University in Washington, DC. Since earning her PhD from the University of Illinois at Urbana-Champaign in 1993, she has published widely in the fields of child welfare policy and economic history. Her research has been funded by the National Science Foundation, the National Institutes of Health, the Institute for New Economic Thinking, and the Alfred P. Sloan Foundation.

Kelsey Hilbrich is a sophomore at the University of Pennsylvania in the Huntsman Program in International Studies and Business, meaning that she is currently a candidate for a bachelor of arts in international studies and a bachelor of science in economics from the Wharton School in 2014. Kelsey is a member of the Wharton Dean's

Advisory Board at UPenn and also works as a research assistant in the Management Department. She hopes to focus her studies more specifically on finance and operations and information management, graduating with concentrations in both subjects. As a junior and senior in high school, Kelsey debated the benefits and costs of both public and private unionization, thereby piquing her continued interest in the subject matter.

John Hoag, PhD, is a professor and associate dean of the College of Business Administration at Bowling Green State University. He was previously chair of the Department of Economics at Bowling Green State University. He has a BA from Purdue University, an MA from Minnesota, and a PhD from the University of Kansas. He has authored or coauthored four books, the most recent, in 2012, *Intermediate Microeconomics*. Additionally, he has some 30 articles, monographs, cases, and book chapters to his credit. His current research interests include various aspects of teaching economics and entrepreneurship.

Shawn Humphrey, PhD, is an associate professor of economics at the University of Mary Washington. His research is focused on the role of violence in the process of economic development, including work on the link between a state's choice of how to organize its military forces and its constitutional design, the role of Article VI in England's Glorious Revolution, and collective action and the pattern of prestate conflict. He earned his PhD at Washington University in St. Louis.

Anna M. Jacob, MEd, is a PhD student in education policy and doctoral academy fellow in the Department of Education Reform at the University of Arkansas. She works as a graduate assistant with the School Choice Demonstration project, an educational research project based within the University of Arkansas's Department of Education Reform. She received her BEd from St, Patrick's College–Dublin, where she graduated with first-class honors, and her MEd through the University of Notre Dame's Alliance for Catholic Education program.

Joyce P. Jacobsen is Andrews Professor of Economics at Wesleyan University. She has an AB in economics from Harvard, an MSc in economics from LSE, and a PhD in economics from Stanford. She has numerous publications in labor economics, with a specialty in the economics of gender, including two textbooks (*The Economics of Gender*, and *Labor Markets and Employment Relationships* with coauthor Gil Skillman) and a reader, *Queer Economics* (with coeditor Adam Zeller).

Lane Kenworthy, PhD, is a professor of sociology and political science at the University of Arizona. He studies the causes and consequences of living standards, poverty, inequality, mobility, employment, economic growth, social policy, taxes, public opinion, and politics in the United States and other affluent countries. He is the author of *Progress for the Poor* (2011), *Jobs with Equality* (2008), *Egalitarian Capitalism* (2004), *In Search of National Economic Success* (1995), and articles in various social science journals. He also writes on these topics at his blog, *Consider the Evidence*.

ChangHwan Kim is assistant professor of sociology at the University of Kansas. His research interests include labor markets, income inequality, racial/ethnic relations, and statistics. His research appears in, among other outlets, *American Sociological Review*, *Annual Review of Sociology*, *Social Forces*, *Sociological Methods & Research*, and *Work & Occupations*.

Kimberley Kinsley, JD, is an assistant professor in the College of Business Department of Accounting and Management Information Systems at the University of Mary Washington (UMW) in Fredericksburg, Virginia. Prior to joining the UMW faculty in 2007, Kinsley worked as a solo law practitioner in Denver, a public defender in San Diego, an in-house counsel for a major defense contractor, and a military attorney in the U.S. Navy. Kinsley is an active member of the California State Bar. She is a certified information privacy professional and was the 2009 recipient of the Outstanding Faculty Award for the Stafford campus at UMW.

Haydar Kurban, PhD, is an associate professor in the Department of Economics at Howard University. Dr. Kurban received his PhD from the University of Illinois at Chicago. Dr. Kurban's research is focused on inequity in property tax-funded public education, urban sprawl, and economics of disasters. His research projects have been funded by the U.S. Department of Housing and Urban Development, the National Science Foundation, and the U.S. Department of Homeland Security. Dr. Kurban's research papers have appeared as book chapters and as journal articles in *Regional Science and Urban Economics*, *Economic Development Quarterly*, *Cityscape*, *International Journal of Critical Infrastructure*, and *The Review of Black Political Economy*.

William Levernier, PhD, is a professor of economics in the College of Business Administration at Georgia Southern University. He received a bachelor of business administration degree in economics at Gonzaga University, a master of arts degree in economics at the University of Tennessee, and a PhD in economics at West Virginia University. His research interests include poverty, income inequality, the role of economic conditions on election outcomes, and sports economics. He is a member of the editorial board of *The Review of Regional Studies*.

Thomas N. Maloney, PhD, is a professor of economics and chair of the Department of Economics at the University of Utah. His research focuses on African American economic history, racial inequality in the United States, the health and socioeconomic status of immigrants in the United States, and related topics in labor and demography. His articles have appeared in the *Journal of Economic History*, *Explorations in Economic History*, *Social Science History*, *Economic Inquiry*, and other leading journals. He is the coeditor, with Kim Korinek, of *Migration in the 21st Century: Rights, Outcomes, and Policy* (Routledge 2010). He holds a PhD and an MA in economics from the University of Michigan and a BA in economics from the University of Dayton.

Kristin Marsh, PhD, is an associate professor in the Department of Sociology and Anthropology at the University of Mary Washington, where she teaches courses on social stratification, gender, work and occupations, and sociological theory. Her current research focuses on the gendered experiences of achievement among professional sociologists and academics. She earned her MA in sociology from Georgia State University and her PhD in sociology from Emory University.

Michael E. Martell, PhD, is a professorial lecturer in the Department of Economics at American University. His current research investigates the determinants of labor market inequalities for gays and lesbians and the impact of public policy on these inequalities. He has also taught at Elizabethtown College and the University of Mary Washington.

Yeva Nersisyan is a visiting instructor of economics at Franklin and Marshall College and a PhD candidate in economics and math and statistics at University of Missouri–Kansas City. She received a BA with honors from Yerevan State University in Armenia in 2006. Her research interests include monetary and fiscal policy, financial economics, and political economy. She has coauthored a number of publications on the topics of financial fragility and instability, financial reform, government deficits and debt, and pension reform. She is currently working on her dissertation exploring a theoretical and statistical link between multifunctional banking and financial fragility.

David Neumark is a professor of economics and director of the Center for Economics & Public Policy at the University of California–Irvine. He is also a research associate of the National Bureau of Economic Research, and a research fellow of IZA. He has held prior positions at the Public Policy Institute of California, Michigan State University, the University of Pennsylvania, and the Federal Reserve Board. He is a labor economist with broad public policy interests including: age, sex, and race discrimination; the economics of aging; affirmative action; minimum wages, living wages, and other antipoverty policies; the economics of education; youth labor markets; and local economic development.

Pia Orrenius is a research officer and senior economist at the Federal Reserve Bank of Dallas and adjunct professor at the Hankamer School of Business, Baylor University. She is also a research fellow of the Tower Center for Political Studies at Southern Methodist University and the Institute for the Study of Labor in Bonn, Germany. Her research focuses on labor, regional and demographic economics. She is coauthor of the book *Beside the Golden Door: U.S. Immigration Reform in a New Era of Globalization* (2010, AEI Press). She received her PhD in economics from the University of California at Los Angeles and BA degrees in economics and Spanish from the University of Illinois at Urbana-Champaign.

Lynn Paringer is a professor of economics at California State University–East Bay and a certified financial planner. She holds a PhD in economics from the University of Wisconsin–Madison. Her areas of expertise include health and labor economics and employee benefits. She has served as a principal investigator on studies that examine such things as the pricing and coverage of long-term care insurance policies in California, the quality of medical care provided by different health plans, the extent of biased selection among plans, the impact of health insurance on medical care use and health status, employer responses to changes in health care policy and regulations, and the impact of health care costs on access to care. She has published numerous articles in professional journals. Lynn has been a Fulbright Fellow at the Prague School of Economics. She also teaches in domestic and international MBA programs as well as in the personal financial planning curriculum through the University of California.

Matt Parrett, PhD, is an assistant professor in the economics department at Bridgewater State University in Bridgewater, Massachusetts. Previous to this, he worked as a transfer pricing manager in the Atlanta office of Deloitte Tax LLP. He earned his BA in economics from the University of Mary Washington and his MA and PhD in economics from Virginia Tech.

Steven Pressman is a professor of economics and finance at Monmouth University in West Long Branch, New Jersey. In addition, he serves as North American editor of the *Review of Political Economy*, as associate editor and book review editor of the *Eastern Economic Journal*, and as treasurer of the Eastern Economic Association. Over the past three decades, Pressman has published more than 150 articles in refereed journals and as book chapters, and has authored or edited 16 books, including *A New Guide to Post Keynesian Economics* (Routledge, 2001), *Alternative Theories of the State* (Palgrave/Macmillan, 2006), and *50 Major Economists*, second edition (Routledge, 2006), which has been translated into five different languages. Pressman is a frequent op-ed contributor to newspapers and to popular economics periodicals such as *Challenge Magazine* and *Dollars and Sense*. He is quoted frequently in local newspapers and magazines as well as major national newspapers such as the *New York Times* and the *Washington Journal*, has been interviewed on the radio, and has made numerous TV appearances, including an appearance on Fox Business News.

David C. Ribar, PhD, is a professor of economics at the University of North Carolina at Greensboro, where he conducts research on disadvantaged families, assistance programs, and household time use. His research has investigated barriers to employment, women's decisions to become young mothers or female heads of families, parents' decisions to purchase or provide care for their children, youths' schooling, work and substance abuse behavior, public and private transfers to alleviate poverty, participation in assistance programs, and families' material well-being. Dr. Ribar was previously a professor at the George Washington University and has served as a research fellow at the U.S. Census Bureau and as an analyst at the Administration for Children and Families. He is currently a research fellow at the Institute for the Study of Labor in Bonn, Germany

Arthur Sakamoto is a professor of sociology at the University of Texas at Austin. He has a BA from Harvard, and MA and PhD degrees from the University of Wisconsin at Madison. His research interests include the sociology of inequality, economic sociology, and race relations. He is affiliated with the Population Research Center and the Center for Asian American Studies at the University of Texas at Austin.

Isabel V. Sawhill, PhD, is a senior fellow in economic studies at the Brookings Institution, where she serves as director of the Budgeting for National Priorities project and codirector of the Center on Children and Families. She has authored and coauthored numerous books, including *Creating an Opportunity Society* and *Getting Ahead: Economic and Social Mobility in America*. Her research has spanned a wide array of economic and social issues, including fiscal policy, economic growth, poverty and inequality, welfare reform, the well-being of children, and changes in the family. Prior to joining Brookings, Dr. Sawhill was a senior fellow at The Urban Institute. She also served as an associate director at the Office of Management and Budget from 1993 to 1995, where her responsibilities included all of the human resource programs of the federal government, accounting for one-third of the federal budget.

Laura J. Templeton, PhD, is a recent graduate of the sociology program at the University of Alberta. Her research centers on the production of economic inequalities for highly skilled immigrants in Canada. Her areas of interest include work and occupations, economic inequalities, status of women, and intimate partner violence. At present, she is the lead research analyst for a community-university partnership project in Edmonton, Alberta, that is exploring more effective ways of delivering services to low-income families with children.

Sally Wallace is a professor of economics and chair, Department of Economics, Andrew Young School of Policy Studies at Georgia State University. She also serves as the director of the Fiscal Research Center. Her work focuses on behavioral aspects of tax and expenditure policy—both domestic and international. Previously she served in the U.S. Department of Treasury. She has worked in a variety of countries including Russia, China, Jamaica, Cote d'Ivoire, Ghana, Uzbekistan, and the Philippines among others.

Karl Widerquist is a visiting associate professor in political philosophy at the Georgetown University School of Foreign Service in Qatar. He holds two doctorates—one in political theory from Oxford University (2006) and one in economics from the City University of New York (1996). He is coauthor of *Economics for Social Workers* (Columbia University Press), coeditor of *The Ethics and Economics of the Basic Income Guarantee* (Ashgate), coeditor of *Basic Income: An Anthology of Contemporary Research* (Blackwell), coeditor of *Alaska's Permanent Fund Dividend: Assessing Its Suitability as a Model* (Palgrave-Macmillan), and coeditor of *Exporting the Alaska Model: Adapting the Permanent Fund Dividend* (Palgrave-Macmillan). He is a founding editor of the journal *Basic Income Studies* and has published scholarly articles on economics, politics, and philosophy in journals such as *Political Studies*, *Utilitas*, the *Eastern Economic Journal*, *Politics and Society*, and *Politics, Philosophy, and Economics*.

Patrick J. Wolf, PhD, is a professor of education reform and 21st Century Endowed Chair in School Choice in the Department of Education Reform at the University of Arkansas. He has authored, coauthored, or coedited three books and more than 75 journal articles, policy reports, and book chapters on school choice, civic values, special education, public management, and campaign finance. He received the Significant Research Award of the University of Arkansas College of Education and Health Professions in 2011 for leading the federal government impact evaluation of the D.C. Opportunity Scholarship Program. He received his BA in political science and philosophy at the University of St. Thomas (St. Paul, Minnesota) summa cum laude and his AM and PhD in government from Harvard University.

Carolyn M. Wolff is a doctoral candidate in economics at the University of North Carolina at Greensboro. Her research interests include applied topics in labor and public economics. Her current research focuses on the impacts of financial incentives and on the employment decisions of welfare recipients. Previous to pursuing her doctoral degree, she worked as an economic consultant. She earned master of arts and bachelor of arts degrees in economics from Boston University.

Edward N. Wolff, PhD, is a professor of economics at New York University, where he has taught since 1974. He received his AB degree from Harvard University in 1968 and his PhD from Yale University in 1974. He is also a senior scholar at the Levy Economics Institute of Bard College, a research associate at the National Bureau of Economic Research, and a council member of the International Association for Research in Income and Wealth since 1987. He served as managing editor of the *Review of Income and Wealth* from 1987 to 2004 and was a visiting scholar at the Russell Sage Foundation in New York (2003–4) and president of the Eastern Economics Association (2002–3). His principal research areas are productivity growth and income and wealth distribution. He is the author (or coauthor) of: *Growth, Accumulation, and Unproductive Activity* (1987); *Productivity and American Leadership* (1989); *Competitiveness, Convergence, and International Specialization* (1993); *TOP HEAVY: A Study of Increasing Inequality of Wealth in America* (1995, 1996, 2002); *Economics of Poverty, Inequality, and Discrimination* (1997, 2009); *Downsizing in America* (2003); and *Does Education Really Help?* (2006).

L. Randall Wray is a professor of economics at the University of Missouri–Kansas City, senior scholar at the Levy Economics Institute of Bard College, and director of research at the Center for Full Employment and Price Stability. He is currently working in the areas of monetary policy, employment, and Social Security. Wray has published widely in academic journals and is the author of *Money and Credit in Capitalist Economies: The Endogenous Money Approach* (Edward Elgar, 1990) and *Understanding Modern Money: The Key to Full Employment and Price Stability* (Edward Elgar, 1998). He is also the editor of *Credit and State Theories of Money: The Contributions of A. Mitchell Innes* (Edward Elgar, 2004) and coeditor (with M. Forstater) of *Keynes for the 21st Century: The Continuing Relevance of The General Theory* (Palgrave Macmillan, 2008). Wray holds a BA from the University of the Pacific and an MA and a PhD from Washington University in St. Louis.

Madeline Zavodny is a professor of economics at Agnes Scott College in Decatur, Georgia. She is also a research fellow of the Institute for the Study of Labor in Bonn, Germany. Her research areas are labor and health economics and economic demography. Much of her recent research has focused on economic issues related to immigration, including *Beside the Golden Door: U.S. Immigration Reform in a New Era of Globalization* (AEI Press, 2010), coauthored with Pia Orrenius. She received an undergraduate degree in economics from Claremont McKenna College and a PhD in economics from the Massachusetts Institute of Technology.

Index

DATE DUE

			PRINTED IN U.S.A.